RHETORIC AND CIVILITY

SUNY Series in Speech Communication

Dudley D. Cahn, Editor

RHETORIC AND CIVILITY

*Human Development, Narcissism,
and the Good Audience*

HAROLD BARRETT

State University of New York Press

Published by
State University of New York Press, Albany

© 1991 State University of New York

For information, address the State University of New York Press,
State University Plaza, Albany, NY 12246

Library of Congress Cataloging-in-Publication Data

Barrett, Harold.
    Rhetoric and civility : human development, narcissism, and the good
audience / Harold Barrett.
        p.   cm. — (SUNY series in speech communication)
    Includes bibliographical references.
    ISBN 0-7914-0483-8 (alk. paper). — ISBN 0-7914-0484-6 (pbk. :
alk. paper)
        1. Oratory. 2. Rhetoric. 3. Persuasion (Rhetoric)
    4. Narcissism. 5. Socialization.   I. Title. II. Series.
    PN4051.B37   1991
808.'.001 — dc20   90-32467
CIP

10 9 8 7 6 5 4 3 2 1

To my students of the annual Seminar in Rhetorical Studies
California State University, Hayward

Contents

Preface

The word narcissism, made permanent in the literature of psychoanalysis by Sigmund Freud, is derived from Narcissus, the name of the beautiful and vain youth of Greek mythology who was so enthralled by his own reflection in a pool that he pined away and died. He was changed into a flower of the same name. Though love of self was Narcissus' problem, we have come to know that, quite reversed, narcissism as a personality problem is characterized by dependence on assurances and attention of others, in an effort to sustain self-regard.

Since the 1970s, narcissism has been popularized as a prevalent human condition, and the general reading public has come to know of so-called *narcissists*. When used in a maladaptive or pathological sense, narcissism refers to inordinate self-absorption: extreme self-interest and limitation in the capacity to care for others.

Applying the topic to my field of specialization, rhetoric, I have made it my chief scholarly interest of the past ten years. The study has provided me with a valuable means of comprehending rhetorical maladaption—how certain narcissistic behavior is a key to explaining ineffectiveness in social interaction, whether on the public platform or in relationships of any sort. Excessive self-occupation works against success in identifying with others—an essential rhetorical function.

But should a rhetorician get involved in psychology and psychoanalysis? Clearly, the answer is yes, if that rhetorician would understand fundamental processes of rhetorical interaction and reasons for both success and failure. As Wayne Booth advised, "Psychoanalysts have dealt with the irrational more effectively . . . than have students of rhetoric, and any new rhetoric must be ready to learn from them."* I have taken Professor Booth's counsel.

*"The Scope of Rhetoric Today: A Polemical Excursion," *The Prospect of Rhetoric,* ed. Lloyd F. Bitzer and Edwin Black (Englewood Cliffs: Prentice-Hall, 1971), 93–114.

ix

In coming to appreciate the causal connection between rhetorical dysfunction and kinds of narcissism, I have found it helpful to conceive of some new terms. The first is *rhetorical disposition*, to represent the condition arising out of favorable narcissism, when the force of self is healthy and strong. The second is *rhetorical indisposition*, to represent the disabling influence of unfavorable, oppressive narcissism. Another useful conception is the *rhetorical imperative*, which, linked to primary biological and social processes that function from birth, is the mighty engine motivating the great quest for representation of self in interacting symbolically with others.

The book begins with a chapter that puts the idea of rhetoric in historical and contemporary perspective, outlines rhetorical functions, forms, and workings, and introduces a psychological framework found to be useful in analysis of rhetorical motivation and strategy.

Following that is a chapter on the infant's development of a rhetorical disposition. Chapter three is an extensive discussion of narcissism and the nature and rhetorical consequences of rhetorical indisposition. The fourth chapter discusses approaches to the task of analyzing and criticizing rhetorical indisposition.

Chapters five through eight illustrate lives of people whose early development did not provide rhetorical adequacy, i.e., who were fundamentally — as seen at last — rhetorically indisposed. Thus their failure is explained.

The final chapter connects the topic of civility to rhetorical disposition — and incivility to indisposition. A dominant representation of incivility in society is the narcissistic individualism that jeopardizes personal success and the public good. An ideal, yet practical, construct and rhetorical solution is proposed: the *good audience*, the model of an active, self-respecting, rhetorically disposed person or group who in their rhetorical maturity selectively confirm and disconfirm the behavior of people with whom they relate. The development of good audiences in influential roles of good parents, good teachers, good officials, good therapists, and good citizens everywhere should be one of the nation's highest educational priorities.

Any decrease in the level of civility threatens fundamental social structures and individual happiness. Acknowledged as indispensable agents in the maintenance of civility, rhetorically disposed persons are among society's most valued resources. Our need of these healthy ones has never been greater.

A number of colleagues — local and distant — contributed significantly to this book. The first person to name is Gale S. Auletta who was extraordinarily generous with her knowledge of new methodologies and information when needed. Others who lent a hand are Wende Black, Karen L. Fritts,

John C. Hammerback, Jamie L. Kauffman, Stephen W. Littlejohn, Anne L. Makus, Daniel S. Prentice, and Alan M. Smith. Sociologist Charles Derber helped too.

Librarian Carol A. Castagnozzi supplied an indispensable bibliography. Thanks to her and all the other dedicated people who work in our university library.

Robert L. Ivie and William F. Eadie read a draft of the manuscript and prepared reviews. Their wisdom guided me each day as I wrote the final draft.

A special word of gratitude goes to Claire Allphin, a trusted friend who listens well and understands.

Jake Barrett again served as proofreader. I value his ready assistance and loving support.

Typist Lorraine Zeyen is still with me, somehow deciphering my penciled insertions and producing professional copy. I am indebted to her.

I want, too, to mention the country of New Zealand, where on sabbatical leave I learned something about civility—both in the libraries there and among the people.

This book is the product of exceptional editorial expertise. Without Dudley D. Cahn's knowledge, intelligence, and vision, certain key topics would not have been treated and certain deficiencies would not have been remedied. I think of competent editors as good audiences. Truly, Professor Cahn is one of these.

Let me acknowledge the essential contribution of the one who coordinated the entire effort and saw to it that it was to be: Priscilla C. Ross, the supportive and effective editor of the State University of New York Press. Thanks, also, to Production Editor Christine M. Lynch who shaped the manuscript into a book.

Now to Carol: What would I do without her bright spirit, constant encouragement, and keen interest in ideas? Whether in testing a line of thought or proofreading a chapter, she was there, always.

1
Rhetoric

AN OLD ART

The idea of rhetoric is as old as civilization. It was systematized as an art in ancient Greece to implement democratic government, since successful citizenship required skill and sophistication in decision-making, reasoning, and speaking—all of which are parts of the rhetorical faculty. After establishment of the polis, the autonomous city-state, came gradual growth of popular government. Athens emerged as the model, with its great legislative Assembly flourishing in the fifth century B.C. In that city, all male citizens were allowed a direct hand in making laws, but enjoyment of democracy depended on effectiveness in speaking. Plaintiffs and defendants in court proceedings also needed rhetorical ability, for they were required to appear and plead their own cases. Other users of rhetorical processes were persons designated to speak on special occasions of the community, e.g., at funerals or festivals.

Aristotle's Definition of Rhetoric

The most noteworthy theory of rhetoric to come out of antiquity—albeit in the century after the flowering of democracy in Greece—was from Aristotle who said that rhetoric is the art or faculty of observing (discovering) in any given case the available means of persuasion.[1] Thus he found rhetoric related to finding the means—arguments, appeals, strategies—for building promising persuasive cases with audiences in situations as they arose.

Enthymeme

Aristotle emphasized *discovery* in his definition—*invention*, as the Romans later called it—and named the *enthymeme* as central in the rhetorical process.

Aristotle's enthymeme is a deductive structure which typifies human thought patterns and therefore is essential in the discovery of the "available means of persuasion." And unlike the formal syllogism which deals in ab-

1

solutes, the enthymeme deals in probabilities—the typical kind of material found in legislative, judicial, and ceremonial speeches. A formal syllogism is grist for scientific or philosophic dialogue, e.g.,

> Major premise: All men are mortal.
> Minor premise: Socrates is a man.
> Conclusion: Socrates is mortal.

But in the Athenian Assembly, deliberations were on debatable questions and ordinary recurring topics like war and peace, ways and means, defense, etc. Thus served the enthymeme, the practical mode of reasoning for addressing matters in *dispute*, for handling *unsettled* questions and *issues*. By definition, an issue is ipso facto an undecided matter, one on which the truth of neither side is established. Therefore, the better cases heard in public speeches were those judged to have the higher degree of probable merit or promise or comparable practicality. Moreover, unlike the learned ones with their syllogisms ("All men are mortal," etc.), speakers in the legislature, courts, or on streets of the Agora, usually found it advisable to build their arguments with some part open or incomplete, allowing for audience participation in the formulation of thought. Enthymemes, therefore, often appeared with only two of the three syllogistic parts—or even one. As he gave his memorable funeral address, proud Pericles doubtless enjoyed full Athenian cooperation in "supplying" the basic and omitted premise of this enthymeme: Fellow Athenians, one reason for our greatness is that "we are originators, not imitators." Pericles did not have to remind those people of the value of originality. He was safe in assuming that he and they shared it; therefore, he could leave the agreed upon major premise *unspoken* ("A great city is one valuing originality"). Talking in this way, Pericles invited audience participation in completing the point; speaker and listeners reasoned together, intimate in spirit. When cultural and social values are shared, speakers' enthymemes are not as complete.

Style and Structure

Orators learned, then, that enthymemes of three complete premises often were unnecessary for persuading audiences. In fact, a full stock of premises in an enthymematic statement could imperil the case, given possible listener impatience with redundancy or seeming condescension. In defense against Aeschines' sweeping indictment of his entire career, Demosthenes pleaded for fair treatment. Formally laid out, one of his points (one enthymeme) can be cast as follows:

> Major premise: Fairness requires that a living person be judged
> in comparison with his contemporaries, not the dead.

Minor premise: I am a living person.
Conclusion: Fairness requires that I be judged in comparison with
 my contemporaries, not the dead.

Here is the point in full, as he structured and expressed it to achieve
his purpose:

> You next call to my remembrance the great men of the past. You
> are right to do so. But it is not right, gentlemen, to take advantage
> in this court of the feeling which exists permanently towards the
> dead in order to examine me, living as I do among you, and com-
> pare me with them. No one can be unaware that there is always
> an undercurrent, deep or shallow, of envy towards the living, while
> the dead are immune from the dislike even of their enemies. In
> view, then, of the character of these gentlemen, am I now to be
> judged and assessed in comparison with my predecessors? I hope
> not. Justice and equity alike forbid it, Aeschines. The standard
> must be you yourself, or any other person still living who shared
> your policies.

Demosthenes' care in organizing and phrasing the elements of his argument contributed to his reasoning and its full effect.

Symbols

Greek orators and theorists, including Aristotle, recognized the power of
language in the rhetorical act. Ancient speech making offers an early
demonstration of the function of symbols, of how humans use and react
to particular meanings given to words — verbal symbols, but also the nonverbal: objects, facial expression and physical movement, dress, designs, etc.
One can imagine the meanings that Greeks attached to the "Olympic
Games" (as term or event experienced), a city called "Sparta," and the word
"arete." The symbols of a culture — with their shared meanings — can have
a tremendous impact on people of the culture. Influencing others requires
selection and effective presentation of appropriate symbols. Demosthenes
saw Philip II of Macedonia as a grave threat to Athenian security, and
in speech after speech he warned that Philip was out to conquer Athens.
But Demosthenes was not successful in causing the people to take arms
against the Macedonian (not until too late). He shaped a spectre symbolizing clear and present danger, yet hard as he tried, he was unable to secure
sufficient agreement on meaning in the symbol.

The Audience

Speakers of any age attempt to lay out their premises skillfully, adjusting form to inclinations of listeners. They embellish their lines of argument with words appealing to ideals and experience, to their listeners' sense of fair play and knowledge of human behavior. In so doing, they exemplify the finding of Aristotle that rhetoric is a popular art — audience-centered, practiced with awareness of the thinking and feeling of recipients. It is "the hearer, that determines the speech's end and object," Aristotle said. In tackling problems of the community, the rhetor's art was in deciding, in choosing theme and thought, structure and style, all elements as dictated by purpose, yes, but also as influenced by audience and occasion.

So it is in democratic meeting places today. The exchange is dialectical, involving adaptation and give-and-take. While free to take issue (and formulate enthymemes) people seeking a hearing are influenced in their approach by situational realities and acceptance or denial by peers. Indeed, rhetoric is viable only when decisions of speaker and listeners are free.

Above all, rhetoric is an activity of *options*. The first choice has to do with goal and strategy: how to succeed in achieving one's purpose. The second choice is relational: how to treat the audience. The latter, as an ethical concern, brings up questions of fairness, integrity, and respect for others. Necessarily, the matter of adherence to moral and social values has always put heavy burdens on speakers who approach an audience and consider the nature of the relationship. From antiquity to the present, ethics and morality have had firm connection to rhetorical theory and practice. In fact, it was Quintilian, the first century Roman teacher, who defined the orator as "the good man speaking well" and who made that idea central in his monumental book on rhetorical training.[2]

Since freedom is related to vulnerability, the risks in addressing an audience in a democratic setting may be extraordinary, sometimes calling for great wisdom and courage. John F. Kennedy's book, *Profiles in Courage,*[3] brings to mind examples. Issues of freedom, risk, and action — all topics of that book — suggest another side to standards of citizenship as related to rhetorical activity. Whose responsiblity is it that appropriate actions be taken in a democracy? It rests with those whose welfare and general happiness are at stake — the people, as members of groups or as individuals. They have the power in both a political and interpersonal sense. Given a rhetorical way of thinking, the people are the *audience*, the source of influence in a free society. In a subsequent chapter we shall start a discussion of the "good audience" and its essential role in the civics of living and relating. And again, whether referring to speaker or audiences, the dimensions of rhetoric are both practical and ethical.

The Appeal of Ethos

Another observation of Aristotle that continues to carry much meaning is on proofs or appeals. Though wishing for sufficiency in rational appeal (logos), and yet acknowledging the force of emotional appeal (pathos) in rhetorical exchange, Aristotle, the good observing scientist that he was, had to conclude that very likely the most telling appeal was in *ethos*: in the rhetor's revealed character, wisdom, and good will—his credibility. Ethos is personal proof. One case in point is found in Winston Churchill's speech before the joint session of the United States Congress in December of 1941, just after the Pearl Harbor attack put America at war in the Pacific. He came to Washington to get assurance that the United States would continue to support the war in his part of the world: in Europe. A prominent feature of the address was his advantageous reference to his legislative and parental identity. "By the way," he remarked in the introduction, "I cannot help for reflecting, that if my father had been American—and my mother British—instead of the other way around, I might have got here on my own." That is ethos!—a brilliant revelation of shared personal substance—true kinship! Who can calculate the unifying effect of those few words on members of Congress whose heads had just been turned from the Atlantic to the Pacific. In that moment of high rhetorical drama and intimacy, the speaker's motives were revealed in audience response—and the listeners' motives in the speaker's choices of symbols and enthymemes. Such is the essential material of persuasion. The force of personal appeal cannot be overestimated.

Role as Strategy

The ethos of rhetors is established by the words they use and the roles they assume in their meanings and varied interactions. Roles are indicators of identity that serve in reaching and affecting others. Everyone, as a rhetorical being, has a repertoire of roles, large or small. In a functional sense, roles are strategies selected and enacted to achieve goals. For example, if we were to reanalyze Winston Churchill's speech, we might be able to assess his effectiveness by taking into account the roles he assumed. Quite clearly, in reminding the American legislators of his American mother, he projected himself as *kinsman*. That is a vital role. Moreover, he was a fellow politician, a *brother*. That, too, can be an effective role. And everybody knew Churchill as *hero*. (Symbols and roles may come together.) Incidentally, in the months ahead, he was to become known and accepted by many as *savior* of the Empire. Certainly on that day in Washington, he acted as *promoter*, a role that may not have carried positive value for some members of the audience who saw him promoting his own cause.

All people, ordinary and great, have in stock numbers of learned and well-practiced roles. An example is the person who relies on a sense of humor and gets on by being *comedian*. That same individual might occasionally play the role of *adviser* with friends, *father* with younger employees at work, or *cheerleader* with a discouraged colleague. The roles chosen vary according to their availability to the person — whether a part of the person's repertoire, and according to the situation faced and the aim of the rhetor.

Intentionality

As rhetorical creatures, we humans act with intention, i.e., with aim and purpose. The influencing of others is accomplished verbally and nonverbally, and it is the position here that messages invented — those of conscious design as well as those arising from below the level of consciousness — ordinarily will reflect the rhetor's feeling and intent. It is a fact that many statements are not truly deliberate, e.g., a nonverbal burst of laughter. Realistically, speakers cannot exercise complete control over all messages sent. Consider the kind of nonverbal statement that contradicts the verbal and thus confuses the receiver of the message, as in the case of a frown accompanying words that sound cheerful. Rhetorical miscues do occur. Momentarily out of touch with an audience, a rhetor may utter a counterproductive phrase or make a gesture that detracts from purpose. But that is not to deny intentionality. It is only to recognize the occurrence of rhetorical lapses, given human fallibility. Generally speaking, then, symbolic behavior is expressive of rhetorical intent.

Identification

Churchill's speech before the Congress *brought speaker and listener together.* The process is identification. In his *Rhetoric,* Aristotle made some mention of this significant process, e.g., in regard to composition of the speech of praise. It is advisable, he said to "take into account the nature of our particular audience," and to be aware of those qualities esteemed by them: observe that "it is not difficult to praise the Athenians to an Athenian audience." But while suggesting the persuasive value of speaker-audience identification, Aristotle left development of the theory to future writers. Notable among those theorists is Kenneth Burke of this century who finds identification of rhetor and audience as both process and end.[4] To identify is to talk another's language. It is to discover and reveal *shared* properties — *common* attributes, values, needs, and feelings. The aim is to find consubstantiality, i.e., to acknowledge common "personal substance," the stuff that makes speaker and audience alike and facilitates intimacy and dialogue: a coming together. Taking this process into account, we can begin to understand a rhetor's motive and an audience's response.

To identify is to make reference, if one is Winston Churchill, to his mother's American birth and other shared interests: or if an ex-New Yorker to reveal the fact of one's New York City childhood when speaking to other ex-New Yorkers; or to locate common community interest while conversing with a neighbor. If people were not separate and distinct, there would be no gaps to bridge, no need for rhetorical action. But alas, we are not of one heart or mind. In great and ordinary interactions, people—all of us as individuals apart from others—strive to make connections. Hence, no human function or goal is more basic than achievement of consubstantiality, be it on grand or mundane level. The fundamental idea of rhetoric, then, can be expressed in terms of persons divided, purposefully seeking union, and finding available means through choice and design of enthymeme, fitting structure, and appropriate style. The rhetorical act is of people affecting others—selecting strategies, roles, places, and times to achieve their ends. Occasions of rhetorical interaction involve audiences of many or one and range from the most formal to the most intimate and personal.

Extending Aristotle

In Aristotle's *Rhetoric*, we have the first treatment of a practical and *relational* dimension in the art, marking a significant departure from the idealistic position of his teacher, Plato. With the audience seen as a central, participating member, Aristotle's rhetoric becomes *rhetorical interaction*; the art of discovering available means of persuasion is deciding on enthymemes, yes—but also it is adapting to audiences. Aristotle's thought, as augmented over time, is the substructure for much modern rhetorical theory. Among the most significant authors of augmentation is Burke who worked up that profound idea of consubstantiality—of locating shared substance as the essential of any rhetorical exchange. New meaning emerged when we began to understand the process of people "being with" others and making their respective selves available in building enthymemes together. Then we saw the application of rhetoric to relationships. We found key conditions to be levels of reciprocity and mutuality in thought, feeling, and attitude. Theorists developed concepts like "confirmation-disconfirmation" to distinguish between productive and supportive messages and those which are not.[5] Trust and sharing of self and ideas became central. While it will be more apparent at a later point, we can conclude now that all communicative states are rhetorical, i.e., functional and instrumental, presented to affect an audience and dependent for success on their potential in bringing about identification. From this position, common attributes in all varieties of rhetorical activity become apparent, whether in references to Demosthenes in the Athenian Assembly, Churchill before Congress, a set of American parents talking over a problem on how to deal with the kids, or the kids themselves interacting with each other in their relationships. Found in all exchanges of people are thoughts to be expressed, influence exerted, choices made, purposes and goals decided and pursued, language used — verbal and nonverbal, courage mustered, roles played, and perceptions of self and audience discovered. Rhetoric involves people in scenes and situations acting purposefully and strategically.

Burke extended the functional Aristotelian view with new social and psychological perspectives on motivation and the workings of human interaction. Conceiving of society as dramatistic, Burke connected motivation to symbolizing. People are moved to act on others with their language, seeking consubstantiality. He theorized that as people reject hierarchy, as they move out of "their proper places" in society, they experience guilt. It is in response to inherent, eternal guilt, said Burke, that people act. They do so to redeem themselves. Guilt, then, provides motivation for action. As moral philosopher and psychological child of a classical psychoanalytic intellectual environment, Burke wrote of humans in conflict who, sensing their guilt and "pollution," are driven to seek purification and redemption. Such are the bases of rhetorical motivation. This Freudian-informed interpretation served for decades. But of late it has become clear that Burke's construct is not fully adequate in characterizing human purpose and rhetorical behavior in this day. These times require further augmentation in theory. Retain principles of Aristotle and Burke, yes, but to understand contemporary motivation, add *self psychology*.

HEINZ KOHUT AND THE PSYCHOLOGY OF THE SELF

Prominent among more recent departures from classical psychoanalytic theory is the well-established self psychology school, founded by Heinz Kohut.[6] Kohut discovered that while certain of Freud's concepts, e.g. on the effects of drives in conflict with one another, served to explain behavioral phenomena apparent at the turn of the century, they do not suffice in addressing phenomena of behavior observed now. Children of Victorian households were intensely involved with family, servants, and others. The stimulation was constant and too great; conflicts resulted. Today, conditions are just the opposite. Adults are emotionally distant, and the family atmosphere is flat and sterile. Thus, children are understimulated.[7] Left to themselves, they feel disconnected, alienated.

Because "man is changing as the world in which he lives changes," a new psychology must be adopted. Freud's so-called "Guilty Man" acted to satisfy drives, while today's "Tragic Man" acts fo fulfill himself, to express the pattern of his individual self.[8] The former was susceptible to neurotic conflict, the latter to a pervasive sense of self-defectiveness. "If guilt be the emotion of Freud's conflicted Guilty Man, shame . . . is . . . central to Kohut's Tragic Man." Shame is evidenced in self-deficit: humiliation, apathy, inner emptiness, isolation, and low self-evaluation—conditions stemming from "failure to live up to an ideal." Shame is the "hallmark of the defeated self."[9]

Guilt arises from transgression; shame from self-deficiency and "flaw in identity representation." The guilty seek forgiveness; the shamed—with their unattainable ideals—seek acceptance.[10] The modern result of failure in the quest of moral perfection or affirmation of ambitions—even among healthy persons—is guiltless despair—i.e., shame.[11]

Reflecting personal imperfection and incapacity, shame is a powerful motivator. It can act as an "internal trigger to the more socially discordant and observable expressions of rage and aggression," or to socially useful expressions of shortcoming and of dissatisfaction with oneself.[12] The career of Jim Jones and the events at Jonestown show how calamity might arise out of childhood injury and resulting shame. The case is discussed fully in Chapter five. On the socially useful side—the creative or heroic side—is the great leadership of Winston Churchill, who may have owned a "persistent, poorly modified grandiose self."[13] In acting on others, the usual motivation of both evildoer and hero is not guilt—not instinctual and biological conflict—but limitation of self.

KOHUT AND BURKE

This is the era of Tragic Man—the age of adverse narcissism, and if the psychology of Kohut and his many adherents is sound, a fundamental condition of people now is not guilt from transgression, but shame from defect—and therefrom are we moved to act and relate to others. Thus, the necessity of rethinking the parts of Burkeian theory that relate to foundations of behavior. Burke's human subject, guilty and polluted, seeks purification (through victimage and mortification) and redemption (forgiveness),[14] while the subject of Heinz Kohut, shameful and deficient, seeks justification of self (through aggression and withdrawal) and perfection (acceptance). The Burkeian subject is limited by inner conflict; the Kohutian by fragmentation of self. Thus in the seeking of conflict resolution or cohesion are they rhetorically motivated.

As guilt has given way to shame, behavior from "sin" has given way to solipsistic inquietude and forms of self-protective accommodation. Needless to say, the hound of guilt remains, but as shall be apparent in subsequent chapters, the exertions of self-criticism provide the driving force of this age. Therefore, rhetoric needs a new psychology, one fit for use in dealing with issues reflecting the tenor of these times: times bearing on material vs. spiritual values, individual interests vs. community interests, and demands of the present vs. uses of the past.[15] Relevant and patently significant, self psychology and related compatible theory promises to be useful in rhetorical investigation—in understanding changes in personal epistemologies and modes of invention, world views, strategic behaviors, and rhetorical styles. Our psychology must be suitable to the current social psyche and cultural conditions. How would this psychology assist the study and criticism of rhetorical acts in this era? A psychological understanding of an enthymeme reflecting deficit, as opposed primarily to moral stricture, is of great value to students of contemporary rhetoric and public address. For example, one American politician's declarations, "You won't have Richard Nixon to kick around anymore," and "I am not a crook," are representative of the voice of injured narcissism, not guilt. Applied to rhetorical behavior, the newer theory facilitates investigation of the rhetor's motivations toward self-justification and keeping the pieces of self together. Mr. Nixon did not seek forgiveness; he was not Guilty Man.

In another case, it is likely that knowledge of the German nation's response to Hitler would be incomplete without benefit of insights on self-depletion in the people and their perceived failure to meet cultural and national ideals. A critic outfitted with an appreciation of self psychology might bolster Kenneth Burke's superb criticism of Hitler's *Mein Kampf*.[16] While Burke is brilliant and convincing in his explication of the use of the Jew as scapegoat, another critic might come to important findings in exploring Hitler's use of the depressed German people ("self-objects," as Kohut would have called the interacting populace) to rediscover his—der Führer's—omnipotent self. Accordingly, the critic would explain the relationship of Hitler and the people as collusion in pursuit of similar ends. It was a self-deficient people with whom the self-deficient Hitler achieved that peculiar empathy: a resonance of injured self on injured self. Both shamed, they became united.

When presidential aspirant George Romney made his fateful trip to Viet Nam in the spring of 1968 and then admitted that he had been "brainwashed" by American generals there, he unintentionally committed political suicide. His was not an admission of guilt but a naive revelation that Americans translated as incompetence: the people concluded that he was not his own man. A simple error may be forgiven, but a sign of incapacity is not the same—not a discrete mistake to be excused. Romney's statement carried great implications and had indelibility, suggesting some deeper predisposition of the man. Once fully revealed and impressed, such an image is likely to persist, despite disclaimer.

The American public's sensing of presidential aspirant Senator Gary Hart's motivation from narcissistic injury[17] may have contributed significantly to his rejection in the presidential primaries of 1988. The central issue was leadership, and Hart's haughtiness and aloof individuality — his self-defeating, *unrhetorical* "my-personal-life-is-my-own-business" message — detracted from positive traits. The dominance of personal code of conduct over social values gave evidence of rhetorical weakness and unpresidential character. Given the stakes and this subject's hauteur and defensiveness, the people were not forgiving. Gary Hart was Kohut's Tragic Man. But the main point is that his rhetorical story — and that of many others — would remain only partially told without utilization of the theory on motivation advanced by the self psychology school.

EVERYONE A RHETOR

When thinking of users of rhetoric, we bring to mind names like Demosthenes, Winston Churchill, Franklin D. Roosevelt, Martin Luther King, and men and women who are public figures of our day. But all persons are rhetors. All have statements to make and influence to exert. All have audiences to address: others who figure decisively in their respective rhetorical environments. All interacting persons face critical rhetorical questions and issues: on credibility, self-disclosure and intimacy, predictions on outcome, costs and rewards, constraints of audience and occasion, reciprocity, values, and norms, etc. To engage rhetorically, whether with hundreds or with but one other, is to take part in discovery, merger, give-and-take, and compromise. Rhetorical interaction involves use of agreed upon symbols, of shared meanings. In a metaphorical sense, it is "playing the game," i.e., recognizing commonly accepted rules; it is appreciating the conventions created for this world of people affecting people. To engage rhetorically is to affect others strategically with acquired roles, going for some gain with — and through — others, and necessarily constrained by *their* rhetorically behaving selves, as they of course, act in *their* own interests. This is a persuasive enterprise of mutual interest and self-interest. Sometimes an adventure and often quite ordinary, it is a civil and dialectical process of social interaction: society's most humane means of implementing essential checks and balances on behavior. Though, as Aristotle noted, violence and economic power can be used to accomplish certain ends. it is through rhetoric that culture is sustained.

A PREVIEW

Now let us remind ourselves of the individual's first rhetorical experience. When does one first get involved with others rhetorically? Surprisingly, the answer is, *at birth*; the newborn infant's first involvement in rhetorical activity begins immediately. In one way or another, the foregoing theoretical discussion applies to the very first relationship, that of infant and parent. Parents have goals to gain, plans to accomplish, and persuasive things to say — as does the infant, which soon becomes evident. Increasingly, week by week, parent-child interactions take on more obvious rhetorical shape, the character of which will have influence on all phases of the new one's entire life with others. That is the first topic of the next chapter.

From the discussion of the infant's earliest social life come a number of other vital topics. One is about the *self* — an individual's unique identity or being — and self-adequacy. A second topic is the *rhetorical imperative*, a conception characterizing the great quest for representation of self through others. The *rhetorical disposition* is another significant topic. Formed in infancy, this is the condition that individuals enjoy when narcissism — sense of self and personal motivating force — is favorable. Underlying this happy state is self-esteem: "the sense each of us has in varying degrees of being a worthwhile, valuable person."[18]

The topic of Chapter three is rhetorical *indisposition*, the unhappy state — that of diminished potential in interaction with others, of motivation from unfavorable narcissism.

But first, the good part.

2
Rhetorical Interaction in Infancy and Establishment of a Rhetorical Disposition[1]

Quintilian was the first student of rhetoric to acknowledge the great effect of childhood experience on future speaking behavior. Even the earliest influences on development are vital, he declared; nothing in the child's rearing "is unnecessary to the art," and training should begin at birth.[2]

The spirit of Quintilian pervades this chapter, enriched by a wealth of relevant data on human development that was unavailable to him. Yes, conditions of infancy are basic to rhetorical adequacy. And further, one's first rhetorical experiences occur in earliest infancy. We shall look into those conditions and experiences.

BEGINNINGS

Every child is born into a life with others, and it is only in exchange with others that personal growth and social competence can come about. Quite clearly, all dimensions of the infant's life — all features of affective (emotional), cognitive, and behavioral makeup — are developed in interaction with people: principally the mother and other primary caregivers. The quality of the early communicative environment is terribly consequential, for the shape of a new human being is at issue. Indeed, the outcome is even more momentous and far-reaching than that, as ego psychologist Esther Menaker concludes: "the internalization of the communicative interaction between mother and child is the primary basis for all personality development, for all social action and interaction, and ultimately for all we know as culture."[3]

Foundations of civility are set in those early interactions. Given the personal, communicative, cultural, and other critical implications, a rhetorician's interest in the subject is understandable, particularly if that interest is in locating origins of rhetorical success and maladaptation.

In review of basic processes of development, we shall see that the human infant's existence requires not only satisfaction of biological needs, but also social effectiveness with caregivers. Thus the *rhetorical imperative:*

13

the great urgency constraining infants to act in their own behalf, influencing the responses of others. If environmental conditions are adequate, grounds exist for the normal infant to develop a rhetorical disposition, features of which are audience consciousness, readiness for healthful consubstantiality, situation awareness, inventional capacity, a wholesome sense of personal power, and acquisition of basic rhetorical skills. If conditions are not adequate, grounds for rhetorical indisposition are laid: narcissistic disablement and consequent problems in meeting rhetorical contingency.

Thus is derived the principal premise of this chapter: *Social events occurring in infant–caregiver interaction during the first months and into the second year will have continuing impact on the infant's growth as a rhetorical being.* Indisposition is the subject of Chapter Three.

As we begin this discussion of the early environment and parental influence, it ought to be observed that disposition and indisposition are relative terms, not absolute. Let us be guided, then, by a rule of probability, noting further that some human growth patterns are reversible. At work in any infant's life are numerous interpersonal and cultural influences on development, not to mention physiological conditions.

DEVELOPMENTAL OVERVIEW

It is now widely held that the baby arrives with definite social potential, equipped to engage and adapt.[4] Though not all cognitive and behavioral patterns that emerge in early weeks and months of interaction — whether innate or learned — are irreversible or destined to have a continuing or long-range effect, some do stay and influence the future. Such lastingness may be especially observable in rhetorically related behaviors. H. R. Schaffer carefully concludes

> that there are at least three senses in which one may talk of continuity: first with regard to the *functions* of communication (the wish to obtain certain objects, to affect the other person's behaviour, and so on); second with regard to the *constituent skills* required for communication (such as intentionality, role alteration, etc.); and third, with regard to the *situation* in which communication occurs.[5]

As we see, Schaffer singles out communicative goal and intent, persuasion, role adjustment, and situation awareness as those elements with continuity. These are elements of rhetoric as well.

Clearly and necessarily, the very nature of the caregiver–infant relationship is rhetorical. Each participant needs to influence the other. Strategists from the beginning, both become increasingly sophisticated in discovering available means of reaching their respective ends through one another — the infant with that first audience and the caregiver with that new audience. Their life together is characterized by moves and responses, repetition, and mastery of assorted methods that bring them success.

Many theorists, like Schaffer, discuss *stages* of growth, noting in each "a particular kind of developmental task that parent and child must jointly confront." The relationship of caregiver and infant is renegotiated at each successive step, as they assume new goals and as maternal involvement becomes less and less direct; "at all stages . . . the nature of her interactive behaviour must change in tandem with his." Theirs is a "mutually accommodative interactive system." By two months, "the regulation of mutual attention and responsiveness in face-to-face situations . . . becomes a central theme." At five months, a new issue is incorporation of objects in social interaction which ensure the couple's "topic sharing." Profound changes occur during the eight to ten months period, e.g., "the emergence of relational and integrative abilities," which "means that the child's behaviour now becomes much more flexible and coordinated. A more symmetrical relationship with the caretaker, based on reciprocity and characterized by intentionality, can thus begin to be established." Then at around eighteen months, as Schaffer discovered, abilities in symbolic representation emerge. After that, exchanges with others take on greater verbal character. As their self-awareness heightens, infants reflect more on their own and others' behavior and come to adjust their behavior accordingly. Their "verbal directives now become increasingly effective as a means of social control."[6]

Daniel Stern, in his writing on infant development frames the action with the idea of *self* rather than stages. It is the *sense of self* that dominates in early social growth, providing the central motif. It and its counterpart, "the sense of other, are universal phenomena that profoundly influence all other social experiences." Stern structures his discussion as much topically as chronologically, naming four different senses of the self. The first, a part of the infant's growth from birth, is the sense of an *emergent self*: the "organization-coming-into-being" from which will develop subsequent senses of self. The sense of *core self*, consolidated as a "separate, cohesive, bounded, physical unit," appears during the period from two to six months and provides the infant with a sense of its own "agency, affectivity, and continuity in time"; the infant becomes increasingly active in creating an interpersonal world. The *subjective self*, formed during the period from seven to fifteen months, roughly, is characterized by the "seeking and creating of intersubjective union with another." The involvement is in "learning that one's subjective life — the contents of one's mind and the qualities of one's feelings — can be shared with another." After that, the *verbal self* forms, featuring the interpersonal activity relevant to language acquisition and negotiation of meaning. The various senses of self remain "fully functioning and active throughout life. All continue to grow and coexist."[7]

Whether focusing on stages or on the sense of self, current work in infant development finds social interaction to be the fundamental and outstanding theme. Prominent among terms used to depict conditions of this wondrous adventure in interaction are mutuality, reciprocity, and joint effort — all associated with the dialogue — a conception of utmost significance.

DIALOGUE

Acting together, caregiver and infant "play out their pretence that the infant is in fact a fully qualified partner, able to take his turn and answer back as though aware of the rules of the game." In this way — and while growing toward equality in status and responsibility — the child comes to acquire social skills.[8] Quite reasonably, "social skills" may be translated as "rhetorical competence," for most such discovered capabilities have suasory relevance or utility. Truly, the infant lives by affecting others. Those "preflight" maneuvers — those rhetorical similations — are to secure response. Events of the dialogue are conducted by *two* determined people; *both* have work to do, as human development studies show. When read from a rhetorical viewpoint, the literature on parent-infant interaction offers a most illuminating perspective — allowing for unique appreciation of the functional quality of activities of the dialogue. The infant's prerhetorical efforts — like those one day to be fully intended and invented — pervade the busy scene. Sometimes like play, but often with unmistakable intensity, happenings in the dialogue are vital and exciting. It is serious business, this corporate enterprise that is the coming to be of an effective somebody.

RHETORICAL DRAMA OF THE DIALOGUE

In those dynamic encounters of parent and infant, actions of both parties are purposive, conducted to achieve respective, specific ends. Both persons aim to get results in their distinct quests, the parent wanting the infant to "accommodate himself to her," and the infant, in part, seeking to handle uncertainty by developing "appropriate techniques for responding to whatever unpleasantness may arise." Each finds strategies to elicit specific behavior from the other.[9] In repeated exchanges, reports John Newson, the baby "begins to offer with some certainty the appropriate actions which are required of him to sustain the chain of reciprocal activity."[10] Stern observes, for example, instrumental use of crying as early as three weeks in the infant's life, instrumental smiling at the third month, and laughing in response to stimuli at the fourth to eighth months. By three months, "the infant is well equipped with a large repertoire of behaviors to engage and disengage his caregivers."[11] Leon Yarrow and his colleagues find that the very young infant is "an active organism who influences people," and receives feedback in an "interactive system of mutual influences."[12] Development is a joint enterprise, and as the relationship grows, each party demonstrates effectiveness in regulating exchanges, the character of which have unmistakable rhetorical features.

Rudimentary modes of mutual influence become quite apparent in the first few weeks. Though such vocal and physical infant behaviors as moving helplessly, sighing, crying, and other acts evoke reaction by caregivers, it is gazing — eye-to-eye contact — that is "the most compelling of infant cues," Joy D. Osofsky and Karen Connors discover. "Eye contact helps mothers feel less strange with their babies," giving "them a sense that the baby is a real person, a social being who can enter into a social relationship with them, and arouses their positive feelings for the baby." A mother reads into eye behavior "intelligence, curiosity, or other personality traits." Her behavior is influenced as much by the presence the child makes as by her past experience. Thus, she or another caregiver interprets signals from the infant and reacts accordingly, but should the infant cut off the caregiver with a break in eye contact or appear unresponsive, the caregiver may feel less attached to or less competent with the infant, or may reduce the frequency of attempts to affect the infant or change the approach.[13] Caregivers are dependent on responses from their infants.

Turn taking, Reciprocity, Strategy

Most significantly, from the beginning, the baby seems to be ready for the invitation to turn taking, as seen in behavior at the breast or bottle, i.e., sucking then stopping, feeling the caregiver's jiggle of nipple, sucking again, and so on in a suck-stop-jiggle-suck alternation. This phenomenon, according to Kenneth Kaye, is a form of dialogue — and "the earliest example of infants and mothers learning to take turns."[14]

Further evidence of the reciprocal nature of the mother-infant relationship is found in facial expression and timing of other behaviors. John and Elizabeth Newson report on observing these natural conversationalists who "look attentive when we speak to them and wait for an appropriate pause or hiatus before they in turn make some gesture, or vocal or pre-vocal response." But the baby's role is self-directed from the outset of this joint effort. Neither mother nor baby ever has sole control of the dialogue.[15] The mother provides the structure — the "scaffolding" to keep the dialogue going and "make the alternating role sequence first possible and then familiar." As the baby becomes more skillful and secure as an active participant in this on going building process, "the props may be gradually removed." Consequently, by approximately nine months, the baby will "almost inevitably have a considerable history of involvement in two-way communication episodes simply as an indirect consequence of being given the minimal care and protection necessary to keep him alive and well."[16]

The infant grows, then, through full involvement in a lively interactive process, and by complicated adaption rather than in a simple or unidirectional way. To understand the process, we must be able to conceive of an *exchange* — of a developing relationship in which parent and infant experience reciprocity of influence. The system becomes more complex as the relationship becomes stronger and more complex. Among the general modes of behavior reflecting that complexity are sequencing, timing and regulating, negotiating, risking denial, moderating, maintaining interaction and terminating it. As early as six months, Stern shows convincingly, caregiver and infant "have evolved their own interactive style and their own interactive fit as a pair."[17] Specific functions of the pair, some of which a rhetorician would want to term "strategies," are eliciting specific reactions from each other, engaging and disengaging each other, fixating each other's eyes, averting their gaze and avoiding eye contact, moving close and pulling back, inviting and cutting off an exchange, tracking each other, using the head or arms in signalling, improvising messages, changing messages, and the like. The parent's efforts to regulate the level of activity are more obvious, yet, notes Stern, "When one watches infants play their role in these mutual regulations, it is difficult not to conclude that they sense the presence of a separate other and sense their capacity to alter the behavior of the other as well as their own experience."[18] Rhetorical consciousness is formed early in life.

INTENTIONALITY

Though behaviors of the infant are strategic from the beginning, activity of those early months constitutes a prerhetorical state. Next is the stage of intentionality. Having found a fit with the environment, e.g., in sensitivity to reciprocity, perception of causation and sequencing of events, and awareness of others' roles in achievement of his or her goals, the infant senses that certain physical or vocal behaviors can be used purposefully to get desired results from others.[19] We can fix the occurrence of one's debut as a rhetorically behaving creature, then, at a point between eight and ten months. Rhetorical cries are not those of earlier months when a pain was felt, but of months later when, for example, the infant asks for treatment of the pain. "The older child has had countless experiences informing him of the contingency between his behaviour and its effects, and as a result he becomes able to signal for his mother in a purposive fashion," acting with an eye to the future.[20] By such action, the child demonstrates appreciation of the idea of futurity and a level of maturity that is essential to rhetorical sophistication.

During the months following birth, the parent imputes meaning to the various cries, smiles, and head turns. Consequently, the responsive infant discovers their meaning — and usefulness in communication. Actions achieve meaningful status "to the extent that they are capable of being used as communication gestures which he knows how to produce, on cue, in the context of a social exchange between himself and someone else. In a real sense, therefore, gestures only acquire their *significance* in so far as they can be utilized as currency within social dialogues." As accepted by infant and caregiver, these behaviors become conventions of communication. Now the infant is able to communicate with specific aims *and* make adjustments as indicated by caregivers' feedback.[21]

Thus does the human baby — still new, less than one year of age — make entry into the world of *relating with intention*. The young one has learned that satisfaction, only possible through another, can be achieved by some nonverbal signal of "I want." After this, all sorts of choices will begin to complicate life, like what to say, how to be, with whom, when, and where. Things will not be as simple from then on. With achievement of a sense of rhetorical power comes loss of innocence. With wanting to influence others' actions and acquisition of the means to do so, the adventuresome but vulnerable infant begins to move out from Eden — from the garden and onto the bustling road beyond.

Another important dimension of intentionality and early rhetorical behavior is social and moral responsibility, features of which are acquired via the many, many instances of parental confirmation of this behavior and disconfirmation of that, etc. From the beginning, the well-nurtured infant begins to build a groundwork for eventual internalization of moral values, the first year being the critical period. With a solid foundation shaped from adequate parental influence, the child in subsequent months and years is ready to learn rules of social conduct,[22] or, as Lawrence Kohlberg would express it, is prepared for vital role-taking opportunities. Such provision is the parent's most important contribution to a child's moral growth.[23] In any case, a caregiver's sensitive ways and love secure "the roots of the infant's personal moral sense." The character of their relationship is a major influence on development of a sense of right and wrong.[24]

GOOD ENOUGH ENVIRONMENT

Under what conditions does the normal baby experience adequate affective, cognitive, and behavioral development? Writers on the subject are now given to less rigidity in naming their criteria, choosing to discuss environmental adequacy in broad terms. While affirming the significance of the relationship of parent and infant in dialogue, students of human development are satisfied to expect "good enough mothering," the "good enough mother," the "good enough environment," and "average expectable environment." As Donald W. Winnicott conceived it, the term "good-enough mother" — not always the infant's mother — "is one who makes active adaptation to the infant's needs, an active adaptation that gradually lessens, according to the infant's growing ability to account for failure of adaptation and to tolerate the results of frustration."[25]

In this sense, an appropriate mothering relationship is defined "within a certain range of adequacy, sufficient to permit reasonably satisfactory development, given a child of normal responsiveness."[26] Ideally, notes Alice Miller, there should be provided "the necessary emotional climate and understanding for the child's needs. But even a mother who is not especially warm-hearted can make this development possible, if she only refrains from preventing it."[27]

Heinz Kohut, too, is realistic in expectation. The healthful environment includes occasional failure. Kohut uses the term "optimally failing parents," to characterize adequacy in the role, particularly as failure relates in a positive sense to "optimal frustration" of the child's narcissistic needs. Optimal frustration as a necessary and good condition may result from brief delays in a parent's empathic response, the parent's "mild deviation" from the "beneficial norm" of the parent-child relationship, or in the discrepancy between experiences of the relationship and actual satisfaction of needs. Kohut distinguishes traumatic from optimal frustration as difference in degree, the difference between one parent's harsh "NO!" and another's kindly "no" — or between an "uncompromising prohibition" and the offering of "acceptable substitutes for the forbidden object or activity." Optimal frustration is founded on a loving attitude rather than counteraggression.[28] Useful, nontraumatic disappointments lead to internalizations of the idealized parent imago. As optimal, they promote reality reckoning. They promote consolidation of the self: the building of self-confidence and self-esteem, the establishment of values and bases of morality, discovery of means for handling life's irritations through positive and nondefensive behavior, and "acquisition of responses that are in harmony with the fact that the world contains real enemies, i.e., other selves whose narcissistic requirements run counter to the survival of one's own self."[29]

Winnicott's view is firm that "incomplete adaptation to need makes objects real." If adaptation is too close to need or is "continued too long" and "not allowed its natural decrease," it "resembles magic," and perfect parents are no better than hallucinations. But first — in the beginning — there must be nearly exact maternal adaptation, to make it possible for the infant "to develop a capacity to experience a relationship to external reality, or even to form a conception of external reality." In other words, a mother must give the infant opportunity for *illusion* — omnipotence in fusion with her — before she can succeed in her next great task, *disillusioning* her infant. Experiencing illusionment and disillusionment is necessary preparation for facing later restraints in living,[30] including those of rhetorical interaction. Indeed, no human being is ever free from the work of dealing with inner and outer reality — of countering forces of dependence, fusion, and invitations to unpromising narcissistic attachment.

As we shall come to see more clearly, establishment of structures for rhetorical success is linked to the quality of the child's early environment.

MIRRORING

Out of the eventful dialogue of mother and infant are produced elements of meaning that have significance for all events in the years of life ahead, especially those that are rhetorical. Extremely consequential in the growth process is *mirroring* in which infants experience a sense of their own being through their caregivers' presence. Through contact with others, they start to become what they will be. Among the first to determine that the self is developed in the process of social experience were Charles Horton Cooley and George Herbert Mead.[31] Others have extended and adapted their conclusions, using them in their own work. For example, as phrased by Arnold H. Modell, "the child's cohesive sense of self is forged through the affective bond that is formed when the mother gazes at the child's face, reflecting the child's affects." Thus a mother mirrors back information to the infant on the infant's emotional state, and gives information on her own as well, setting the foundations of empathy.[32]

Heinz Lichtenstein specifically includes in this critical proceeding the sensory elements of touch, smell, and other primitive sensations that constitute a mirror of dimly emerging "outlines of the child's own image as reflected by the mother's unconscious needs with regard to the child." Out of the child's infinite potentialities is actualized "one way of being, in the child, namely being the child for this particular mother, responding to her unique and individual needs." Thus is reflected back to the child a vision of his or her own presence.[33] Far from innocent, a mother acts from personal interest; while following her will, she "tells" her child about itself and herself. The infant is thereby served, as used by a caregiver's exercise of will.

As Lichtenstein would put it, the "organizational principle" for developmental differentiation is set in this interaction. In relating with adults, the infant receives an identity theme which in life is developed into "an infinite variety of identity transformations, as a simple musical theme is developed into a symphony." But the development is reversible, for in life

one achieves and maintains a sense of identity not by "pure reflective mirroring" but by "the capacity to select types of actions which will bring a
corresponding reaction from the other."[34] Such a perspective suggests profound rhetorical implications, e.g., as regards requirements of self-esteem
in relating satisfactorily to others and uses of personal identity in effecting
identification with others.

Mirroring is a consequence, the incidental, unsought result — the precious byproduct — of the parent's harkening to the child's and the parent's
own mundane importunation. In active answer to the child's demand, the
parent makes a presence allowing the infant to experience self-identification
not only through physical self-exploration but also through social and
psychological interaction with the parent.

That special self of the parent, as the parent attends to the infant, is
a sender and receiver of persuasive messages. Needless to say, the tone and
texture of the messages as transmitted and interpreted by both parties depend on all that the parent has become and wants now, as well as the infant's peculiar inclinations and immediate needs. The mirroring occurring
out of the transactions of one unique pair will be of messages different
from those of another unique pair. Great variance exists in behavior of
infants and others — in their asking and answering. Indeed, for one child
to ask little from a parent may be to receive little; for another child, it
may be to motivate intense response. Notwithstanding the seeming
paradoxes and unexpected content of messages transmitted, many clues
on an infant's formation of self and development of characteristic behaviors
are to be found in observation of the dialogue of these two goal-oriented
agents, and specifically in the rhetorical dynamics featured in the mirroring process.

One more environmental dimension must be added. Although the
primary caregiver's influence is critical, that person may not be acting alone
in affecting the child. Anyone's effectiveness can be reduced or increased
by a third party's presence. Schaffer reports that "mother and father do
not impinge on the child separately, with additive effects, but have a combined influence to which the child responds." As in other rhetorical scenes,
the nature and effect of one person's care may be altered in the presence
of others, e.g., it has been found that parental touching of the baby will
be lessened when both parents are present.[35]

Affect Attunement

Stern provides a fascinating discussion on a particular critical dimension
of mirroring in the dialogue. In exploring intersubjectivity — the sharing
and affecting of subjective experience that characterizes the infant-caregiver
relationship — he finds a new term — "affect attunement" — to name a spe-

cific process in their relating. Though seeming to be like parental imitat-
ing of the child's behavior, affect attunement is a distinct, more advanced
mode of connecting. When the infant is about nine months old, the caregiver occasionally is constrained to move beyond mere imitation and into
an affective *matching* of personal behavior with the infant's. The result
is a motivated, concordant sharing of the quality of feeling that is manifested by the child. One of Stern's examples is a nine-month-old girl who

> becomes very excited about a toy and reaches for it. As she grabs
> it, she lets out an exuberant "aaaah!" and looks at her mother.
> Her mother looks back, scrunches up her shoulders, and performs
> a terrific shimmy with her upper body, like a go-go dancer. The
> shimmy lasts only about as long as her daughter's "aaaah!" but
> is equally excited, joyful, and intense.[36]

Whether imbedded in other actions or standing alone, attunements
are interpersonal communion — a state of "feeling-connectedness," of "being with,"[37] perhaps on the order of unions that a rhetorician might perceive
in Burkeian and idealistic terms as exceptional consubstantiality. Though
possibly a common event in lives of good enough caregivers and their infants, an attunement serves as a key reinforcer and validator of an infant's
feeling states. At this point, a rhetorician must speculate that adequacy
of affect tuning in infancy may very well be a major predictor of satisfaction in achievement of identification with others later in life.

Of course, parents are selective in their attunements, as in all behaviors.
It is this selectivity of parental behavior, that gives special significance to
the process. Through selective attunement, parents possess great power in
shaping a child's subjective and interpersonal life. In that process, parental behavior "tells" the child which subjective experiences of the parent
are to be shared, and which are out of bounds and unacceptable. Thus
in their selective attunements, parents "create corresponding intrapsychic
experiences in the child. It is in this way that parents' desires, fears, pro-
hibitions, and fantasies contour the psychic experiences of the child." Just
by "being themselves, parents inevitably exert some degree of selective bias
in their attunement behaviors." Acting together, parent and child form
"characteristic patterns that may last a lifetime."[38] A father's self-needs
may work to direct his daughter toward development of a sense of right
and wrong or an interest in liberal social causes or communication ap-
prehension, etc.

In a large and vital measure, the good enough environment is a function of good enough attunements. And in such a rhetorical climate is the
formation of adequate rhetorical structures favored.

A RHETORICAL IMPERATIVE

Central in the mirroring process is the act of the caregiver making a peculiar presence in reaction to the infant's expressed need; the infant's existence and importunate demands give rise to the caregiver's functions. With this understanding, the story of first motives begins. Next to be acknowledged is the influence of the most basic force of all: survival. Current theory finds a critical link between the infant's mechanisms for survival and the earliest social activity. Staying alive depends on human association. And it is that association which provides the ground for discovery, practice, and development of social behaviors — behaviors which eventually evolve as agencies of rhetorical interaction. In clarifying this essential biological-social link, Schaffer tells how the infant, by means of the rooting response discovers an object of stimulation (usually the nipple) and turns naturally and automatically to it whenever his or her cheek is touched. Also vital are such innate responses as sucking and swallowing. Other behaviors are less specific in purpose, e.g., crying and smiling, but they do serve to secure the caregiver's attention and to influence continued interest in the child. The compelling stimuli of these social systems work to make caregivers available and ready to initiate interaction with the infant. Rooting, smiling, crying, and sucking — all function to protect the young, and all lead to the promotion and maintenance of proximity with caregivers. They are genetically biased attachment behaviors, set patterns of action that are activated by stimulation.[39] Without success as a stimulator — as an instigator of response — the infant will not prosper.

The little one, then, arrives with means of getting on as an agent acting on others: to assure being seen, heard, and attended to. More than merely available for excitement, the normal infant is endowed with the purpose of creating it. Observed as vocalizations and bodily movements, the baby's assorted kinds of persuasive conduct represent an ulterior motive of survival. That is the prime issue. As days become weeks, patterns are formed which lend predictability to the infant's behavior and help facilitate an enmeshing of infant and parent behavior. These ingrained patterns are revealed in the specific ways that infants stimulate caregivers. In turn, the caregivers, in their sensitivity to stimulation by the infant, make response. But success in this cooperative enterprise depends on the participants responding *appropriately* to each other.[40] As communication theorists would put it, their critical interaction must provide mutual *confirmation*. When appropriate, the messages of both say "You exist" and "We are relating" and "To me, you are significant" and "Your way of experiencing your world is valid."[41] Needless to say, when one of the parties *disconfirms* the other, e.g., by denying the other's existence through a certain gesture or in any other way pronouncing the other as insignificant, the relationship is put in jeopardy and the infant's development is at risk. The crucial physical and psychological linkages are accomplished through intersubjectivity, and failures therein can result in social rupture. Maladaptive results are a topic of Chapter three.

Thus do biological constraints — survival needs — dictate social performance and set off the beginnings of the socialization process.

Thus do biological inevitability and social necessity serve as foundations of the *rhetorical imperative*: the great quest for representation of self through symbolic interaction with others. To *be with* others — identified with and affectively tuned — and through others to receive evidence of one's being and personal power is an irrepressible and constant goal. The basic urgency of the self to be confirmed — the absolute need to unite with other living beings — to touch, engage and merge — this phenomenal force in everyone's life, is in evidence from the beginning. The required transactions with others become sustained by rudimentary forms of *speech*: speech — rhetorical interaction — the prime medium of "individual human mental growth and the essential ingredient of civilised society," as Colwyn Trevarthen, authority on infant growth, affirms.[42] In this process, the rhetorical imperative is made manifest: from biological mandate, to stimulation and social response, to pre-rhetorical gesture and pattern, to intentional acts of symbolic influence. Over time, development continues; rhetorical maturity increases, and the growing person comes to appreciate common social ends. If all goes well enough, this remarkable rhetorical force continues to motivate productive interaction in all eras of an individual's life, thereby assuring maintenance of the self and continuation of society.

COGNITIVE AND BEHAVIORAL GROWTH

It is assumed that given normal promise and adequate environment, an infant will grow satisfactorily. Important cognitive structures, e.g., learnings, when internalized, come to represent the infant's total being and are vital to its future successful functioning. Involved in continual social interaction, the infant gains enormous knowledge and many forms of understanding, becoming an intellectual creature and more cognitive than sensory in orientation. The infant learns elements of problem solving, invents and tests hypotheses, and acquires powers of prediction and ideas of contingency, i.e., in anticipating the future and comprehending that one action leads to another.[43] All of these behaviors and acquisitions are related to rhetorical functions.

Flourishing in an adequate environment, in mutually beneficial interaction, the infant is helped to consider new behaviors and expand its outlook. Extremely significant in growth is visual interplay and freedom in expression of scopophilic impulses, those relating to joy in looking. *Looking* without inhibition is basic to cognitive development and the formation of healthful behavioral patterns. David W. Allen writes persuasively on the connection of visual free play and growth: "Vision is the core part of perception and knowing. It affects our attitudes about power and curiosity and our attitudes about ourselves and others. It becomes a central organizing modality for other kinds of knowing. The way we see the world is the way we see ourselves, and the way we see ourselves is the way we see ourselves being seen."[44] Allowed to explore — visually and in all other useful ways — the infant is induced to remain intellectually open and responsive, to establish a conflict-free and active curiosity, and to come to a positive personal and social view.

OTHER RHETORICALLY RELATED COMPONENTS

Below is a list of rhetorically related elements built up in early infant development, some more cognitive than behavioral and vice versa. All have an emotional dimension, and none is exclusive of any other. As Yarrow reminds us in regard to infant competence, "cognitive, motivational, and social behaviors are inextricably linked." They depend on and influence each other. For example, "The capacity to make perceptual discriminations is basic to the discrimination of persons; memory and the development of object permanence are necessary for the development of trust in the mother; these same functions influence the capacity to distance oneself from objects and represent them symbolically."[45] All components that follow are elemental features of what will become a highly prized human resource: a rhetorical disposition.

Dialectical sense: As the good enough caregiver follows individual interests — and is unwilling to let the infant go his or her own way — and as the infant seeks to go that way, two strong persons engage and develop patterns of give-and-take that assume continuity. Dialectical behaviors for the future are founded in this way, as well as a related positive outlook on interaction.

Empathic sense: The capacity to participate in another's affective state — to feel it as another feels it — is a vital product of healthful social exchange.[46]

Significant progress toward individuation: The stage is set for the infant's becoming an autonomous, self-sufficient, independent being. Features of a distinct and accepted identity are formed. Paralleling a clear, separate sense of self is development of a sense of others as distinguished from oneself.[47]

Foundations of ideals and values: These important cognitive structures are the results of internalizing the idealized parent imago.[48]

A sense of power and effectiveness: Among developing sources of power are the infant's success in imposing an organization on his or her environment and in influencing others. Appropriate, consistent, well-timed maternal responses serve to confirm the infant's growing belief in being able to affect the environment.[49] A good enough mother will confirm and integrate the child's basic desires and impulses, cues, and incomplete actions, and by so doing will show "the child that he is alive and can have a positive effect on the object world."[50]

Strategies of influence: Enjoying social success, the infant discovers actions that will evoke corresponding reactions from another. Patterns of social behavior for coping with primary caregivers are developed and confirmed, e.g., roles of the communicator, including uses of joking, pleasing, and identifying with another. The infant becomes relatively expert in reading cues, signals, and other actions — and in discriminating among them. Persuasive behavior tried in the dialogue and found useful becomes available for future use and refinement.[51]

Roots of creative functioning: Along with curiosity, as mentioned above, and the investigative spirit and natural experimental tendencies that are cultivated, the infant learns ways of using frustration as a force for positive functioning. Enjoying success in his or her environment, the baby is reinforced in continuation of exploratory behavior and use of acquired skills.[52]

Grounds of self-esteem (sense of self-worth and value) and inner sense of security[53]

Body awareness and sense of personal vitality[54]

Acceptance of certain "realities of life": For example, the infant learns to tolerate delay and adapt to others' systems.[55]

Techniques for handling contingencies: Among such techniques are means of dealing with uncertainty and unpleasantness in the world.[56]

Recognition of differences among situations[57]

Codes of behavior, rules, conventions, and consequences of violation[58]

Potential for transfer of skills beyond the dialogue[59]

THE RHETORICAL DISPOSITION

The child's great adventure in rhetorical becoming is both critical and exciting. Among the rudimentary formations, as we have seen, are precepts and bases of rhetorical consciousness, knowledge, skills, understandings, and various learnings — all necessary to effectiveness in interaction with others. Through true empathic mirroring and idealization in the many instances of dialectical and interpersonal exchange — with myriad occasions of waiting and proceeding, asking and receiving, inviting and denying, infantile pretending-to-be and maternal accepting as-is, and other interactive behaviors of both parties—the infant takes on particular ways of being with others and makes preparations for a life of relating, of affecting and being affected. The process *and* end are rhetorical. On the point of quality in the process, it should be restated here that parents cannot be perfect. But let us go farther and acknowledge that all offspring will experience injury and inadequate levels of support, e.g., too little stimulation or confirmation. It is bound to happen, given human nature, peculiar parental fallibility, stress and pressures of living, etc. A result is the development of narcissism: *favorable* forms that arise from optimal frustration and beneficial disillusionment; and *unfavorable* forms that arise from an environment that in serious ways is abusive, neglectful, or overindulgent. While this topic will be explored thoroughly in Chapter three, it needs to be observed here that a rhetorical disposition is fostered by useful adversity—which produces favorable narcissism—and that unfavorable narcissism is a base of rhetorical indisposition.

What yield of benefits are of greater value to a child than the rhetorical? In their important essay, "Rhetorical Sensitivity and Social Interaction," Roderick P. Hart and Don M. Burks[60] lay out five characteristics of rhetorical sensitivity. The rhetorically sensitive person tries to accept roletaking as a part of life, tries to avoid counterproductive stylized language, is willing to adapt to existing conditions, seeks to distinguish between information that is useful and that which is not, and tries to understand that an idea may be rendered in a number of ways. In acquiring rhetorical sensitivity, those who have enjoyed a good start in life are favored.

To be added to rhetorical sensitivity are the following six groupings of rhetorical structures built up during the first year or so. These are major and momentous gains, which if held and advanced in subsequent formative years, will continue to mark the rhetorically disposed person.

Audience Consciousness (Other-Awareness). In traditional psychoanalytic terms, the growing infant seeks to maintain omnipotence through continuation of symbiotic fusion—*perfect identification*—with the mother.[61] But to whatever extent it operates, it is a *childish* notion, and not to be. In an environment that includes healthy people in healthful pursuit of their own goals, reality checks are provided. The infant comes to know how far to go: what behavior is acceptable and what is not.

In developing an awareness of others' responses and a sensitivity to their intentions and feelings, the infant acquires the capacity to anticipate their behavior. Thus the infant becomes a predicting and adapting creature, one who from extensive experience in turn taking and mutual cuing learns accommodation, reciprocity, and ease in visual, vocal, and physical contact. "How we experience ourselves in relation to others provides a basic organizing perspective for all interpersonal events."[62]

Readiness for Consubstantiality. Between the seventh and ninth months, infants discover that they have minds and that others have their separate minds. "Only when infants can sense that others distinct from themselves can hold or entertain a mental state that is similar to one they sense themselves to be holding is the sharing of subjective experience or inter-subjectivity possible." The process may be something like "what is going on in my mind may be similar enough to what is going on in your mind that we can somehow communicate this (without words) and thereby experience intersubjectivity." This kind of experience depends on the sharing of a "framework of meaning" and modes of communication, e.g., gesture, posture, or facial expression. With the shift from regulation by another person to the sharing and influencing of each other's subjective experience,[63] a big step in rhetorical development is taken. Parenthetically, it is impossible to resist repeating Kenneth Burke's "simplest case of persuasion" which occurs when you talk another's language "by speech, gesture, tonality, order, image, attitude, idea, *identifying* your way with his."[64]

And so it is that from promising beginnings—the crucial social training of good mirroring and modeling—the infant sets the ground for finding kinship with humanity. Early on, the infant knows a need for others' warmth and caring, and not long thereafter of others' needs of responses in return. Thus, bonds are made. Healthful attachments in infancy increase the probability of healthful attachments in later years, with family, friends, and other "audiences." Satisfying experience in consubstantiality foretells realization of the same throughout life. The secure infant enjoys the prospect of coming to be at home with future audiences as an assured, tolerant, trusting and credible, self-caring, empathic, alert, and effective individual.

Situation Awareness. The baby learns early of the propriety and relative usefulness of certain modes of action as called for by circumstance. With recurrence, specific scenes or predicaments become catalogued as situations. Awareness of situational demand leads to differentiation among the classification of constraints, and one might project, to beginnings of a sense of genré. One game or type of behaving might be appropriate at a given time but not at others. Certain rules of conduct will be seen as obligatory under given conditions. Thus many constraining and diverse experiences with others result in an emerging understanding of convention and distinction of occasion. Through learning—repetition, reinforcement, confirmation, increasingly greater social perception—infants acquire sensitivity to binding and changing circumstance. In this manner do they prepare to function rhetorically, with flexibility and sophistication, outside the parent-infant unit.

Inventional Capacity. While receiving encouragement and support of natural curiosity, the infant builds up a capacity for rhetorical discovery, a fundamental resource in speaking to others and relating. When ready and daring enough to move away from the caregiver's immediate holding, the child steadily expands personal horizons in energetic exploration. Not only are breadth and new perspectives added, but also faith in processes of inquiry. Secure and imaginative in questing, the new one is primed to be the intelligent and vigorous investigator, and with sufficient and confirmed experience, the role is fixed.

Under the influence of beneficial environmental factors that serve as organizers of their minds, infants advance basic processes of thinking which are essential to reaching rhetorical goals. They have their first lessons in objectivity, as they make tries at distancing themselves from others. By one year of age infants have enough practical rhetorical experience to equip themselves with rudiments of deductive and inductive reasoning. In addition, they discover causation, elements of which have been facts of life in all interactions since the earliest days.

Vicissitudes of the dialogue also provide for formation of beliefs, ideals, and values: the stuff of strength in living, the major premises of rhetorical exchange. Babies build a stock of reliable ideas and premises, holding to what is useful and good for them — and also sensing others' conceptions of the good: values. Quite obviously, infants — from the beginning, at the onset of social life — start to shape and store functional *topoi* and roles. Once acquired, these are available for use in continued discovery and effective interaction.

Sense of Personal Power. Healthy babies enjoy awareness and acceptance of self. They appreciate both their uniqueness and relation to others. Their state of well-being offers the promise of becoming persons with lasting respect for personal freedoms, dignity, worth, and responsibility. They have reason to expect resilience in relations with others and the ability to predict possibilities therein. They become conscious of personal intent and purpose, while discovering that they can affect the immediate environment. They begin to perceive that their acts carry information and can be called up for use with others in achieving rhetorical ends.

One extremely vital power developed in the early dialogues is as respondent. The optimally frustrated infant begins to acquire the skills and strength not only for listening and attending but also for usefully denying others' unrealistic or egocentric behavior. Given a well-internalized sense of self and associated values — evidenced in what others may preceive as reliability, confidence, good humor, courage, congruence and consistency, etc. — the infant has opportunity to become a receptive and confirming audience who while sensitive to available cues and whole meaning, sets fair limits on others' behavior. Adequate growth outfits the child with the potential of usefully representing reality to others, while interacting successfully with others. Reliable mirroring is a mark of the *good audience*[65] and an admirable attribute of ethos. Taking great steps toward independence, the infant reaches phase-expected rhetorical maturity, daring to foreswear innocence and inexpedient protection, becoming an influential, self-assured individual.

Functions of Rhetoric. As recipient of extensive training, the little one learns rhetorical strategy: ways of effectively influencing others. Skill in the use of fundamental symbolic behaviors is developed, e.g., in starting, maintaining, and terminating interaction, not to mention the many varieties of each and styles in representation. One sign of rhetorical promise is role development. When confirmed in experimental tries, the infant masters roles to suit various ends and is caused to face and solve essential rhetorical problems: to make decisions relating to time, place, topic, and audience, etc. The new rhetor finds competence in using humor, defending and supporting premises, along with innumerable ways of coping with contingencies. The infant learns the value and uses of order: the security of structure, effects of sequencing events or actions, priorities and placement.

In the first year a memory is acquired. Indeed, between the second and seventh months, infants become able to recall certain of their motor experiences, perceptions, and affective experiences. Stern notes that they can perform acts of cued memory recall as early as the third month and that their memories serve significantly to integrate elements of the developing self.[66]

In good growth, the infant builds a self that is prepared to resolve a classic, ever-existent issue of rhetorical interaction: self-disclosure. At a point in life — not in early infancy — each human becomes aware of two opposing forces operating. On the one side is the necessity to show feelings and beliefs, etc.: consubstantiality depends on it. On the other side is the fact of risk and the need to protect the self against injurious disconfirmation. Normal children who enjoy a supportive environment come to accept this perilous part of life and to resolve the problem in each new situation. They set down foundations of prudence — and courage — and start to shape guidelines for decisions on making an effective presence to others and using rhetorical opportunity, while aware of the hazards involved in relating.

Early in the second year, the sense of verbal self forms, as language acquisition advances. Functioning alertly in dialogue, the infant observes symbolic patterns of others and employs skills of imitation, while furnishing a repertoire of gesture, vocal intonation, facial expression, verbal expression, etc. Clarity, precision, and directness in uses of verbal and nonverbal symbols bespeak the baby's development as a social, responsive, and purposeful individual.

IN A WORD

Linked to the human survival mechanism, the rhetorical imperative is a necessary outgrowth of the infant's innate social responsiveness. From the earliest moments of life, the infant seeks sensory stimulation, in quest of food and comfort. First in evidence as primitive motive, the incipient imperative appears in all periods of growth. But it is after the time of archaic, "prerhetorical" behaviors — and development of intentionality — that life-sustaining social expression becomes manifest in unmistakable rhetorical terms. We see suasory behavior as arising patently from an imperative: an urgent requirement of the self to be with others and purposefully influence them.

Existing at one time as no more than generic social power, the rhetorical imperative becomes particularlized in accord with the infant's discovering each new contingency. Interacting in a healthful setting as all goes well, the normal infant will grow steadily, while becoming increasingly sophisticated in inventing and refining strategies that are essential to experiencing effectiveness with others.

Thus is the rhetorical disposition established — and continuation of human culture assured.

3
Rhetorical Indisposition[1]

USES OF ADVERSITY

Impelled at the outset of life by the biologically linked and socially mandated rhetorical imperative, infants interact with others. That is their necessary business. Closely involved with people of needs and various degrees of mental health and interpersonal sensitivity, these new humans must learn to deal with behaviors of all intent and tone, some of which contribute to productive mirroring and optimal attunement and some of which are disruptive. Whether influenced by satisfactory or poor environmental conditions, the urgency to thrive motivates. And infants acquire coping strategies, some good and some bad. To be sure, all environments are imperfect, and emotional stress is known to all babies — including the most fortunate, whose parents consistently seem to make ideal responses to their young ones' expressions of the rhetorical imperative. Given the fact that parents are fallible, mismatchings and mistakes are certain to happen. Rhetorical implications are vital.

Adversity experienced in the dialogue contributes to narcissistic injury and loss. As a sense of self and awareness of the constraining presence of others form in critical daily interaction, so does vulnerability increase, from which frustrations and disillusionments follow. Adding great energy to the basic rhetorical motivation, then, is the pressing need arising out of unhappy experience: the demand of self to meet the "damage" sustained interpersonally along the way. While these deficits and hurts are necessary and normal, the infant's unwitting goal is to make up for them. Out of flawed mirroring occurs invention of means for meeting losses and functioning. Enter the *force of narcissism*. It is in the attempt at restitution — to restore the self and preserve self-esteem — that narcissism is manifest, throughout life.[2]

A Narcissistic Continuum

Narcissism — the great force of self — is a relative term. All persons are "narcissistic," for all have known early discontent and pain; all come to possess a self to care for and in which to invest interest. It is principally in response to urgings of a needy self by which humans become creative, compete usefully, work productively, and interact successfully—and by which they suffer impairment of these same processes. Narcissism is favorable or detrimental, depending on the direction and character of its force. It "may promote growth" or "support regression."[3] Violence and racism, philanthrophy and martyrdom, magnanimity and meanness—all flow from the narcissistic well. The lives and deeds of few, if any, historical figures will be understood adequately without acknowledgment of the energy of their narcissism at work. Among notable examples are Winston Churchill and his leadership, Martin Luther and his reforms, Eugene O'Neill and his plays—and the acts of Adolf Hitler. Let us add to the list the names of any or all of us, as we review sources of our personal power or reasons for our successes and failures. Human endeavor, whether grand in design or ordinary, is fueled by the unrelenting need to maintain and reaffirm the self, to certify worth.

Favorable narcissism mobilizes behavior to beneficial purpose and is represented by normal self-concern and an adequate level of self-esteem: productive pride, we might call it. Persons supported by a healthy ego are socially responsible and rhetorically aware: able and free to involve themselves in interactions of daily living, maturely accepting and prudently revealing attributes of a well-regarded self and making other appropriate and strategic choices in relating to others. They respect the rhetorical process and know its risks, recognize demands of time and place, and remain relatively free of distracting defense behaviors. Theirs is useful or "good" narcissism.[4] Unfavorable narcissism, a major topic of this chapter, leads to rhetorical indisposition of one form or another.

NOT GOOD ENOUGH

Narcissistic problems can arise in infant development when all does not go well enough in the interpersonal relationship with the caregiver. It is the early dialogue and critical mirroring process to which we should look first in tracing beginnings of functional difficulty, including rhetorical dysfunction.

Stimulation

In infant growth, intensity of stimulation is a highly significant variable. Appropriate degrees are fundamental to development of a rhetorical disposition, in that they promote sound exploratory and social engagement behaviors. When levels of arousal are suitable, roots of industry and initiative grow, and children are able to discover that they have some control over their world. Further, to succeed in the all-important process of taking in

INTERRELATEDNESS OF
POWERS AT WORK IN RHETORICAL DEVELOPMENT
The First Year or Two

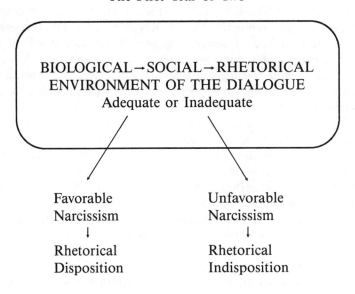

BIOLOGICAL → SOCIAL → RHETORICAL
ENVIRONMENT OF THE DIALOGUE
Adequate or Inadequate

Favorable	Unfavorable
Narcissism	Narcissism
↓	↓
Rhetorical	Rhetorical
Disposition	Indisposition

Fig. 1 Biological necessity constrains social performance; from social urgency, the rhetorical imperative facilitates participation in the dialogue in development of the self; interaction in that environment yields a unique self, the character of which is revealed in its narcissism; adequacy in the environment is predictive of favorable narcissim and rhetorical disposition, while inadequacy is predictive of unfavorable narcissism and rhetorical indisposition.

information, babies must be neither too lethargic nor too tense.[5] (See Chapter five for discussion of effects of stimulation patterns on Jim Jones' development.) Thus, too little or too much stimulation are basic determinants of rhetorical dysfunction.

Understimulation is insufficient excitement: the level of intensity and affect falls below an optimal point, e.g., when a mother in depression is unable to muster the energy or brightness sufficient to excite the child and thereby promote interaction. Understimulation may result from caregiver lethargy, inhibition, fear of denial by the infant, or a limited repertoire of interactive strategies. In any event, the infant's needs for stimulation from others are neglected. The consequences of understimulation are possible misregulation and disruption of the socialization process.[6] In turn, rhetorical growth is stunted. It must be remembered, too, that misregulation may stem from infant passivity, for caregivers also need stimulation to do their part. Each must motivate the other. It is a matter of simple reciprocity: if unaffected by the infant and perhaps feeling incompetent and rejected, caregivers will not reach an excitement level that is necessary to elicit responses from the infant. Understimulated, with unmet self needs, the infant comes to feel powerless, isolated, or unincluded and then may — in narcissistic protectiveness — give up on involvement in rhetorical activity, thereby missing out on opportunity for growth, including rhetorical development.

Overstimulation, such as insistent, intrusive behavior and forms of excessive control, also leads to maladaptation. A mother who in lively interaction attempts to meet her child's distress by sharply escalating the intensity of her presentations risks adding to the distress. Another instance is the parent's ignoring the infant's averted gaze that signals a need to terminate the interaction. In such cases the infant is deprived of the chance of making a choice and experiencing effectiveness. When these moments become chronic, the infant may learn, Daniel N. Stern observes, "either that his facial displays of emotion are not relevant communicative events to change the world or, worse, that they are, but will make matters worse." Without information on success — without confirmation, the infant will stop trying. Mismatching of behavior as a result of unpredictability and overenthusiastic maternal behavior intrudes upon development of self-regulating processes. If babies are not able to succeed in regulation by tuning out the excessive behavior and establishing comfortable distance, they may need to resort to a self-protective strategy such as going limp.[7] One consequence of mismatching is life-long reliance on others in regulation of well-being — and rage, as an outgrowth of that.[8] As we shall see, such dependence and narcissistic defensiveness reduce rhetorical productivity.

Predictable, confident, caring, and active mirroring behavior by the primary caregivers gives promise of adequate social and cognitive growth in normal infants: a wholesome sense of self, i.e., useful narcissism. On the other hand, insecurities and other narcissistic deficiencies of caregivers may yield related symptoms of unhealth in their children: an uncertain sense of self, i.e., unfavorable narcissism. Competency in the mirroring role is required in the establishment of self-assurance and realization of personal worth. The healthy and empathic parent, while participating as a target for idealization — albeit unwittingly — promotes cohesion of self and social responsiveness. Insensitivity in attunement and other miscarriages in mirroring, as discussed in Chapter two, can lead to arrested development and aberrations of many sorts: malformations of values, ideals, identity, and views on life.[9]

A Functional Self and the False Self

A healthy, functional self results from parental adequacy in illusioning and disillusioning, as Donald W. Winnicott observed.[10] In appropriate illusioning, the parent encourages and supports the child's uniqueness and individuality, confirming grandiosity; in appropriate disillusioning, the parent provides reality checks, fostering internalization of social norms and disconfirming the infant in unrealistic expectations. The expected result of adequate parental influence is an integrated, self-respecting person who accepts others and is prepared for necessary social adaptation. The self is strong: the quality of narcissism is healthy and favorable. In this sense, a socially constrained self is an essential feature of the mature, rhetorically disposed person; it represents a happy compromise between sought omnipotence and social requirement. It is a good adjustment, for a certain holding back of feelings or minor denial of needs of the self will serve both personal and social ends. Thus the functional self is adaptive, truly a *rhetorical* self, one continually engaged in discovery and use of means needed in getting on satisfactorily with others.

Now to the unhappy eventuality: the ill-conditioned false self. Herein are found origins of unfavorable narcissism. Caregivers whose behaviors with infants are characterized by neglect, overcontrol, or abuse, etc., are deficient in creation of an environment that is needed for acquisition of a wholesome sense of self; they are inadequate providers of reliable models for sound idealizations and ethical awareness. Consequently, their children often suffer in rhetorical development. Under the meanness of their narcissistic motivation, they make a presence that may be too close to their children or too distant; these caregivers are too frightened, or too preoccupied, or too bewildered.

Parents who themselves were deprived of adequate mirroring in infancy, often seek it through their children. In so doing, they reverse roles of the relationship, using the infant for *their own* needs in mirroring, rather than allowing themselves to be used advantageously by the infant. When exploited in this way, infants may come to realize that expressions of their needs are not welcome; consequently, they learn to suppress or conceal them immoderately, yielding to parental power. It was in studying this condition that Winnicott conceived of inadequate mothering — and the opposite the "good enough mother." Caregivers who are not good enough are "not able to implement the infant's omnipotence." They repeatedly fail to "meet the infant gesture" and instead substitute their own gesture "which is to be given sense by the compliance of the infant." Winnicott called this the earliest stage of the false self: *the self represented by the child's attempt to be who the parent needs him or her to be.*[11]

With claim to the "real self" repudiated, the rejected, vulnerable child will make a role adaptation, foregoing fundamental self-interest "in order to hold onto the mother. Living up to her idealized expectations and ministering to her narcissistic needs, he denies and loses himself."[12] Consequently, an overly conforming, unhealthy self develops. A child so used must keep up, at great personal cost, an elaborate system of self-representation. When ruled by these oppressive, self-imposed requirements on how to relate to others, the child becomes a desperate, excessively accommodative — but resentful — rhetor, striving to avoid disapproval and scorn, wanting to be somebody, knowing that the only way of getting on is through assiduous perfection of means to justify the self.

OPPRESSIVE NARCISSISM AND RHETORICAL DYSFUNCTION

Unfavorable expressions of the false self appear widely in life. Examples are in physical violence, disregard for person or property, greed, intolerance and bigotry, waste of natural resources, and neglect of the elderly. When ruled by baneful narcissism, people occupy themselves in supreme self-interest — determinedly in quest of support and approval, maintenance of pride, avoidance of liability, achievement of certainty and absolute security, etc. But they do not find much real satisfaction in the pursuit, for their needs are difficult to meet. Many are given to vivid imaginings of grandeur, remaining dependent and vulnerable, suffering severely from criticism and slight. While symptoms of unfavorable narcissism vary from person to person, the following are common: depression, inordinate fear of change, feelings of emptiness, lack of empathy, inappropriate aggression, rigidity, delinquency, promiscuity, humorlessness, moodiness, feelings of not belonging, lying, hypochondria, and deficiency in genuine feelings of sadness and longing. Though their need for being loved is keen, the poorly adapted person's ability to care and love may be limited, if existent.[13]

Quite clearly, whether in greater or lesser degree, and whether constant or of the moment, unhealthful narcissistic influences are likely to have negative impact on rhetorical processes. Disturbances can be classified as cognitive, perceptual, and behavioral.

Cognitive Disturbances

Burdensome narcissism may lead to limitation in cognitive exploration and capricious reaction to challenges of discovery. Effects vary from person to person, and what one individual may experience as an occasional episode, another endures without relief.

The Spirit and Process of Discovery. In watching a happy child seek information, e.g., in pulling a flower apart piece-by-piece or manipulating a nest of boxes, one is reminded that discovery is a common human function. The process of looking, asking, examining — and finding — continues through life, whether centered on mechanical concepts, aesthetic design, political ideology, religious precepts, or other interest. Such mental activity contributes to well-being — and perhaps is dependent on it. The rhetorical relevance is profound, as we shall see. Unfortunately, the process of discovery is circumscribed in the lives of many people. Persons of an unfavorable narcissistic inclination are constricted in explorations and inconsistent in reaction to the challenge of discovery. Indisposed to spend resources in seeking out, alienated from pursuits of inquiry, they lack what Thomas Hobbes called "lust of the mind," to know how and why.

The condition may be observed as deficiency in creativity and mental vigor, incapacity to initiate and carry out inventive activity, as well as failure in appreciation of the past. In some instances, the spirit of exploration is erratic, "on-and-off," highly individual and selective. What appears as apathy, low motivation, weak self-discipline, enervation, or disinterest in learning, can be explained as the working of overwhelming naricissism, the kind that narrows self-sufficiency and blocks productiveness.

The mind of a person when narcissistically withdrawn responds primarily to stimuli of self-relevance. When "fundamentally uninterested in others," attests Janet Karsten Larson, "he lacks the spring of genuine intellectual curiosity."[14] This is a parochial mentality. In Jurgen Reusch's words, "That which happens in the body, inside of people, or inside of an organization is more understandable to such a person than that which happens outside of his organism or outside of his organization."[15] Among other symptoms are diminished listening and reading abilities or other skills of learning, impatience in learning, heedlessness, poor concentration, and peculiar responses to information.[16]

Also prominent in serious cases is an extraordinary need of support and nourishment, the inability to acquire for themselves, along with the expectation that others will supply them and do things for them. Many experience depression, a disorder that contributes greatly to their mental straits, bringing on intellectual lethargy and sluggishness. Sufferers block out material that is external to them or find themselves unable to muster the mind for productive activity.[17] Depression, Gregory Rochlin explains with Freud's words, forces "abrogation of interest in the outside world" and "inhibition of all activity."[18]

Since processes of discovery may shut down when depression sets in, the topic has epistemological relevance: when one's self becomes one's principal burden, to know oneself becomes "an end, instead of a means through which one knows the world."[19] Self-absorption creates a tight personal realm; it resists exterior stimulation and cripples inquiry. In personalizing information, people make *themselves* the necessary subjects of the textbooks and novels that they read, as well as the plays, Gothic cathedrals, athletic contests, and other objects they encounter. Though extraordinarily dependent on another person's beliefs or attitudes, many cannot know the beliefs or attitudes *as known by that person*. Instead, their cognition is subjective and insensitive.

When narcissistic self-censoring, insecurity, depression, deflation, and other personality features work to diminish useful mental engagement with others, information from outside objects becomes either useless or unavailable. While probable that few of the affected truly recognize the extent of their solipsism — the belief that the self is the only thing that exists and can only know itself — it is the philosophy defining their spirit and mental operations in discovery. And it defines their corresponding rhetorical activity.

Rhetorical Implications

Certain rhetorical implications seem obvious, for effectiveness in rhetorical interaction is dependent on discovery, on invention of useful material: the mental activity of locating reasons and arguments, thoughts and feelings, ideas and facts. Among the sources of content is the individual's own mind, available as both store and generator of material. Minds of others contribute to discovery and development through direct contact and indirectly as their products are acquired in print or oral form. Impairment of these functions may be reflected in outcome.

The central influencing element in the inventional process is the audience — the other. Practical theory holds that selection of content should be made with the other person in mind, i.e., in "consultation" with the eventual receiver(s) of the message. Rhetorical success — and health — require a kind of dialogue with others: engaging them and coming to know the stuff of their independent minds. This act involves the rhetor in risking contact with unfamiliar thought and testing it against favored personal thought. Daring a comparative analysis or challenge of one's long-held and ingrained ideas may indeed require real courage, a rhetorical virtue to be respected. But courage is not a common characteristic of those oppressed by narcissism.[20]

Adequate invention in the rhetorical act calls for a certain vigor and spirit, qualities that some persons are unable to bring to bear with regularity. Mental emptiness, lack of direction, narcissistic ennui or "funk" — all associated with depression — are hindrances to rhetorical effectiveness. In "down" periods, judgment powers are curbed or impaired; choicemaking is unreliable. Such rhetorical demands as purposefulness, perspicuity, appropriate organization, and careful screening of ideas are not met consistently by depressed individuals. Moreover in depression, people forego rhetorical opportunity, misjudge constraints of audience and occasion, and neglect other requirements in preparation. When the malaise is upon them, productive cerebration and active invention may be seriously limited. Not uncommon is the plight of a forty-year-old, intelligent, depressed, and indecisive psychiatric client named Linda who, although professionally successful, eventually came to feel overwhelmed and defeated by seemingly unresolvable goal conflicts and a life that she concluded was going nowhere.[21] She is one of those who sometimes finds rhetorical chores "too much." "What's the use?" they ask. "What's worthwhile in life?"

Relatedly, discovery of the means of functioning effectively with others calls for independence and willingness of participants to "move out on their own," to rely on themselves in quest of answers and perspectives. It calls for a sense of future and a positive attitude toward planning events and making preparations to influence events.

Rhetorical success requires motivation not only to seek and engage but also to test and weigh the bits of potential content that turn up. Patently, this entails looking outside of the self, recognizing and transcending the oppressiveness of the mirror of self. Those who see only themselves in others find only themselves — and talk only to themselves. The iron rule of unfavorable narcissism enforces fixation on the model of self — the provincial mind — and an inability to value and utilize precious available information. When indisposed to make contact with the world, to chance challenge of their personal cognitive selves, people know little of it. They are rhetorically disabled.

Cases of inventional incapacity may be classic or quite common. Literature provides relevant examples. One is the alienated, brooding, irresolute, and ineffective Hamlet who was unable to discover a solution to his predicament and "introduce organization and control over his life."[22] Another is Paul Morel of D. H. Lawrence's *Sons and Lovers* whose spirit became passive and empty, precluding discovery of adult ways of being effective with others. Paul's predicament is treated fully in Chapter seven.

Primary process thinking. Infantile ideation that appears in daily communication of adults has been a subject of interest to psychoanalysts since Freud. It is characterized as regression, childish return to the earliest — the most primitive — patterns of mental activity, those marked by contradictions, absence of logical thought, and strange or aberrant connection of ideas. In primary process thinking, reports Gregory Rochlin, individuals rely on "childish principles of causality" and "resort to magical thinking and wishing." This infantile turn of mind is a cognitive liability, sometimes appearing as pining away or doubting, and becomes in Freud's words, "the prototype of all later intellectual work directed toward the solution of problems."[23] It can appear as fantasy. In the narcissistic mentality of Lawrence's character Paul Morel is a strong pull to retreat from the real world: of some-day living with his mother in a cozy cottage — just the two of them, alone (see Chapter seven).

Primary process thinking may show up as incapacity to know one's mental state. Affected persons "often do not know when they are angry, frightened, or unhappy," Joyce McDougall finds. As dependent individuals they are unable to assess themselves and their condition. And factors such as others' individuality, the "impossibility of magic fulfillment of wishes," and "the inevitability of death" do not have meaning.[24] When the self is under threat, as it is in the burdensome narcissistic state, use of reason may be replaced by the world of magic. Such can happen at any point in life — when rational thinking reaches "its bounds in failing to provide gratification that is sought for wishes that narcissism requires." Regardless of one's level of intelligence and reasoning powers, the archaic — primary process — system is never relinquished entirely.[25]

Rhetorical Implications

In rhetorical situations, the individual in his or her narcissistic immaturity reverts inordinately to mental structures of infancy for criteria of judg-ment, material, and argument. Such is the childish thinking of the hus-band driven to operate from the premise that his wife's first duty is to meet *his* needs. A psychoanalytically informed rhetorician might call this nar-cissistic mode of discovery "regressive invention," or "reliance on the ar-chaic enthymeme," for it represents a return to the individual's primitive con-ceptions. Narcissistically infused content can spoil rhetorical interactions.

Regressive invention often will lead to choices that are unsuited to rhetorical exchange. The narcissistic enthymeme represents naivete, childish self-interest, possibly fantasy, reflecting the rhetorical maturity level of its creator. Confusion in invention, moreover, may be traced to activation of such primary processes. Sheldon Bach cites the case of one narcissistic pa-tient, a lawyer, who told of his regression and resulting inability to work. "When I'm talking and lose the gist of my thought," he complained, "I can't get back on the track — I become incredibly simple-minded — if you told me a joke I wouldn't understand it!"[26] Ordinarily, it is an adult men-tality that marks a reliable rhetorical standard for setting goals and invent-ing useful lines of thought or action; while reversion to magical thinking or unreal hopes may lead to unfavorable outcome. Related instances are fabrications and other deceptions of the type that arise from narcissistic immaturity. Janet Cooke's hoax is viewed that way by Richard Restak. A *Washington Post* journalist until forced to resign in 1981, Cooke reportedly "constructed her Pulitzer Prize-winning story on a lie in order to win a prize she hoped would provide the self-confirmation that was missing and unobtainable by honest effort."[27] In this instance, cognitive folly had devastating effects.

Beliefs, Values, and Ideals. Peculiarity in formulation and maintenance of beliefs, values, and ideals is another product of disadvantageous narcissism. It is evidenced in narrow personal perspectives and horizons, subjectivity, dependence, distortions of reality, lethargy, and solipsism generally. Uniqueness, inconstancy in belief and commitment, rigidity, delusion on self, loss of the spirit of play, lack of rhetorical appreciation, and faulty views on identification are characteristic patterns.

Patterns and Rhetorical Implications

Often cited in reference to narcissism is belief in personal *uniqueness*. The power of this way of thinking enforces a mental set that holds affected individuals apart from others—above and special. The narcissism of Shakespeare's Hamlet may be understood as a model of human alienation and uniqueness. His is a great individuality, a painful self-defined singularity.

There are people who have scant knowledge of their position and influence in others' existence. As McDougall notes, they are unaware that "they too occupy a psychic space in the minds of others," while "screaming out" the "right to become alive," assuming that the world owes them this.[28] A connected belief amounts to what might be termed a narcissistic "code of justice." Called *entitlement*, its expression is simple, represented by the assertion: "I deserve special treatment." Very clear, though not always verbalized, this personal thesis obliges others to show partiality, to acknowledge the special person's self-appointed roles, or grant extraordinary latitude in conduct. To "holders," entitlement is assumed as a tenet on personal impunity; it is a working premise that ordinary statutes or conventions somehow do not apply to them. In this mentality, self-derived status creates exemption from penalty: of primitive origin, "I can get away with it" is the tacit call. An example is the narcissistic assumption that if one abuses another in a tirade, all will be forgotten by the next day: it never happened, really. Again, the narcissistically confused seem unable to know their potential for affecting or being brutish—or perhaps not until their victim provides feedback sufficient to register a feeling.

Keen feelings of personal uniqueness create barriers that may be insurmountable, for audiences are often harsh judges of people who seem firm in convictions of peerlessness and are reluctant to respect others' individuality. Postures appearing as aloof, unbending, unfriendly, and imperious are hardly promoters of good ethos. A positive reaction ordinarily requires a generous offering of self to others, along with appropriate acknowledgment and accommodation. When commanded instead by grandiosity and a belief that one is made of better stuff, the result is likely to be arousal of others' defensiveness.[29]

Narcissistic entitlement can prove a liability for the same reasons. It was a sense of entitlement — and possibly uniqueness — that lay behind young and proud Tiberius Gracchus' pique when he was denied a good soldier's welcome and honor upon his return home from an ill-fated military engagement in Spain. He believed that he — the son of illustrious Romans — deserved accolades, not derision. It was this mistaken assumption of special status that marked the beginning — if not the entire course — of his tragic downfall. The case is discussed at length in Chapter eight.

Another cognitive problem of ill-favored narcissism is *inconstancy*: a lack of steady resolve, particularly in adhering to social values, moral precepts, or philosophic outlook. Carl Goldberg illustrates bases of narcissistic values and convictions through the gauge of the legendary Don Juan, one who accepts as valid or true "that which falls in with what he would like to believe is true."[30] In this case, pressures of self-interest can lead to adjustment of principle. Or said without euphemism, the conscience and value system are corruptible. Needs of self-cohesion or public image may dominate truthful argument, for in certain patterns of narcissistic thinking, appearance has priority over substance.

When under the sway of pernicious narcissism, many are not given to consistency in maintaining positions or to keeping commitments over time, except in adherence to criteria of personal benefit. Shakiness in conviction — or not knowing what to believe — is a characteristic cognitive deficiency. Another is indifference to abstract thought and careless dismissal of ideas listlessly judged as irrelevant or insignificant. Furthermore, the affected person may hold two opposing views simultaneously, favoring one and then the other — or unable to appreciate the contradiction, find self-satisfying logic in defense of it.

Rhetorical effectiveness calls for some measure of consistency in expenditure of intellectual energy and constancy in belief. Stability and uniformity of view are expected by others, and needless to elaborate here, a message is weakened when its creator is known to hold a contradicting opinion. The life of Senator Joseph McCarthy illustrates the result of anomalous self-interest and grandiosity, obliviousness to social norms, and deterioration of credibility. With "no truth in him," this narcissistically injured, unhappy man ran rough shod over ordinary values and principles of human decency. Deceitfully presenting himself as a war hero and acting as "tough-guy" communist fighter, he sent out messages flawed by "flim-flam, hypocrisy and knavery, brutality, obscenity, and moral depravity." (See Chapter six.) Another who operated from cynical premises was Jim Jones of the Peoples Temple, an ethically unrestrained user of people. He was a con artist who learned all roles necessary to his ends, the dominant being omnipotent father. Revealing cognitive structures that seem to have been built from childhood abuse, he came to view the world as alien and hostile and to act from values that ran counter to the social good. His beliefs and values were reflected in his rhetorical choices. Jones' story is told in Chapter five.

Rather opposite to inconstancy, but also detrimental, is *rigidity*, e.g. in belief, literalism, and incapacity or refusal to make proper adjustments in thought as reality may dictate. One example is a peculiar and dogged loyalty to favored theories.[31] When inflexibly bound to the "letter of the law," so to speak—to a strict construction of messages—people in interaction can miss nuances and fullness of meaning and consequently lead themselves to inappropriate, rhetorically unmotivated statements. Prudent adaptation is a useful and approved procedure in rhetorical interaction, for change and challenge are constant features of any activity involving the impact of mind on mind.

One form of rigidity, a general inability to suspend disbelief, rules out the enjoyment of an inconceivable drama or improbable narrative. The indisposition of some persons to respond to others' fantastic stories or incredible adventure tales can be taken as a listening deficiency. Related is narcissistic literal-mindedness, i.e., the excessive bent toward taking comments from a standard of exactness. For example, a person may interpret an employer's minor and basically inoffensive directive on company policy as an ultimatum. Or a person may overinvest in another's casual word and hold it as a pledge. In specific reference to the "as if" personality, Rochlin reports on "an overliteral interpretation and uncritical devotion to manuals on how to entertain properly, control anger, influence people, or raise children."[32]

Delusion on self may be rhetorically disastrous, perhaps as much as ignorance of the audience. Stressing the personal quality in communication, Charles M. Rossiter and W. Barnet Pearce note that the self-estranged person—one who really does not know herself or himself—cannot communicate "with maximum personalness." Confusion may be the result. Self-awareness, a constituent of "personal communication," influences others to provide useful feedback.[33] Without personal communication, useful responses would not be evoked and utilized; narcissistic deficiency would not be checked. Reusch recognizes the need of self-knowledge in interactions, holding that disturbances arise "when an individual's identity is ill-defined or when a person feels that he does not possess an identity at all." Knowledge on identity is a "prerequisite for successful communication. In all expressions of the individual, this awareness is transmitted to the receiver; it primes him with regard to the interpretation of messages and in a subtle way defines form, timing, and content of the statement."[34] What people believe about themselves seems to tell others what is being said, and guides others in formulating a response. Thus persons deluded on self-identity, cannot faithfully direct audience interpretation of their messages or gauge their ethical appeal. Likely results are incongruity, ambiguity, and failure. Not knowing himself — and building his presence on false values — Willy Loman of Arthur Miller's *Death of a Salesman* sustained an illusion of success and personal power. When these yielded to the sad realization of his long-held self-delusion, he chose to kill himself. At long last, he found his identity; then he destroyed it.

Loss of the spirit of play is another factor. The inability to appreciate the abandonment and selflessness, release of imagination, and positive response to illusion required in playing with others is a part of the pattern of disadvantageous narcissism. Directed by excessive self-concern and exhaustive, self-conscious calculations on measures for personal security, affected persons are blocked in healthful expressive behavior. They know not the joy of play. In rejecting the quality of play, by internalizing a distorted version of reality, they diminish their potential for relating and, commensurately, their social effectiveness.[35]

Further, good players insist on playing by rules of the game. Deviations are not condoned. And so it is in most rhetorical action. "Audiences" — the one or many with whom one interacts — generally are conventional groups or individuals, holding to expectations and set notions on acceptability of aim, content, strategy, etc. The "rules of play" are constraints of audience and occasion. People respond positively to certain ways of saying things, e.g., to words that acknowledge their self-image. They respond negatively to others, e.g., to inadequate substantiation of ideas. Conventions of rhetoric, then, are matters of form, social agreements, and various ad hoc understandings. In this sense, people who successfully interact abide by a spirit of "play." Speaking metaphorically, we say that they follow rhetorical "rules of the game." These are social agreements — rules enforced by audiences. For a more formal interpretation of rules, see Chapter four.

Thus, individuals are rhetorically deficient, as far as they are unwilling or incapable in play. The code of being a "law unto myself" conflicts sharply with general social codes and with accepted ways of playing, and incapability or unwillingness in play are gauges of rhetorical deficiency. Joseph McCarthy and Jim Jones, subjects of subsequent chapters, are obvious examples. The former found it difficult to play by rules of the game, both on the playground as a child and later in the field of politics. Contemptuously yearning for omnipotence, he bypassed convention, finding his power outside common canons. Jones' pattern, as child and adult, was to seduce people out of the larger society into his own and impose rules by which all were to play *his* game.

Those who reject social and rhetorical requirements as useless or "unauthentic" put themselves outside the arena of active life with others. Dismissing convention, they risk alienation and rhetorical failure, for their act is to repudiate their identity as rhetorical creatures and disclaim the function that is necessary to success with others.

Lack of rhetorical appreciation is another pattern. Palpably, the narcissistic individuals who are the subject here cannot have a true and steady rhetorical sense, albeit they may be keenly sensitive at times to points of others' vulnerability. Their regressive tendencies and low levels of awareness of the values and functions of rhetorical usages incline them to neglect opportunity or favor coercion — and sometimes violence — over persuasion. Respected by its service to civil society, persuasion is a humane mode of influence that acknowledges another's distinct identity and freedom to accept or refuse a presentation. Accordingly, rhetoric is a civil power, resting on choice in behavior. To coerce is to restrain by force, to deny choice; it is to repress or overpower. Persuasion and coercion differ in the amount or degree of genuine regard for another that is to be found in any specific act of interpersonal influence. Persuasion depends on a positive and free response from the audience, while coercion may succeed with power alone. Thus caring people persuade; uncaring people coerce. Those who in their narcissism care less are less given to trying persuasion. The heavier the self-absorption, the less the predisposition to work at use of the arts of persuasion. Though one must acknowledge indeed that coercion and physical power can be employed effectively to influence behavior, values of this society put those usages outside the field of rhetoric and condemn their use. In the final analysis, both McCarthy and Jones showed little faith in rhetorical forms of power, resorting instead to well-perfected extrarhetorical strategy, e.g., the lying and bullying of McCarthy. Stunted or regressed, certainly indisposed rhetorically, Lee Harvey Oswald was a socially feeble being who quietly contrived personal effectiveness through violence. He accomplished his act in secret: alone and safely sequestered, far removed from the target of his grieving self, undisturbed by intimacy, his rhetorical impotence covered.

Faulty views on identification also appear in unfavorable narcissism. A positive response to social values is seen in the identification of people, one with another. This is a Burkeian lesson. But ironically, severe narcissism makes people into sovereign and special human islands — those who cannot identify with others in the necessary and ordinary rhetorical sense of the term. It is such narcissistic lack to which Bach refers, saying, that "if the partner in the dialogue responds to one's feelings, then a link is forged between feelings and events, but if the response is consistently irrelevant, then the worlds of feeling and events remain separated, meaningless, and frightening."[36] When under the sway of oppressive narcissism, people cannot connect feelings to events, or themselves healthily to others. Yet, impelled to "identify," i.e., to control, they force self-serving linkages or ad hoc relations or symbiotic arrangements of fusion to suit their personal ends. For a period, imposed connections may seem to work satisfactorily, but good social health and sustained success with others are dependent on recognition and acceptance of others' individuality. Not willing to be held captive, most people eventually resist extremes of fusion and will not relate on those terms. The other extreme, dissociation, is as significant because persons denied access to interaction are alienated, lost as potential audience.

Also notable as a rhetorical liability is that kind of narcissistic behavior involving control by assumption. Its effect is to disallow distinction in others. This characteristic — a rhetorician might want to call it "begging the question" — is an insensitive inclination to impose personal preconceived premises in exchanges with others[37] and attempting to control events therefrom. Certain that their premises are shared, some narcissistic people tend to present themselves as possessors of solid syllogistic certainty rather than enthymematic probability. Ignoring others' positions, they want to control the completion of others' thought — to deny partnership in the enterprise — and otherwise force others to conform to their peculiar outlook. Appearing as obstinate or authoritarian, this mentality brought to relationships is rhetorically unpromising.

"I refuse to adapt or civilize" was the wishful declaration of one business executive. Stiffening at identifying with others and carefully "weighing and measuring" the self shared with others, he resisted placing "a value beyond himself on others" and felt that "to take others into account" and accommodate them would show his deficiency.[38] As McDougall notes, there is a tendency in some to *create* "the meaning that the other person has for them without taking too much account of the Other's reality." Such cases are not uncommon.[39]

Serious narcissistic injury or threat leads to doubts on adequacy and subsequent impaired rhetorical functioning, in that feelings of impotence — powerlessness — detract from efforts toward identification. Moreover, corrective and defensive measures often are self-defeating, for they involve intense concentration on the self apart from others and grim determination to prevail. A classic example is Captain Ahab in desperate pursuit of the great white whale. Preoccupation with strategies of personal performance promises defeat in rhetorical relating, for self-interest dominates, ruling out reasonable interactive accommodation and connection: the behavior necessary for success. In interaction with others, benefits are realized through incorporation of a vision of interpersonal union and exchange.

This, then, is the solipsistic tone of heavily narcissistic cognitive structures and processes. Extended, it depicts a view which, in Peter Marin's account, is "centered solely on the self and with individual survival as its sole good." It is a retreat from "morality and history, an unembarrassed denial of human reciprocity and community."[40] It represents a mind that cannot apperceive a culture's past or future. That mind is in an altered state of consciousness, unable to distinguish between the objective world and the subjective, no longer sharing the cultural world view.[41] Formulation and maintenance of beliefs, values, and ideals reflect this state of consciousness and show bases of rhetorical indisposition.

Disturbances in Perception

One obtrusive feature of restrictive narcissism is peculiarity in perceptions of persons, events, and ideas. Dominating is the formidable premise of self-absorption: "I see only what *I* see." All but personal relevance is blocked out. This kind of screening, McDougall reports, leads people to "perceive only what accords with their preconceived notion of the Other, and of the world in general, and to eliminate perceptions and observations which do not fit with the existing idea."[42] Reckonings on reality are entirely personal. When under such influence, people do not "really see and hear and feel who we are and, to the extent that we are narcissistic, we do not really see and hear and feel the true presence of others."[43]

Descriptions and understandings are subjective, when unrefreshed by information exterior to the self. Historian Carl L. Becker probably would have agreed that the intensely narcissistic cannot qualify as good historians, for they are not equipped to enlarge and enrich what he called the "specious present." Cognitively, they are unable to "push back the narrow confines of the fleeting present moment so that what we are doing may be judged in the light of what we have done and what we hope to do."[44] As Richard Sennett puts it, such narcissism stimulates "the belief that this experience at each moment is absolute."[45] Indisposed to capitalize on rich external resources, rigidly "on their own," narcissistically focused individuals conduct themselves under limitations not shared by more mature persons.

Such infant adults are unable to perceive the impact of their presence on others. They are rhetorically blinded. McDougall reports the case of a woman who was relatively unaware that her hostile remarks and observations might possibly affect others in her life. Constrained by a narcissistic perceptive deficiency, she knew others to be alive, to be existent; therefore they needed little else.[46] As children may be oblivious to the effect of their hostility against a parent — seeming to assume that a parental function is to accept attack stoically—so childlike persons of any age misjudge the emotional vulnerability of others, including those whom they idolize.

Anomie, an oppressive narcissistic state characterized by lack of purpose and disorientation, indefinite ethical values, rootlessness, and other cognitive incapacities, influences perception by putting up a misshapen lens for viewing life. Herbert McClosky and John H. Schaar found that anomic persons are strongly governed by "aversive motivational and affective states" and suffer "from a tendency to distort their perceptions of social 'reality,' to accommodate poorly to social change, complexity, and ambiguity, and —through the projection of their anxieties, fears, and uncertainties —to perceive the world as hostile and anxiety-ridden."[47] These narcissistic mental operations conflict with objective reality, producing unreliable images and faulty judgments.

Rhetorical Implications

Rhetorically mature and effective persons are open to a range of perspectives "in any given case"; they use their understanding to create options. Thus enabled to choose from among a variety of possible responses, they can make realistic and sound decisions on structuring messages. They accept the fact of audience, i.e., that outside themselves are others to be acknowledged and addressed: people to be thought of as partners—and necessary resources—in the conduct of a rewarding exchange. The rhetorically sophisticated are responsive to their audiences' perceptions. In a colloquial word, rhetorical adequacy includes "seeing it as they see it." This means knowing where the audience stands—not to mention encouraging the audience's participation—and benefiting from their view of the occasion in which both are involved. Writing of the reticence syndrome (in which narcissism would seem to be a significant factor), Gerald M. Phillips and Nancy J. Metzger point to awareness of the meaning of others' behavior as crucial in developing competence in communication: "The individual who does not have the ability to perceive or interpret the cues of others cannot use the cues of others as guides to his own behavior."[48] The competence to sense and translate feedback is a sine qua non in rhetorical interaction. In a related but broader view, McCloskey and Schaar note that certain narcissistic dispositions, in particular the anomic, reduce "chances for effective interaction and communication," and in consequence hamper further the "opportunity to learn the norms and to achieve a more coherent sense of how the society works."[49] The experience of success is basic to social growth and, it should be added, to rhetorical ability.

One specific rhetorical problem is dependency in perception. Bach cites the case of a narcissistic woman who confessed, "I can't tell when anybody's kidding or not."[50] We sometimes call this behavior "dumb" or childish, indicative of rhetorical incapacity and potential handicap. A thirty-year-old professional man, given to relying too heavily on others' perceptions and appreciation of his activities, was very excited when asked to lecture on his hobby, for which he was renowned. After the speech, he enjoyed a "heady feeling," thinking he had done a "superlative job." But on this occasion he was not with people who knew him and his personal needs, and upon overhearing one audience member roundly discredit the speech and speaker, he was "mortified and tried to disregard the feeling but it remained." In that foreign setting, the "narcissistic objects" needed to support his perception were not available.[51] A different facet of the problem is seen in the instance of a very successful business executive who, as he advanced in the company, became increasingly fearful of revealing the shy, hostile self that he had concealed so well. He perceived himself as "only self-serving" and "a menace to others." Projecting such perceptions, he felt vulnerable and expected hositility in return. His narcissism threatened rhetorical success.[52]

Fundamental to rhetorical maturity are clear perception of reality and the mental disposition to visualize the self in healthful alliance with others; no condition would seem more damaging to rhetorical purpose than a narcissistically clouded vision. The promise of good results is diminished, given a narrow and provincial individuality that prevents acknowledgment of individuality in others or is unable to sense the effect of its presence on others.

Behavioral Disturbances

In behavioral terms, unfavorable narcissism is observed both as inward and outward expression. Clear examples of the former are evasion, withdrawal, and depression; of the latter are hostility and rage.

Avoidance—Resentment—Anger. Narcissistic concerns about worth of self are never-ceasing. One sign is interpersonal conservatism: stinginess in giving of self. In strategic avoidance of personal loss, many hold back until sure of favorable odds on outcome. There is a type of narcissistic behavior, reports Rochlin, typified by a wish to do nothing and a waiting to be told what to do. Included in the pattern is resentment of what others require while pretending to do it. Beneath the passivity are feelings of anger that will be expressed eventually. Aggressive and destructive behavior may complete the pattern — of which low self-esteem is the motivating condition.[53]

Out of insecurity arises reluctance to assume community responsibilities and obligations of friendship, disinterest in proposing change or taking the lead in groups or organizations, and general regressive behaviors. Making choices may be avoided, particularly when alternatives are sensed as personally threatening. Existent is an inclination to dodge decisions, to wait for the situation "to become either perfect or hopeless," or to postpone opening the mail. Even elementary discriminations may be difficult to make.[54] Thus some individuals keep themselves outside the flow of significant areas of life. Afraid—and possessed of a sense of futility and an absence of purpose—they shy away from any commitment, except to meet needs of self in the here and now. They are unwilling to dedicate with any regularity a reasonable portion of themselves or their time to activity that is other than personal.

Of all modes of narcissistic withdrawal, depression is the most crippling, given its overwhelming power in sapping energy and defeating interest in being up and doing. Stemming from wounds to the self, depression is a common enforcer of behavioral paralysis. Loss of confidence leads to diminished ability to "cope in the *outer* world" or "to negotiate." Preoccupied and befuddled, sufferers—whose numbers are large—become "totally absorbed by . . . efforts to retain some equilibrium."[55] Moreover, depression begets depression: "The depressed person's inability to respond to us—our incapacity to infect him with even a minimum of joy in response to our presence and to our efforts in his behalf—inevitably creates a lowering of self-esteem in ourselves, and, feeling narcissistically injured, we react to it with depression and/or rage."[56] Others' narcissism can activate our own.

Notwithstanding their problems, the narcissistically unhealthy may appear to behave quite satisfactorily, and one cannot judge entirely by appearances. As Bach puts it, they have "learned *techniques* for living, instead of learning how to be human."[57] The "as if" personality is exemplary in the extreme of this form of narcissistic behavior. Helene Deutsch writes of the person whose "whole relationship to life has something about it which is lacking in genuineness and yet outwardly runs along 'as if' it were complete." The person "conducts his life as if he possessed a complete and sensitive emotional capacity," but the entire performance, though "an ostensibly good adaptation to the world of reality," is mimicry and "corresponds to a child's imitativeness."[58] Maintenance is unsteady—and costly.

General Rhetorical Implications

Success in any rhetorical interaction does not occur magically. Unwillingness to exert management in pursuit of goals is a reason for rhetorical failure.[59] For example, desired results usually depend on decisions in organizing ideas, on putting this point here and that there. And it is essential *to do* something—to act in order to achieve an end (and, indeed, to be able to *set* a definite end).

A rhetorical contingency necessitates relevant and adequate response. Of course, no response—inaction—is a choice and by default will yield a result of some kind. Ignoring and withdrawing are common narcissistic responses to rhetorical invitation. Whether in passivity or aggression, narcissistic individuals are directed by self-absorption, caught between personal confinement and rhetorical demand. The result is rhetorical inexpedience or costly torpor. An attorney in his forties, reportedly not possessing "a firmly integrated sense of self" and unable to feel real love, devoted most of his energies to work. But occasionally he became infatuated with a woman – and then obsessed by her and tormented by fears of losing his identity in her. At such times, his work suffered severely, becoming "trivial and not worthwhile," he said. "I couldn't keep my mind on my clients or the cases I was arguing. After months and months of preparation, my arguments seemed empty and lifeless. So what if I was prepared for the case? So what if I won or if I lost?"[60]

Another behavioral phenomenon is impotence. Here an interesting analogy exists between sexual and rhetorical behavior. Serious narcissistic injury or threat leads to lowered self-esteem and often to impaired social functioning, including loss of rhetorical effectiveness. Such "impotence" may be the epitome of narcissistic incapacitation.[61] As with sexual impotence, corrective and defensive measures frequently are self-defeating, in that they involve intense narcissistic concentration on the self apart from others and grim determination to control the self in that situation and thereby succeed. "*I* can do it!" is the recurring but empty resolution. Such was the case of the man whose extremely intense resolve to overcome public speaking deficiencies only heightened his problems. All energy went to individualistic self-perfection, none to developing ease in relating to audiences.

Given doubts on adequacy and consequent inordinate preoccupation with strategies of personal performance, rhetorical relating is defeated (as is loving); unmitigated self-interest controls, ruling out interactive accommodation, the behavior necessary to success. Highly motivated to prove themselves or avoid shame, affected persons struggle for themselves, incapable at key times of incorporating and holding to a vision of reciprocity in doing things or to seeking realization of mutual satisfaction. Single-minded striving for effect only worsens the problem, since in human interaction, including the rhetorical, goals are reached only through and with others.

When narcissistically impoverished, people cannot hold constantly to balanced behavioral patterns. They can perform productively no longer than resistance to regression and dependency will allow, no longer than their more adult goals, ideals, and stabilizing forces stand fast, or sometimes, it may be said, no longer than the attention or applause or special favor last.

In relationships. Centering on unfavorable narcissism in relationships, the discussion now assumes full social dimension. It is in the interpersonal scene that the condition finds most graphic expression, for as Rochlin states in the negative, "With an increase of narcissism, interest in others is correspondingly lowered."[62] Again, as Sydney E. Pulver notes, the issue is self-esteem: "Individuals with high self-esteem are precisely those most able to be more interested in others, while those with low self-esteem are most likely to concentrate upon themselves."[63] Carl Goldberg, psychotherapist and author, in reporting on his own narcissistic experience, includes reference to "manifestations of a deep distress of self-esteem" and "frequently a sheer refusal to function socially."[64]

Narcissistic feelings, secured in early infancy, have immense power in influencing relationships. For example, infantile regressions appearing in daily exchanges with others can lead to expressions of envy, hate, resentment, etc. They also can result in peculiar classifications, one of which we might call the dysjunctive, for as Otto F. Kernberg finds, affected persons "divide the world into famous, rich, and great people on the one hand, and the despicable, worthless, 'mediocrity' on the other." They will admire some hero or outstanding individual, using the person as an agent of themselves. But devaluation of the idol will occur if they come to perceive themselves as rejected or if the idol disappears or is "dethroned." To become classified as mediocre is a fearful prospect.[65] Vacillation between over-idealization and devaluation is representative counterproductive behavior.

Threatening relationships, the weight of negative narcissism enforces insensitivity to others' states of being. Sufferers are deficient in self-awareness. "Out of touch with important aspects of themselves," observes McDougall, they "have difficulty in accepting that others are equally prone to anxiety, depression, frustration and irritation." Relationships conducted from this primary process model, in which the reality of others is devalued, "are by no means rare in the world at large."[66]

The behavior may show itself as domination by a single issue in the individual's life — a "self-issue," actually: a binding fixation leading to inordinate emphasis on one idea or affiliation. Identification with the theme — whether professional, ethnic, religious, regional, etc. — is overwhelming, to the point that self-presentations are persistently and entirely of but one signature. They "wear it on their sleeves," so to speak, and expect special acknowledgment accordingly, while blind to the wider social good. A type is the "divinely chosen" zealot, or the likes of the "Mau Mau" extremist of the 1960s whose method of civil reform was coercion, or any whose fierce personal attachments or supreme pride intrudes upon community interest.[67]

Though acknowledging that some narcissistically plagued people on the surface may be "engaging and attractive" and "quite likable," Kernberg reminds us that their social adaptation is only superficially smooth and effective. Their internal relations with others are seriously distorted, for it is narcissistic supplies that they seek: offerings of special attention and favor that others can provide them. But many resent being dependent on others, are intensely envious, and when finished with a person will contemptuously move on — like "squeezing a lemon and then dropping the remains."[68] Annie Reich's findings on "as if" narcissistic persons are similar to Kernberg's on the narcissistic generality. She reports, they are "incapable of loving anybody" and relate "via a primitive form of identification," and without continuity.[69]

In dealings with others, narcissistically maladapted persons can be exploitative and parasitic, feeling "they have the right to control and possess others." Too, they often "feel sexual excitement for people considered valuable or attractive by others, or for those who seem unattainable and withhold their bodies." They "want to spoil, depreciate, and degrade what others have and they lack, particularly others' capacity to give and to love."[70]

Aaron Stern's conclusion on the socially inadequate narcissistic person's plight is colloquial as expressed, but apt: "He is the dependent human being, adopting postures of ingratiation to be sure that others love him. . . . This constant effort to win the support and approval of others is a hell of a way to go through life — never being able to be one's self for fear of possible rejection. It leaves little margin for loving."[71]

Given these data, it is evident that those who have experienced severe narcissistic injury are likely to be impoverished of empathy and interpersonally shallow. Whether enraged, solitary, arrogant, dictatorial, or ostensibly social, they have difficulty in conducting friendships, marriages, interactions with their children, and other relationships.

Rhetorical Implications

Penalties of extreme narcissism are most evident in the rhetorical transactions of relationships. Successful exchange of messages is dependent upon the quality of the participants' association. As Ruesch reports, "the content of a message is a function of the human relationship."[72] In successful relationships, compensations of relating parties are distributed. But the benefits accrue only through choices of rhetorically sensitive persons: those whose behavior is marked by trust, healthful reciprocity, adaptability, and willingness to make investment of self in the enterprise.[73]

In contrast, relationships involving a deprived and narcissistic person are likely to be imbalanced, tilted by force of personal exaction. Throwing their weight to the side of self, often oblivious to social needs, these individuals are inclined to be highly defensive and rigid, unconcerned with others' welfare, and rhetorically parsimonious. Their behavior demonstrates the necessary connection of cognitive to relational elements, lacking the rhetorical consciousness needed in seeking sufficient and sound information on others, their audiences. Information, if somehow discovered, may never be absorbed or put to use, given the rivalry of self-preoccupation. Overwhelming and constant personal interest conflicts with awareness of others' interests and dominates in uneven competition.

Symbiosis. A necessary topic to be treated at this point is the unhealthful "symbiotic" relationship, mentioned in psychiatric literature in explanation of both the beginnings and perpetuation of problems in narcissism. When people are dependent upon each other and reinforce one another's unfavorable narcissistic tendencies, their growth potentialities and functioning are constricted. Finding the condition a threat to human relationships generally, Aaron Stern writes that "the narcissist provides vicarious outlets for our own suppressed, natural, and constantly available narcissistic interests. The more narcissistic we are, the greater is our attraction for narcissists." We serve as foils because it suits our purposes. "We look to act out our own feelings of specialness and our self-centered interest in pleasure through him, trying to hide our narcissism behind his, while posing as the innocent victims of his selfishness."[74] Harry Stack Sullivan describes the exploitative strategies of the "passive-dependent" person of low self-esteem who skillfully and suavely uses personal inferiority feelings to evoke philanthropic concern from others. If the others are given to finding their security in "domineering and vassalizing their fellows," the one of poor self-opinion will "fall very readily into the orbit of these others, and all concerned do a great deal for one another without any particular satisfaction."[75]

It is difficult for one to imagine a more stifling relationship than narcissistic symbiosis. Let us take two persons who in their dependency make themselves present to each other at all moments, and who consequently are constant influences on all their respective movements. Neither has achieved individuation: independence as a person apart. In desperate reciprocity, they keep themselves in a closed system — each other's captive, trapped, held back, rhetorically stagnant in an interpersonal backwater. Together, there is no real freedom, no chance of development of positive rhetorical interaction. They are content in their rewarding confirmations. But the price of validation and security is high, for given their mutually imposed despotism, these collaborators prevent themselves from stepping aside to assess conditions and come to free choices on relating, or deciding whether to continue. Pathologically intimate, enduring from need and a history of despair, they never come to know what is rhetorically better for them. Such is the self-imposed lot of Gertrude and Paul Morel, mother and son in symbiotic collusion (See Chapter seven).

Unrelievedly interdependent in an alliance for mutual, albeit antagonistic validation, George and Martha of Edward Albee's *Who's Afraid of Virginia Woolf?* verbally punish each other in ferocious and morbid reciprocity, giving display of heavy deficits felt in themselves. George's contributions to the arrangement arise from dissatisfaction with an unfulfilled life, as evidenced in emptiness, insecurity, compromise, and withdrawal. Martha's plight, as Anita Marie Stenz views it, relates to her quest for "identity and self-esteem in the person and life of the man she married and in the career she planned for him." Her "love" for him — her symbiotic use of him — "is a form of narcissism"[76] — as is his use of her. Both are rhetorically incapacitated, unable to realize maturity and dignity.

The circumstance of Madeleine and Manny, a real married couple, typifies the cost of symbiosis. Bright, energetic, loyal Madeleine emotionally and financially supported her passive, indecisive, irresponsible, alcoholic husband. Oblivious "to her own stifling dependency," she earned dubious rewards of the "good woman," while sustaining Manny's "fantasy that he was in charge of things." Yielding to overpowering narcissistic demand, each diminished the other, misspending twenty-two years together.[77] In terms of current theory on such relationships, Madeleine was a "co-dependent." Codependence is *"any suffering and/or dysfunctioning that is associated with or results from focusing on the needs and behavior of others,"*[78] e.g., alcoholics or others with chronic needs. The dysfunction eventually will affect negatively the co-dependent's behavior in other relationships.[79] The co-dependent, ruled by a dictatorial false self, denies personal needs and feelings, while overly accommodating others and seeking to control.

A general case of reduced ability to exert rhetorical force against their own inclinations is exemplified in the general membership of the Peoples Temple. Unsure of their status in society, doubtful of the future, and limited in personal power, typical members of that community were vulnerable seekers of refuge and the benevolent protection of caring, effective authority. Narcissistically restrained by their long-existing woe and debility, they never came to enjoyment of self-determination, to full social membership. Their condition was complementary narcissism, perhaps a form of mass codependence. Though the traditional "complementary narcissist" was the self-sacrificing woman in a union with a dominant narcissistic man, the complementer may be a partner in any kind of close relationship. The chosen role is as sacrificer of self and exalter of the other. In complete merger with the idealized other, the complementer seeks to gain an idealized self from the other. In the case of cults, the leader secures adherents who endow him or her with messianic qualities, are at the leader's beck and call, and who fight along side him or her in their quasi-holy war against their selected enemy. Responsive to their idol's conception of a powerful force that is out to destroy him or her, the complementers are unconditionally faithful.[80] Chapter six discusses fully the case of Jim Jones and members of the Peoples Temple.

Defensiveness. In concrete language, Harry Guntrip provides an interesting and rather comprehensive overview of ordinary defensive behavior:

> The multifarious ways in which people are on the defensive against one another, in business, social life, marriage, and parenthood, and even leisure activities, suggests that the one omnipresent fear is the fear of being and appearing weak, inadequate, less of a person than others or less than equal to the demands of the situation, a failure: the fear of letting oneself down and looking a fool in the face of an unsupportive and even hostile world. This fear lies behind all the rationalized self-assertiveness, the subtle exhibitionism, the disguised boasting, the competitiveness or avoidance of competition, the need of praise, reassurance and approval, the safety-first tactics and security-seeking, and a multitude of other defensive reactions to life . . . .[81]

Such behavior is pervasive, to be sure. And in a sense, all narcissistic patterns of thinking and behaving can be seen as defensive: in the service of self-security. Whether favorable or unfavorable, narcissism is about adaptation and survival.[82] But for clarity and emphasis, it is appropriate here to set up a separate grouping on defensiveness.

Defenses are strategies to meet contingency, invented under influence of the rhetorical imperative, as are all suasory behaviors. They reveal personal despair and social or work-related impairment, sometimes quite deep. Such defensiveness works against rhetorical interest. Given conditions of this age in which avoidance of shame and affirmation of self are notably high-order goals, individuals tend to devote themselves diligently to achievement of personal security. Defensiveness, negative narcissism, and the dogmatic false self are of one cloth. Indeed, as Arthur H. Modell notes, narcissism "is a reflection of the sense of one's safety in the world,"[83] and the false self—that peculiarly crafted substitute—is the defending self. While certain modes of protection may be considered useful in ordinary maintenance of self-interest—even rhetorically functional—many are maladaptive. When preoccupied in self-defense, individuals are unable to attend to the cultivation of relationships, i.e., to spend resources of self positively. Recall Abraham H. Maslow's placement of needs on a hierarchy. When basic survival needs are not met, individuals may neglect those of a higher order, e.g., the social.[84]

Maladaptive defensiveness, then, is myriad use of the false self as a cover for shame, that *"inner sense of being completely diminished or insufficient as a person, . . . the self judging the self."*[85] Shame occurs, Carl A. Whitaker observes sympathetically, "when you haven't been able to get away with the 'who' you want people to think you are."[86] And it is in this circumstance that the protection alarm sounds, demanding action to shelter the self and prevent its devastation. For some people, responding to that alarm is a way of life: the conduct of an often ill-fated mission of seeking secure bases in others. Reactions may be directed inward as in self-criticism or withdrawal—or outward as in haughtiness or belligerence.

Four principal classifications of defensive measures are control, perfection, blame, and denial.[87] The categories are nondiscrete. For example, a given act of lying may reflect an exercise in control or perfection—or blaming or denying, for that matter.

The first defensive measure, *control*, is about power. One answer to feelings of shame is striving to be in command of all situations, to have power over self and others. Of course, some such strategies of control can be useful, for example, careful organization of ideas in speechmaking or use of personal authority in protecting a child. Examples of other types are bullying, seduction, influencing with real or imagined illness, talking in abstract or esoteric language, identifying with power figures, use of threat, and doing all else to reduce shame through personal regulation or to have the upperhand.

Outward-directed defenses of control range from physical aggression to lying. Rage, occuring when compensations of the false self dissolve, represents an attempt to increase self-esteem. Lordly and imperious behavior are typical defensive responses of the grandiose self.

Lying is an often-used defense of narcissistic manipulation. In Kohut's observations, narcissistic resort to lying is due to pressures exerted by the grandiose self or the need for an idealized self object, e.g., lying to exalt a favored person. Under influence of the grandiose self with its long-held conviction of omniscience, one may lie with a "yes" answer when asked if he or she has read a certain book. So doing, the person holds to an old "principle" of personal distinction. Reliant on others for self-worth, some individuals may seek personal aggrandizement by lying about an achievement of a respected person to whom they have attached themselves.[88]

Seemingly passive in defensive maneuvers, some individuals contain their aggression, directing feelings inward. Basic modes are withdrawal, avoidance, and evasion. One means of exerting self-control is, as Kernberg puts it, to withdraw into "splendid isolation," to take leave, remain silent, fantasize, rely on formal language, etc.[89] A characteristic of such narcissism is defensive retreat from a threatening social exchange, e.g., in avoidance of potentially demeaning competition. Depression is a common response to major narcissistic injury or felt vulnerability.

Defensive striving for *perfection* is related to controlling. As in lying, it is a slavish and unrelenting imposition on the self of a standard of performance. It is to be right in others' eyes and to secure one's self-esteem. Perfectionists are the narcissistic overachievers: those who suffer greatly when receiving an A-minus grade on an examination or who have absolute need to dress in the latest fashion or whose every utterance is cast to meet rigid self-shaped criteria of precision or propriety. Perfectionists are ones who must be "good girls and boys," well into middle life or beyond—those still striving to meet parental expectation. In the poem "Richard Cory," Edwin Arlington Robinson portrays his defensive subject as "Clean favored, and imperially slim. . . . admirably schooled in every grace," a most impressive and enviable person. But what happened to him? "Richard Cory one calm summer night, Went home and put a bullet through his head." Daily the people had seen his perfection—but not his shame. That tragic revelation came later.

As a defense, *blaming* results from self-perceived miscues and failure, upsetting or surprise defeats. One primary purpose of blame is to cover shame by making someone else responsible for what happened. It may involve harsh indictment, contemptuousness, subtle evaluation, or scornful comparison. Blaming oneself is another way of meeting shame; it is an attempt to handle the suddenness or shock of error, thereby using judgment of a parental false self to maintain equilibrium.

The strategy of *denial* is adopted to escape pain, to avoid feeling hurt or lonely or embarrassed. It may be seen in efforts to ignore or tune out others. A familiar example is the child's erroneous declaration, "Sticks and stones may break my bones, but words will never hurt me." Denial is blocking out reality or not acknowledging one's real feelings, being insensitive to personally hazardous and unacceptable facts or conditions: "I don't want to talk about it"—"My divorce hasn't affected me one little bit!"—"You're looking at Mr. Invincible; I can take all the crap those guys at the office can throw at me!" To deny is to reveal personal insecurity. It is to be out of touch with the affective substance of the inner self and that of others. It is to be at a distance always—removed from one's and others' feelings.

Defensive postures are narcissistic, assumed to counter felt weakness— to enhance effectiveness. But they often fail in that purpose, for defensiveness defeats effectiveness. It forces retirement of the very resources needed to relate with success: trust, for example, the absence of which imperils an exchange. It creates barriers and it alienates, thus making identification with others difficult or impossible. The defender's attention is fixed on self-protective strategy. Jack Gibb, in his often-cited study,[90] notes that when devoting an "appreciable portion of his energy to defending himself," the defensive person "thinks about how he appears to others, how he may be seen more favorably, how he may win, dominate, impress, or escape punishment, and/or how he may avoid or mitigate a perceived or an anticipated attack." A result is creation of "similarly defensive postures in others" and possibly increasingly destructive interaction. Listening becomes defensive, promoting distraction and distortion of messages. The greater the defensiveness, the less the ability "to perceive accurately the motives, the values, and the emotions of the sender." Analysis reveals "that increases in defensive behavior were correlated positively with losses in efficiency in communication." Clear thinking, useful identification, and awareness and utilization of feedback are impossible to achieve when defensiveness rules in a relationship.

Whether inward or outward, many forms of defense are rhetorically hazardous. Experienced teachers know of behavioral patterns of some students, who, in anticipation of embarrassment or humiliation, i.e., narcissistic injury, will defend themselves by choosing to be absent from class on the day of a scheduled oral report. A case of aggressive defense – one illustrating forms of control, perfection, blame and denial – has to do with a sensitive thirty-year-old student, who "stung" by the teacher's criticism of his writing style, was enraged and wanted revenge. His response was a skillfully composed and trenchant public challenge of the teacher's priorities. Indeed, his aim was to assume control of class attitude and "destroy" the person who had inflicted the wound. Tension in the group lasted the entire term. At the end of the term, assuming that all could be forgotten, the student asked the teacher for a letter of recommendation.

Defensiveness and Ethos. In rhetorical interaction, no particular is more consequential than ethos. Depreciated ethos, for instance, can be disastrous. A prompt and forthright response by Richard Nixon to facts of the Watergate incident might have saved his presidency. His evasions and other defensive acts only weakened his position. America learned that shame can constrain the behavior of presidents as well as the ordinary citizenry – and become a political issue. Behavior that is perceptively evasive, uncaring, self-abasing, spiteful, envious, abusive, and tyrannical, etc, contributes to tarnished credibility; with mature audiences, it returns only rhetorical loss. Soiled ethos lies at the bottom of numberless instances of rhetorical dysfunction deriving from self-protective strategy.

The case of a former United States senator, Gary Hart, is relevant here. Would candor regarding his alleged relationship with Donna Rice have served to keep his presidential hopes alive in 1988? Very likely not, for the people seemed to take a pragmatic view, judging leadership – not morality – to be the overriding issue. Besides having to deal with the linking of his name to Ms. Rice's, Hart had begun to establish a pattern of self-occupation. For example, he set his birth date ahead one year and changed his name from Hartpence. Then there were other rumors of relations with women. Stories would not die. Moreover, a perception was developing of Hart as rather grim and self-conscious in his quest for acceptance and "perfection," i.e., in his intent on being *right* with the people but without a necessary light heart. Challenging the press to trail after him, to see if he was misbehaving seems to have been an act of denying ordinary vulnerability. His appearance with Ms. Rice on the yacht is another instance of denial: "Nobody can see *Gary Hart* here!" he appeared foolishly to have said — or just as puerile, "Gary Hart is above public judgment." He was not able to relieve his rhetoric — nonverbal as well as verbal — of his own insecurities and consequent defenses. Where was the infectious and disarming humor that public persons need when they err? Where the early and easy allowance for personal mistake? Blaming the press seemed a weak defense. Where was the ease of the healthy but human candidate? "Lighten up, Gary," a rhetorician might have advised; "show that you can laugh at yourself!" But Gary Hart, a proud and determined man, doubtless suffering, and spurred by urgent, self-exacting demands, expressed himself with a kind of arrogance, while ignoring values and expectations of the people who would confirm or reject him. They did reject him.

Vocal and Linguistic Distraction. Relevant vocal and linguistic characteristics deserve mention as possible sources of rhetorical deficiency. Depression, for example, carries with it certain vocal peculiarities that may prove to be obstacles in interaction with others. Reusch tells of distracting manifestations, e.g., "uniform phonation; narrow vocal range; falling rhythm," and monotonous voice which may "trail off." [91] Maggic Scarf notes that forms of depression are evidenced in "pressured, repetitive speech." When depressed, some people "will often speak in sentences that are slow and halting"; too, their facial expressions tend to be "flat, fixed, and unchanging." [92]

A narcissistic tendency in language use is to protect with distance, e.g., through formal usage, or, in seeming avoidance of responsibility for thought, through ambiguous usage. Ambiguity allows the user to escape the confines of explicit declaration and fixed, unalterable meaning. Passive voice and euphemism, too, provide the safety of imprecision and adjustability of meaning according to personal need. But while it might be argued that linguistic defenses of narcissism are rhetorically useful upon occasion, the perspective here is wider. While momentarily valuable perhaps, they prove unreliable as permanent resources. For example, though prudence occasionally may call for gentle euphemism rather than clear and direct assertion, equivocal, flaccid, safely veiled language does not allow for a strong, credible presence that others often expect.

McDougall has discovered that certain relationships "may well give rise to a form of personal esperanto," an "idiosyncratic use of language" that is "to be understood, through and in spite of one's way of communicating." It is a way of relating to selected others — of following a primary process model of dependence on others' peculiarities.[93]

MOTIVATION: PRIMAL FORCES AND NARCISSISM

A great force directing each person's way of being with others is a unique, personally fashioned rhetorical imperative. Essential to the character of that imperative at any social moment is healthy or unhealthy narcissism and behavior that may be rhetorically disposed or indisposed. Does the imperative prescribe heavy self-protection, or does it call for gestures of trust? What rhetorical choices does it empower? The growth of each human being is through a process that necessarily is social, for "the child is from the start embedded in a social world; without others he has no existence."[94] Thus the powerful demand for success with others; thus the rhetorical imperative. The mighty engine that drives the self in all interaction is abetted by the individual's inimitable stock of narcissistic energy, the primary expenditure of which is to effect recovery from unavoidable personal deficit. In this combine — of the primal force for survival and good or bad narcissism — is found peculiar motivation. And from that is rhetorical disposition determined.

The rhetorical imperative thereby becomes motivationally associated with one's narcissism: both the salutary influences that promote prosperity and the pernicious that work against it. But the ever-operative imperative carries on, no matter the consequence, pushing for effective representation of the self — regardless of qualitative values in the striving for self-fulfillment and repair. In this sense, the rhetorical imperative works disinterestedly, demanding action on others but blind to narcissistic bias. Basically, it is narcissistic quality — whether favorable or unfavorable — that makes the difference between a rhetorical and unrhetorical statement. And as is the tone of one's narcissism so is the thrust of the rhetorical imperative. One's rhetorical disposition — or indisposition — is revealed in exertions of the imperative. And to what effect? The audience will be the final judge on that.

TEMPORARY, INCONSISTENT, OR
PARTIAL RHETORICAL SUCCESS

In the great adventure of living and dealing with others, the healthy, normal person upon occasion will experience transitory oppressive narcissism and consequent rhetorical dysfunction, and the unhealthy at times will experience narcissistic maturity — or what passes for that — and consequent rhetorical success.

The Healthy Do Fail

In the instance of the healthy one failing, consider the factor of spontaneity, a quality often held up as virtuous and beneficial in interaction with others. But what of the effect of spontaneity on rhetorical purpose? It can be disadvantageous. Now, the well-adapted individual, with a soundly internalized rhetorical sense, has a built-in checking system to mediate judgments. And yet every such mature person will err, e.g., when in a moment of expressive excitement — in innocence or regression — he or she blurts out something in public that is taken by another as a breach of trust. "How could you have told everybody that!" is the response of the offended person. A rhetorical lapse disturbed a relationship.

Along with momentary imprudence and unchecked spontaneity, other instances of rhetorical failure known to the well-adapted person result from various kinds of triggering influence, e.g., stress, fatigue, grief, and anxiety. Also to be noted are periods of greater vulnerability, of which adolescence, middle age, and old age are examples. Any condition in which reduced self-esteem is a factor may be instrumental in instances of rhetorical mishap.

The Unhealthy Do Succeed

Conversely, narcissistic, rhetorically indisposed persons will know temporary rhetorical success — to a certain degree or at a certain level or with certain audiences. That is, they enjoy momentary effectiveness — infrequent and inconsistent or superficial and partial or mechanical or pseudo identification,[95] with some people, some of the time.

For Instance— When feeling adequate and gratified, in receipt of enough narcissistic supplies during a given day, e.g., a word of praise, a person may adapt satisfactorily and meet others with sensitivity sufficient to the instant.

When addressing similarly inclined others, the narcissistically needy may sense correctly that the others think or feel as he or she; effectiveness may be felt. This is fortuitous narcissistic unity: the locating of others in personal mirrors and generalizing about them therefrom. On occasion, this deduction of kinship will outfit people with relevant information to use in enforcing a connection to others. We must remember that any ordinary, loving person does have narcissitic interests to be met — and who readier to step in to satisfy the interests than attractive narcissists in need. They find some quality in that person that serves their purposes well.[96] Though typically limited by indisposition, the individual discovers the responsiveness of another — and uses that person, while being used. When played out symbiotically, the name of the exercise is narcissistic collusion. Success lies in choice of audience. One selects another as partner — friend or lover, perhaps employee or colleague — on the basis of symbiotic promise. Thus the individual sets up associations to suit personal narcissistic needs, *choosing* to be with others whose needs will ensure accommodation to his or her peculiar narcissism. The partners unconsciously play into each other's hands.[97]

When expressive, rhetorically careless, or naive individuals are found attractive by certain audiences, the appeal may arise from their charm, compelling grandiosity, or novel individualism. It is much as an adolescent's showing off may be appreciated by parents or friends. Though limited in number, particular audiences sometimes will respond admiringly and indulge displays of self-centeredness.

When an indisposed person is able to enforce peculiar personal behaviors, having others come to him or her and for some reason accept the person's individualism and inaccessibility, the narcissistic person may feel rhetorically adequate. Examples are seen in employment situations of one person dominating another, imbalanced marital arrangements, exploitative parent-child relationships, among others. In these cases, the indisposed person has structured a climate of deference and submission. Outside of that limited area of jurisdiction, rhetorical inadequacy may curb the person's power.

When a dream of being effective is experienced as reality, a sense of success is achieved. Kohut wrote of a client who in fantasy acquired a kind of "power and perfection" and realized "a temporary feeling of narcissistic balance" that presumably offered temporary social utility.[98] Perhaps a sense of rhetorical power can be so known.

When skill alone is all there is, it may do to a point. Use of mere rhetorical technique may influence, with resulting audience satisfaction of a sort, e.g., as achieved through dazzling style, impressive statistical display, or captivating nonverbal accountrement of dress, jewelry, or coiffure. But to what purpose and for how long?

When one displays the *likeness* of a substantive self to which audiences may choose to respond, identification may ostensibly result. But indeed it is a likeness! The relating is incomplete or "unreal," not an engagement or sharing. It is a perfunctory meeting that lacks intimacy; the gap remains, unbridged. Though someone does say something to another and the message is received and understood, distance stands. Someone *does* something *to* another; another is *serviced,* not united in consubstantiality. Call it *rhetorical servicing.* Sometimes that may be all that needs to be done, as in giving directions on catching the bus; sometimes it is the best one can do, e.g., when functioning in grief; sometimes it is not enough, e.g., when he needs a warm, soothing word, and she is capable of no more than a cool "You'll feel OK."

The "as if" phenomenon is a peculiar form of servicing. That particular behavior, given prominence in the literature by Deutsch,[99] may help to explain uneven or partial rhetorical success. In the instance of "as if" behavior, the performance may be well ordered, technically sound in other ways, and appearing to be adaptive to realities of audience and situation, and, indeed, results may be positive now and again. Through great need and effort to appear as others want them, these narcissistic, imitative artists adapt their rhetorical behaviors, sometimes brilliantly; in a cynical sense, they "identify" with audiences, giving them "what they want," so to speak, "as if" identifying with them. Understandably, their relationships lack continuity.

Aside from momentary and partial sufficiency or mechanical rhetorical servicing, rhetorical achievement of self-absorbed persons is limited.

4

Approaching the Analysis and Criticism of Rhetorical Indisposition

The purpose of this chapter is to create interest in the study of rhetorical dysfunction and offer guidance on approaching the work. The topics here are rubrics of investigation, steps in investigation, and alternative or augmentative methods.

RUBRICS OF INVESTIGATION

Following are eight points of guidance, mostly to do with setting and maintaining a focus for study. Also, they are reminders of some key concepts of prior chapters.

1. It should be kept in mind that ours is the study of rhetorical *interaction*. It is a dynamic model, of action and response. No one participant in any instance of rhetorical activity ever stands alone, even if standing alone is the participant's desire and purpose. One cannot not affect others, nor can one be unaffected by others. All human agents are rhetors, and all are audiences. Indeed, it is something of a fallacy to classify members of a rhetorical exchange as *either* speakers or listeners. All are audiences; all are rhetorical inventors; all are people who send and receive messages — and all the time — as long as they are together. All make choices in selecting and arranging material, in style and mode of presentation, roles to assume, rules to follow or ignore, etc. — to the end of being effective with others and acting on others, confirming and disconfirming. All are people of influence. Those who would study rhetorical behavior must appreciate these rudiments of the process of interaction.

2. But the investigator of rhetorical indisposition operates from an unusual, perhaps unique direction. This kind of critic is something of a rhetorical pathologist, one who specializes in exploration of impairment. While a chief pursuit of much criticism is to account for the realization of consubstantiality, in this work it is quite the opposite. If in agreement with Burkeian theory, the investigator must believe that the most basic

source of limitation on rhetorical success is unremediated apartness — in distance, difference, resistance — that exists and perhaps persists. In this, the self of the individual is the key variable. And the fundamental condition preventing achievement of consubstantiality is excessive *self*-occupation of some nature. It is this phenomenon to which the investigator is attracted. The guiding standard in investigation of rhetorical indisposition is a perception of health — of healthful identification and civility by which the investigator measures unhealth (see Chapter nine).

3. A critical part of this study, then, is discovery and analysis of messages: what people say with words or other symbols. Examination of speeches, a traditional method in rhetorical criticism, may be part of the necessary work, particularly if public figures are involved. An example is the speechmaking of Joseph McCarthy discussed in Chapter six. In some inquiries, conversations of interacting parties would be given attention. In others, press conferences enter in, or personal memos, interviews, and other types of primary data.

Among principal indicators of individualistic, unrhetorical behavior are messages showing disregard for social agreements and rules of interaction. Now, roles as played constitute messages, and a person's assumption of an unsocial — unrhetorical — role gives off a certain statement, e.g., about goal.[1] It *says* something to an audience and is available for the critic to interpret and analyze. General indicators are patterns of inappropriate confirming and disconfirming. Moreover, unrhetorical behaviors may be reflected in enthymemes, e.g., those that seek to enforce fusion and dependency or those that show no energy for positive engagement of another — no hope for intimacy.

But whatever the scene or occasion, a piece of verbal discourse is particularly valuable in rhetorical criticism, and when possible one wants to get the text or recording. Such is the tangible stuff from which to isolate chief enthymemes or name roles assumed, etc. With a taped or written record, the researcher has an edge and can begin the analysis with enviable confidence. Consider the following datum, taken word-for-word, let us assume. The employee said to the company manager:

> No I don't think I should have to "learn the ropes," as you put
> it. I didn't come here as just another run-of-the-mill technician
> who needs all this silly training like the rest of those people.

An enthymeme testifying to personal uniqueness is embedded in that comment. And if the manager responds defensively, e.g., by saying "I don't make the god-damned rules; go talk to the president," his or her message is also clear and perhaps could be analyzed as adoption of a role of self-exoneration.

Also primary in character, and often important, are non-verbal message components. In reference to critical essays in this book, consider the message on community tension implicit in Tiberius Gracchus' departing from custom by carrying a sword when political hostility mounted in Rome (see Chapter eight). Consider the nonverbal message sent by members of the Peoples Temple in their delivering surprise home-baked cakes to the doorsteps of influential community figures (Chapter five). Or consider the one occasion on which Paul Morel lapsed into use of his father's dialect. Why did he? (see Chapter seven). These are statements of rhetorical import, to be noted and assayed.

What of General Patton's silver helmet and fancy pistols strapped to his waist? Of someone's reluctance to make eye contact with a co-worker? Of a child's inaudibility in the principal's office? Of a job interviewee's overdressing? Or her arriving too early? What are implicit meanings? What is their relation to verbal components?

Reading extraverbal messages are a challenge to the researcher. All modes of behavior may be telling — some as vital as a speech. What is the message in the behavior of a financial adviser who in his individuality decides on a certain occasion to ignore Step Four of very strict company policy on handling retired persons' accounts? It may be "I can get away with it this time," and doubtless is laden with much information relevant to that person's rhetorical profile. Many such messages give evidence of peculiar inclination or personal motivation. Others are relational, revealing the character of the interacting members' feelings for each other and parts that each plays in the relationship.

One point here — on the *absence* of activity. In studying Richard Nixon's apparent rhetorical indisposition as revealed in his part in the unfolding of events during the last months of his presidency, we can learn as much from what he did not say or do as from his speeches, e.g., from the "stonewalling" and other specific avoidance behaviors. The critic's job is to discern what such choices "tell" audiences about the man, his purpose, and his view of his relationship with others — the people, in Nixon's case. The message appears in many forms; we have but to find it.

4. It must be kept in mind that rhetorical interaction is a study of human motivation. Indeed, in one sense, it is the study of the quest for social survival and personal prosperity, since rhetoric is the agency that provides means for discovery of identity, of acquiring confirmation of one's being. Acting to effect personal prosperity, the mighty rhetorical imperative constrains strategic action upon others. To account for rhetorical indisposition is to determine direction of the rhetorical imperative's mandates. A review of basic theory will serve to refresh scholars on motivation (readers may want to revisit Chapter one).

5. Given the centrality of motivation to the process of rhetorical interaction, it would seem that a biographical awareness is essential to analysis of rhetorical indisposition. Personal biography will receive primary focus, perhaps not in all cases, but in most. In earliest rhetorical experience, rhetors develop identities. They carry these with them, as seen in their characteristic playing of roles, development of rhetorical skill or deficiency, self-assessments, social outlook, and goals, etc. Consequently, scholars seek to discover, interpret, and use all relevant personal information on their subjects: rearing and home environment, schooling, associations, accomplishments and key events in life, problems encountered, etc. — everything bearing on their rhetorical development and experience. What is the nature of his rhetorical wherewithal or lack of it? What is hers? Who are they when interacting? What are relevant factors of positive and negative ethos? What are their expressions of unfavorable narcissism? These are the kinds of biographical questions that may be raised initially.

6. In these studies, it must be kept in mind that all humans have had less than perfect upbringing. Full and unceasing confirmation of omnipotence by caregivers is well nigh impossible. Furthermore, it is undesirable. Thus narcissism arises, the favorable and needed, that which may be traceable to adequate parental illusioning and disillusioning — and the unfavorable, from some measure of inadequacy. The former inclines workings of the rhetorical imperative toward mature rhetorical practice; the influence of the latter — as revealed in behaviors of the false self — are toward expressions of rage, depression, avoidance, and defenses generally, some of which can be classified as extrarhetorical.

7. One must remember, too, the investigation of rhetorical indisposition may be interdisciplinary. It very often requires knowledge of other fields and intelligent borrowing, e.g., from child development, psychoanalysis and psychology, possibly history or sociology or political science. Of course, there is reciprocity here, for representatives of those other disciplines occasionally may make use of rhetorical theory. But what do we use? Burke had an answer: "all there is to use." We use what we need — and what we can handle.

Let us look further into this. One should come to feel comfortable in reading literature on infancy and the child's interactions with caregivers. This is not to ask for acquaintance with all theories, but it is to insist on a certain mastery of material comprising relevant findings in at least one established theoretical perspective — one that will serve satisfactorily as a structure for understanding rhetorical implications. Without such, one may end up with a critically incomplete or shaky interpretation of those implications. Incidentally, much of contemporary theory on infant development fits nicely with theories of rhetorical interaction. The emphasis now is on social influences in the infant's life, on interaction with caregivers. Among the numerous highly valued works on child development that contributed to preparation of this book were those of H. R. Schaffer, Daniel N. Stern, and Donald W. Winnicott.

A comfortable working knowledge of useful psychoanalytic theory is strongly recommended also. This achievement will take time and serious study, but adequacy in coming to grips with behavioral motivation depends on a sound psychoanalytic and psychological grounding. Theories of Sigmund Freud, the founder of psychoanalysis, once were the most authoritative, and many remain as a foundation of writing today. But his monumental work is being enriched steadily and extended in interesting new directions. Thinkers are going beyond the master, inventing and adapting in accord with psychological phenomena of this age. Among those who may help rhetoricians and who themselves enjoy the highest respect of their peers are representatives of the so-called object relations school, e.g., Melanie Klein, W. R. D. Fairbairn, Harry Guntrip, Margaret Mahler, Heinz Hartman, and Otto Kernberg. Erik H. Erikson is another writer of repute. This book is indebted to some of those authorities but especially to Heinz Kohut and his followers in the self psychology school of psychoanalysis. Further the works of Gregory Rochlin and Donald W. Winnicott, pediatrician *and* psychoanalyst, have been especially instructive. Encompassing and utilizing psychoanalytic material will call for more than ordinary scholarly maturity and ability.

Though the discussion of narcissism in Chapter three is extensive, it may help to be reminded of works of prominent writers on that subject. Among the authors, besides Kohut, Kernberg, and Rochlin, are Alexander Lowen, James F. Masterson, Alice Miller, Richard M. Restak, Nathan Schwartz-Salant, and Jürg Willi. A particularly illuminating treatment is Stephen M. Johnson's *Humanizing the Narcissistic Style.*[2]

Reading on applicable theories and critiques of culture is also recommended. Rhetorical interaction takes place in scenes contoured by cultural forces, the character of which must be determined and interpreted. Particularly useful in preparation of this book were works of Robert N. Bellah et al., Robert Coles, Willard Gaylin, Christopher Lasch, and Richard Sennett.

8. Though they utilize others' research and ideas, scholars in rhetoric who investigate rhetorical indisposition ought to be aware of their own strength and purpose. As rhetoricians, we operate from a point of vantage: a unique and favorable perspective. When carefully trained in observation and analysis of messages and the dynamics of rhetorical interaction, we are ready to discover and report on significant dimensions in human behavior, some of which are less likely to be appreciated by persons outside

the discipline. Rhetoricians are the ones prepared to do that work — and there is much to be done. The counsel to rhetoricians, then, is to use their expertise, keep their focus on rhetorical interaction. And when in other scholars' fields, the advice is to be studiously circumspect in making applications and to generalize only as allowed by those other scholars' findings. They know the ice of their territorial ponds, the safe places and the thin. Follow their lead.

STEPS IN INVESTIGATION

Addressed directly to the researcher, the following advice is given on steps to take in doing the work.

1. Learn about narcissism and its relevance to rhetorical study. Read widely on the topic. Become acquainted with the literature, both the scholarly and more popular. Compare and contrast theories on the condition. Note the prevalence of unfavorable narcissism and its manifestations, e.g., the inward defensive expressions of depression and evasion, as well as the outward expressions of rage and grandiosity. Note the operation of unfavorable narcissism as a self-defeating behavioral condition. One reason for learning distinctions between the favorable and the unfavorable is that many writers use the terms "narcissism" and "narcissistic" without discrimination and often only pejoratively or in reference to pathology. Writers do have their purposes in their usages and their peculiar meanings to convey. But narcissism is universal, and, to a point or in a measure, it is adaptive and useful in one's life. Indeed, a so-called healthy ego is to be valued. Therefore, in the interest of clarity, the suggestion is to attach an appropriate adjective to the noun, e.g., call it *"oppressive* narcissism" or *"distracting* narcissism." When using the adjective "narcissistic," make clear the sense of the term as used, i.e., note whether you are referring to an unfavorable condition. In most instances, we probably should avoid adoption of the term "narcissist," for the connotation has become negative. Sometimes the context or a writer's obvious intent takes care of the problem of confusion in meaning.

Observe the connection of unfavorable narcissism to rhetorical indisposition. Public instances can be spotted. For example, note the momentary defensiveness of a public official who "lost his cool" and publicly berated members of an audience. Or note a certain celebrity's failure to maintain relationships with intimate partners and others. Interpersonal relationships are less accessible to scholars than public behaviors, but one must not give up because it is in relationships that most of the ordinary narcissistic "damage" occurs. For ideas on analysis of ordinary conversation and personal narrative, see the last section of this chapter. Accessibility is one reason for valuing fictional sources: novels, short stories, films, plays, and television drama. Think back to your reading and viewing experiences, recalling scenes or descriptions of relevant behavior.

2. Identify promising subjects. Perhaps observations have led you to consider investigating a certain subject. But what is a good subject? In deciding on cases for this book, the author asked questions like these about each prospect:

Does it seem to have rhetorical relevance?

Can behaviors of persons involved be classified as rhetorically indisposed, i.e., are the patterns and events of rhetorical maladaptation clear?

Does unfavorable narcissism seem to be an etiological factor?

Are biographical and historical materials and other bibliographic resources available for a satisfactory tracing out and analysis of the relevant patterns and events?

Has the subject not yet been examined for its rhetorical import?

Should it be? And if so, why?

Is it a subject that I can handle, i.e., do I have the scholarly preparation for carrying it out?

And if not, can I make adequate preparations?

Here is an example—a skeletal case, the story of a real person, who, though not famous in the usual sense of the term, was very well known in his field. He was a university professor and scholar. Let's see if one could—or should—study this case.

As Professor Doe's scholarly writing began to receive acclaim, his reputation grew; his future was bright, to be sure. Now, what does it take to put a successful academic career together, besides intelligence, good training, ample knowledge, etc.? Motivation, for one thing: keen interest in making significant contributions and being acknowledged by peers. Nothing wrong with that. Thus does favorable narcissism motivate. But this person's needs—the rhetorical imperative as it worked on him—pushed him to take risks, to violate professional rules. His interest in academic advancement became so pressing that he plagiarized material for one of his studies and submitted the manuscript for publication in a scholarly journal. The tacit, essentially extraverbal message to the journal editor was, "This is all mine." Knowing the scholar's good reputation, the trusting editor took the message as honest and accepted the essay. But soon after publication, the deceit was discovered. Professor Doe left the profession and has not returned. What lies behind this man's professional failure, his rhetorical indisposition? One day, someone may want to investigate the case and report findings. The profession would be richer for it. But does it have rhetorical relevance? Can it be done?

Professor Doe's case does have rhetorical relevance; it involves a person interacting with others — in an imprudent quest for confirmation from others. In narcissistic desperation, he invented improperly — he broke the rules, and he suffered loss of all essential ethos. Yes, his act revealed rhetorical indisposition. But are data available for studying the case? That is a key question. How does one secure sufficient, relevant, and reliable biographical data, e.g., on personal background, feelings and pressures, and specific motivation? The personal interview would seem to be the best instrument for use in this. Consent is needed, and only the subject himself has the answer to his availability. Like this one, probably every subject has at least one big challenge connected to it, but often it can be met in some way.

Among celebrities, e.g., in the entertainment and sports worlds, are to be found many cases of rhetorical indisposition, perhaps because of vulnerability of self and related hazards faced by the populants. These people are in the public eye and dependent on acclaim. Some have been verbally and nonverbally told of their special talents for a long time. That is, messages to them have confirmed their illusion on personal omnipotence. And responses to that kind of information often lead to peculiar problems. Can they sustain the identity? Will the confirmation last? For some, age becomes a factor or waning talent. Also, fans are fickle. In any event, they will suffer loss eventually, and it may be devastating: when they are not sought after anymore — when the bookings fall off, when they do not "make the cut," when a supporter walks out and lets them down. Some are able to keep self together; others fail in that, sustaining painful injury and major impairment in relating. The latter are people who have never grown up; the interpersonal forces were too much to meet. Until the time of the shock, they may have had no realization of their indisposition. For they had been carried by attentions of others, and now they are on their own. The result is a deep, deep hurt — as their fury, despair, and myriad defensive reactions demonstrate. For others, celebrities *and* ordinary people, the rhetorical indisposition may appear much earlier, a consequence of hurts received along the way; they have felt the problem daily and for a long time.

Amid the many cases is one of a successful major league baseball pitcher who after some years began to "lose his stuff." A sportswriter told of his numerous awards and excellent win-loss record and how his arm got sore. Then "all went sour." He began to "blame everybody but himself for his problems, and he transmitted that attitude to those around him. . . . He thought everybody should love him just as much" as when he was winning sixteen games. His moaning began to undermine team morale. He was a person who "had grown well into his 20s without ever having to shoulder responsibility for his actions." Athletes are "shielded from reality and thus unable to deal with adversity," the sports writer claims. Star athletes are coddled from a very early age. "It is not surprising that they come to think they are indeed special and don't have to conform to the rules that govern others."

On a somewhat related topic, another writer quoted a former professional basketball star on his retirement: "You get depressed — like you're falling off a cliff — and there's nothing that seems to excite you enough or makes you interested enough for a long period of time. You're kind of in a malaise." That malaise signals narcissistic injury and as such is predictive of rhetorical maladaptation. One indicator is abuse of others; another is abuse of self, e.g., through alcohol or drug use. Research opportunities in this area are extensive and exciting.

A different kind of narcissism is sometimes seen in the business world. Consider the case of a well-known, highly individualistic and swashbuckling airline executive who typifies in some eyes a kind of capitalistic arrogance. An early sign of this man's intense need to dominate was his involvement in election fraud in college days, a charge to which he eventually confessed. Reportedly, he is an extremely private man and insensitive to others' needs, e.g., of organized workers. He is a vicious competitor. One business journalist declares that "He has proved himself to be a person who will say or do whatever is necessary to get his way." Are his successes the result of extrarhetorical strategy, e.g., brute dictatorial force? The direction of the rhetorical imperative as it works on him might intrigue a student of rhetoric. Or perhaps the investigative scope of this case should be expanded — into organization communications and to include message-sending among all relevant sources: colleagues, business competitors, labor unions, government agencies, etc.

Are there rhetorical implications in the case of a talented American distance runner whose much discussed narcissistic wounding in childhood apparently is reflected in her insolence and maltreatment of co-competitors? Known as "Whiny Ms. Doe," she seems to be working against herself, hurting her career and failing in creating productive relationships. Sports columnists like to write about her, but is her behavior a subject for rhetorical research?

Below is a sampling of prominent names, each representing — on the surface and according to report — ostensible and varying degrees of narcissistic oppression. These are individuals whose rhetorical experience might be studied with profit. Some biographical data are available, e.g., in books, periodicals, and perhaps in their direct testimony or others'. Do they seem to be satisfactory subjects? After this listing will come some fictional subjects.

Real People

William Saroyan: According to his son Aram in the book *Last Rites*, this celebrated author was an angry, unforgiving man whose problems in childhood twisted him emotionally. As young Saroyan tells it, evidence of his father's nature was apparent in his relations with others, where worked the "black poisons" of his soul.

Joan Crawford: Is her story similar to Saroyan's? Read daughter Christina's *Mommie Dearest*. What are rhetorical ramifications?

John Derek: Is his daughter's story similar to Christina's? Catherine Derek's book is called *Cast of Characters*.

Yul Brynner: The embittered Rock Brynner is yet another celebrity's offspring to write about the relationship with a parent. In his *Yul: The Man Who Would Be King*, he tells of his father's disaffecting "pompous, outspoken, cold, and domineering manner."

Richard Nixon: His despair, reputation as a loner, self-absorption, general protective behavior, and related attributes might help to explain his part in the Watergate cover-up and his defensive speechmaking. Could the real "cancer on the presidency" have been the president's unfavorable narcissism?

Brenda Frazier: This famous rich woman and socialite felt unwanted in her childhood; her life included many fractured relationships. "I have never known the meaning of true love," she said. Wealth is no substitute for a rhetorical disposition.

William Jennings Bryan: Bryan ran unsuccessfully for the presidency three times. He died five days after the conclusion of the Scopes trial in which he was opposed — and embarrassed — by Clarence Darrow. What did Kathleen Jamieson mean when she said that Bryan "was the victim of a definition of himself."?[3]

Max Robinson: the first black television anchor person in America, Robinson was under tremendous pressure on the job. Carrying a heavy burden as role model, he suffered severe depression and had trouble in relationships. He died of AIDS at age forty-nine, presumably from drug use. One senses a very important rhetorical story here.

Gary Hart: The case of this beleaguered politician who once was the leading candidate for presidential nomination by his party is referred to in prior chapters. Some interested scholar of rhetorical indisposition ought to investigate further.

Lee Harvey Oswald: What shaping of this life ruled out uses of rhetoric to accomplish ends? Certain persons, in their rhetorical indisposition, are drawn to use of extrarhetorical strategy, including violence and other acts that bespeak unfavorable narcissistic motivation.

General George Patton: Is the evidence of his physical and verbal abuse of soldiers suggestive of a pattern of rhetorical indisposition in his life? Do biographical data include material on the workings of his narcissism?

Harold Griffin: What are rhetorical implications in the life of a man who rose from ghetto life to become a star football player at UCLA, receive a Rhodes scholarship, and amass a fortune as an investment counselor and real estate promoter—but who reportedly had only one ideal: "to become rich and powerful and famous"? Bankrupt, guilty of tax evasion, and characterized as "very clever, very smooth, and . . . totally asocial," he is charged with bilking his clients out of many millions of dollars. And what motivated the clients—the wealthy and professional business people who harkened to his messages of opportunity? "Greed covers it very well," admitted one of the clients who lost heavily. The clients themselves must be included as subjects of study in this case.

Pete Rose: The outstanding professional record of one of the most talented baseball players of modern day is marred by rule violations: e.g., unacceptable physical contact with an umpire and gambling on sporting events, and income tax evasion—not to mention reported acts of incivility in other relations. Does his individualism constitute rhetorical dysfunction? How is narcissistic motivation to be explored in his case? To what extent will society indulge behavior of the sort represented?

Perhaps the subjects outlined above will suggest others—prominent and ordinary.

Fictional Subjects

Chapter seven is an analysis of fictional rhetorical dysfunction. D. H. Lawrence's novel *Sons and Lovers*, while excellent in its own right as a piece of literature, is an unusually realistic and informative study of narcissistic collusion and rhetorical incapacitation. Such a work reminds us that some well-written literary examples may be superior to actual ones. For one thing, all needed data are there, laid out between the covers of the book or between the start and finish of the movie or play. And the "findings" therein are reliable, e.g., on behavior motivation, the demonstration of which is a mark of quality in fiction. In large part, the trained researcher has but to read carefully, interpret, and analyze to the end of explicating rhetorical meaning.

Here are some promising titles, first of novels.

The Brothers Karamazov by Fyodor Dostoevsky. One brother represents narcissistic depravity; another is narcissistically healthy and rhetorically mature; the direction of the third is undecided.

Les Miserables by Victor Hugo. This is another study of contrasts: of the rhetorically disposed Jean Valjean and the uncivil, narcissistically wounded Inspector Javert.

I Look Divine by Christopher Coe. Here is a modern story of narcissistic confinement and sacrifice for an ideal self-image.

Some other interesting novels are James Baldwin's *Go Tell It on the Mountain*, Richard Wright's *Black Boy*, Leo Tolstoy's *Death of Ivan Ilych*, and Georges Simenon's *The Cat*.

Plays and movies offer many possibilities.

Who's Afraid of Virginia Woolf? by Edward Albee. This is a classic of verbal brutality, of George and Martha and their narcissistic aggression.

That Championship Season by Jason Miller is about the lives and interactions of five narcissistically defective people. Their abusiveness, dependence, and insecurity exemplify rhetorical inadequacy.

Ordinary People. In this movie, the mother stands out as the case for study.

Nothing in Common. This movie details the relationship of a son with his rhetorically indisposed father.

Death of a Salesman by Arthur Miller. Either a film version or play is excellent for study of false values, social abandonment, denial of reality, and impoverishment of soul.

The Color of Money presents a fascinating contrast between the narcissistic problems of the "has been" and those of the brash and insecure young pool player who is dominated by the need to be confirmed a winner.

Among other movies with relevant themes and behaviors are *Twelve Angry Men*, *Days of Wine and Roses*, *Desperately Seeking Susan*, and *The Breakfast Club*.

A number of Sam Shepard's plays are promising, as are Samuel Beckett's. Ingmar Bergman's *Scenes from a Marriage* is rich in possibilities. Among topical short stories are Kurt Vonnegut's, "Who Am I This Time?" and John Cheever's "The 5:48."

Heinz Kohut of the self psychology school of psychoanalysis found literature to be a plenteous and reliable source for study of human behavior. In his *Self Psychology and the Humanities*, he refers to a number of illustrative fictional works. Included are O'Neill's *A Long Day's Journey into Night* and *The Great God Brown*, Melville's *Moby Dick*, *Hamlet*, and Heinrich von Kleist's *Michael Kohlhaas*.

3. Formulate a thesis to guide the investigation. The thesis of the study of Jim Jones and the members of the Peoples Temple (Chapter five) is that Jones and the people were willing partners in their disastrous nar-

cissistic relationship. The thesis of the report on Tiberius Gracchus (Chapter eight) is that his story is not one of oratorical greatness but of rhetorical indisposition. Sometimes a question serves well as thesis, e.g., "Can Hamlet's problem be called rhetorical indisposition?"

4. Decide on a research procedure. The case method is the research procedure used in this book; people's lives are studied (see Chapters five through eight). The subjects are individuals interacting. In exploration of three of the cases, the discussion extends to the involvement of many others, e.g., groups or nations. In two cases, the larger groups become co-subjects: Joseph McCarthy *and* the American people; Jim Jones *and* the membership of the Peoples Temple.

A variety of kinds of material are sought by one using the case method. Among those found useful in building the cases here were historical and sociological data, biographical data, texts of speeches, and newspaper reports. From one view, such case studies may seem to represent traditional rhetorical criticism. A closer look will show differences, e.g., the necessary use of psychoanalytic theory to account for rhetors' epistemologies and world views, motivations, and strategies. At a later point we shall consider certain alternative or augmentative methods to case study investigation.

5. Conduct the investigation, staying close to the thesis and main areas of focus, e.g., in seeking evidence of impairment to self and the unfavorable narcissism that lies behind the rhetorical indisposition. Consult all accessible sources of data.

Seek out primary sources, those standing as first witness to events, e.g., speech texts and conversations or other exchanges (noting both verbal and nonverbal components). Other primary sources include diaries, letters, public records, autobiographies, and relevant contemporary newspaper or periodical accounts. Evidence is classed as secondary, if one or more persons has "come between" the primary source and the one doing the research, e.g., a critic who has written *about* someone's speaking practices. Thus biographies, histories, and criticisms — as well as sundry interpretations, translations, or reviews — are secondary. Though the researcher places high value on primary materials, certain second-level data may also be very useful — and indispensable, e.g., well-founded assessments of events and actions prepared by reliable writers who had peculiar access to primary sources.

Two case studies of this book, Chapter five on Jim Jones and the Peoples Temple membership and six on Joseph McCarthy and the American people, make use of both primary and secondary sources. In that, they represent standard methodology in rhetorical criticism: utilization of speeches and public pronouncements, printed news stories, testimony of individuals, and biography. Chapter eight on Tiberius Gracchus, like many treatments of ancient events, is based entirely on secondary historical and biographical material. The old accounts of Appian and Plutarch are the best we have, and indeed, serve satisfactorily in the hands of competent modern scholars. The fact that respected historians who write on the late Roman Republic, like Alvin H. Bernstein and David Stockton, draw heavily on them may be their strongest recommendation. The case of Paul Morel and family, subject of Chapter seven, is fictional; therefore, evidence is not an issue. A novelist presumable "knows all," and if an accomplished writer like D. H. Lawrence, his or her "evidence" will be sound and convincing.

In testing data, there are three main questions to ask: First, "Do I have enough material to allow for drawing conclusions on my subjects' behaviors?"; second, "Are all pieces of material relevant to my thesis and main points of development?"; third, "Is the material reliable?" The third test requires checking on qualifications of sources, finding corroboration, and ferreting out discrepancies and inaccuracies.

Sources used will depend on topic. Preparation of the study of the Peoples Temple required the use of a number of journalistic reports, including book-length treatments, newspapers, and magazines. A key source was Tim Reiterman's (with John Jacobs) biography of Jim Jones. It is always comforting to have at least one particularly sound source like that. Besides supplying needed data, it can be utilized as a gauge against which to check other material.

In going about their work, researchers seek evidence bearing on central issues, e.g., what behaviors seem to be dysfunctional? In what ways are they rhetorically dysfunctional? Are dysfunctional behaviors representative? What is their incidence? And in what scenes do they appear, typically? One needs vital information about all key persons involved, e.g., data on background, schooling, family status, chosen roles and occupational status, personality traits, etc. In what kind of environment were they reared? Does it appear that caregivers provided adequately? Are evidences of regressive behavior to be found, e.g., in adolescence? Some topics will require the raising of different or additional questions. For example, the topic of lying as strategic protective behavior would have the researcher ask about the uses of lying in that era as opposed to prior or later eras or about the place of lying in the culture, etc.

6. Finally, comes the writing of the report. In concluding, ask and answer this question: So what? In the final analysis what have you accomplished in this report? What is the significance of the study? Have you constructed a model for others' use? Do you have some broad implications to lay out? A lesson to draw? An application to make? The Jim Jones study found lack of vigilance among many people and agencies to have contributed to the Jonestown tragedy. The Tiberius study discovered a

possible connection between Tiberius' rhetorical indisposition and the eventual fall of the Roman Republic. What stands out as your chief finding or point of consequence?

ALTERNATIVE OR AUGMENTATIVE METHODS

In the event that the case method of investigating rhetorical indisposition is not applicable to the researcher's task, or if augmentation of a case study is indicated, other methods are available. Discussed below is a variety of qualitative methods, most of which may require direct observation. All can be applied to rhetorical interaction. The treatment is intended to be suggestive of possibilities only and by no means exhaustive or detailed. The purpose here is to stimulate thinking, generate ideas, and offer a heuristic perspective. Some of the approaches can be put in the participant-observer category, since the researcher becomes situated as observer and possibly question-asker and note-taker—in an outside field, e.g., public meeting or workplace. Further, the methods overlap, e.g., to analyze conversation may be to inquire into functions of rules.

Conversation Analysis

One alternative is close analysis of rhetorical elements of two or more persons in conversation. The content of those interactions often is highly complex activity. Special tools have been shaped and refined for use in determining participants' purposes, meanings, and ways of managing their behavior in conversation. How do selected people conduct turn taking? What are discernible patterns of eye contact? Of physical distance from others? Of defensive behavior? Which verbal and nonverbal expressions are "scripted," i.e., well-learned and practiced over time, perhaps from infancy? Which are spontaneous? Which contrived? And what does any given rhetorical act—instance of specific behavior—mean? And, for example, what, in a certain context, is the character of a given rhetorical act's narcissistic component? And, from that, what is its rhetorical value?

A useful introduction to conversation analysis is to be found in Kathleen K. Reardon's treatment.[4] Among topics discussed are structure, management of conversations, and approaches to the study of conversation, e.g., Erving Goffman's self-presentation approach. Also, she includes Thomas S. Frentz's model of conversational structure. Each of its five phases suggests lines of inquiry.

1. Initiation phase: a phase when people exchange greetings.

2. Rule definition phase: a period of negotiation about the type of interaction or amount of time needed for it.

3. Rule confirmation phase: a phase of agreement between the communicators concerning the type of interaction and amount of time that will be allocated to it.

4. Strategic development phase: a period during which the conversation topic is discussed.

5. Termination phase: a phase that includes farewells or changes of topic.

Topics for investigation are numerous. For instance, what behaviors of the initiation phase in a given interaction might constitute rhetorical indisposition? How does the intrusion of unfavorable narcissism affect rule definition? Is rhetorical maladaptation more apparent in the rule confirmation phase than in the strategic development phase?

Shift-Response and Support-Response

In exploration of forms of "conversational narcissism," Charles Derber has conceived two kinds of attention getting response: the shift-response and the support-response.[5] He gives these examples:

John: I'm feeling really starved.
Mary: Oh, I just ate. (shift-response)
John: I'm feeling really starved.
Mary: When was the last time you ate? (support-response)

When people use a shift-response, they shift attention to themselves; when they use a support-response, they focus attention on the other. As Derber notes, "Conversational narcissism involves preferential use of the shift-response and underutilization of the support-response."

Too, there are both active and passive moves: the former being seen in frequent use of the shift-response strategy so as to turn others' topics to those about oneself and the latter seen in infrequent use of the support-response strategy so as to withhold reinforcement of others' topics. Success in the art of attention getting — a narcissistic art as Derber discusses it — may require great subtlety, for "The effectiveness of the shift-response as an attention-getting device lies partly in the difficulty in distinguishing whether a given response is a sharing one or a narcissistic initiative."

How common is this "narcissistic" practice? Quite common, Derber would answer. Does it reveal rhetorical indisposition in the user? The main test is loss of effectiveness with others. Keeping in mind that rhetorical success depends on effecting consubstantiality and on confirmation, etc., the investigator of rhetorical indisposition might use Derber's structures in analysis of interactions, e.g., conversations and group discussions. In studying cases of rhetorical indisposition, one might find employment of the shift-response as a way of life with certain subjects—perhaps to be seen as a metaphor for their ways of being with others.

Rules Research

Rules theory, as suggested above, may be used in conversation analysis, but it has wider applications. In rhetorical interaction, certain behaviors in given social contexts are required; others are preferred; some are disallowed. "When in Rome, do as the Romans do" is a general rule of behavior, but with clear rhetorical implications. In some situations, women are by rule of traditional cultures prohibited from use of profanity and men are not. A child who accepts a treat may be required by family or cultural rules to say "Thank you"—and in a specified way. Of course, people often relate to one another without being conscious of rules while at other times they are highly conscious of rule observance, e.g., in a new social situation or if a topic of conversation is controversial.

This is but a bare introduction to an understanding of rules theory and methodology. Interested persons should consult a more complete source, e.g., Donald P. Cushman's article on rules perspective or Susan B. Shimanoff's book.[6] One will discover many applications to the study of rhetorical maladaptation. For example, a mark of rhetorical indisposition is rule breaking, hearing the sound of one's own narcissistic drummer, e.g., in changing the topic of conversation at will, to suit oneself. In effect, the person says, "I make my own rules." Conversely and interestingly, another mark of rhetorical indisposition is rigid adherence to rules, e.g., when a person as co-dependent goes along with the other person's rules without questioning.

One could use rules theory to substitute for or augment the main case studies of this book. For example, one might undertake an extensive study of Jim Jones' imposition of his rules and the faithful compliance of the Peoples Temple membership (see Chapter five). The American people sanctioned Joseph McCarthy's rules (see Chapter six). Gertrude and Paul Morel worked out rules for their relationship (see Chapter seven), and Tiberius Gracchus violated long-standing rules of Roman political practice (see Chapter eight). In each case, the issue of rules was significant.

Can it be said that the study of rhetorical interaction is the study of rules, and their use? From one significant perspective, yes.

Narrative Analysis

In recent years, the literatures of many academic disciplines have reminded us that people are storytellers. Stories tell who we are and give order to experience. And in relating them, we involve others in our lives and share ourselves.[7] Out of daily living flow narratives, told and retold, in old ways and new.

Narratives are messages sent and received. They are the stuff of our selves: ordinary and informal representations of personal interest, of motivation and social and personal values. They are heard and told wherever people interact (of course, some are intrapersonal and private), wherever people find the responsive presence of others: in bars, supermarkets, hair-dressers' shops, self-service laundries, at picnics and ballgames, on buses and airplanes — everywhere. Some we hear or see created as fiction; people who write novels or plays tell stories of people's stories. And in a real sense, *all* books — all behaviors! — are stories, or parts thereof. Narratives are self-expressive, products of one's total being for others to experience: relayed to declare one's self, to justify a life or an act, to realize satisfaction of self. They reveal the tellers' self-conceptions, the roles they favor, their sense of rules in communication, and the grounding of their enthymemes. Each one's story is unique in substance, style, and mode of presentation. Each is indicative of a peculiar individuality, of motivation in message sending, and of responses sought from others.

Stories told are the result of the rhetorical imperative, different in form from individual to individual and from contingency to contingency. Some stories succeed and others fail, thereby revealing a teller's rhetorical disposition or indisposition and the influence of other constraining forces.

Certain stories that work with one person will not work with another. Rationality is one variable. Walter R. Fisher writes of two essential criteria of rationality: *narrative probability* — whether the story hangs together and is free of contradiction; and *narrative fidelity* — whether the message constitutes a "good reason," i.e., is taken as a "*warrant for accepting or adhering to the advice*" of the message. The decisions on probability and fidelity rest with the receiver, e.g., whether the story is "a mask for ulterior motives."[8]

Indeed, some stories do "turn others off." among such narrative messages are those that seem to challenge the receiver's values, violate certain rules of communication of the time and place, or require the receiver to assume an uncomfortable role. For example, a receiver may resist a teller's inclination to assign the receiver the therapist role — or scapegoat or punching bag.

But it must be noted that some stories condemned by an objective observer *do* work with others. Take, for example, the co-dependent who is ready to certify narrative probability and fidelity in an intimate's unhealthy story. A needy person is likely to embrace a "bad story." Madeleine, whose case was mentioned in Chapter three, doubtless did that for years with her alcoholic husband Manny. Healthful rival narratives that Madeleine may have heard elsewhere, e.g., of a friend or neighbor, could have helped her, but they were not effective, for she and Manny did not change. They stayed together for twenty-two years. Madeleine conceived of herself as one to be there for Manny; that was the way to be a "good wife." Thus she denied any stories that would negate her self-conception.[9]

One approach to studying rhetorical indisposition is to collect and analyze people's stories: to judge the narcissistic quotient of a message's warrant, the maturity level of an enthymeme, the assumed character of the relationship as suggested by message content, the personal values reflected in story exchanging. What warrants, enthymemes, roles, or themes of messages are suggestive of self-aggrandizement or extraordinary self-interest — and therefore seem indicative of rhetorical ineffectiveness? Stories giving evidence of rhetorical indisposition are those revealing insensitivity to others' needs and feelings, and unwillingness to engage cooperatively, intolerance and disrespect, lack of interpersonal courage, a low level of rhetorical ability, dependence, lacks in appreciation of freedom, and a diminished sense of responsibility (see Chapter nine).

Ethnography

Characterizations of ethnographic research are diverse. But Stephen W. Littlejohn's view appears to be representative. He concludes that "Ethnography is a kind of cultural study in which an interpreter from outside the culture attempts to make sense of the actions of the group being studied."[10] The goal in ethnography, as advanced here, is to describe rhetorical behaviors and construct an interpretative model for use in coming to understand them.

James P. Spradley names six steps in the work: selecting an ethnographic project, asking ethnographic questions, collecting ethnographic data, making an ethnographic record, analyzing ethnographic data, and writing an ethnography.[11]

The selected project can be rather large in scope or narrow, involving observations of an entire community or of the few employees of a retail store. Let us say that one is interested in studying rhetorical indisposition as seen in defensive behavior. One might decide to observe relevant interactive patterns among members of a given family or package handlers at United Parcel Service or the customer service department at Macy's. At Macy's, the researcher observes interactions of employees with customers and among themselves, seeking to account for all relevant factors and conditions, including verbal and nonverbal parts of messages exchanged. In carrying out the project, the researcher has lots of questions. What are notable physical features of the scene? Who took part in a given rhetorical episode? Who initiated a given interaction? What did he or she say, with and without words? What was the response? Careful records are kept. If properly done, the study might yield useful data on how defensive behavior is triggered, the types of defensive strategies chosen in that environment, and the maladaptive character of the strategies.

Many helpful materials are available to introduce persons to ethnoraphic methods of investigation.[12]

Other Methods

Marcus L. Armbrester and Glynis Holm Strause in their book *A Rhetoric of Interpersonal Communication*[13] develop a number of provocative approaches to the analysis of rhetorical interaction, some of which can be adapted to the study of dysfunction. In discussing the creation and maintenance of roles — "rhetorical means of becoming socialized" — they note that each assumed role is maintained by its own set of rules, characteristics, and strategies. How might this conception be used in investigating rhetorical indisposition? First, one would turn the entire framework upside down, changing the focus to *un*socialization, i.e., to location of self-serving narcissistic functions. Then, following the adapted research design, one would collect samples of rhetorical exchanges. One might approach the analysis of selected messages of self-absorption by identifying roles played and peculiar personal rules adhered to, naming each role, and determining specific characteristics for each as well as the implementing strategies. Depending on the researcher's interests, one purpose might be to begin shaping a profile of an individual's — or group's — rhetorical indisposition.

Another of Armbrester and Strause's ideas requires classifying "Stereotypic Rhetorical Personality Types," e.g., as "Super-Mom" or "Super-Macho." For each type, the authors identify stereotypic nonverbal behaviors, vocal traits, typical phrases, and rhetorical motives.[14] Though reliance on stereotypic categories is problematic in research, the idea is interesting and may serve heuristically in devising a system of analysis, e.g., for constructing model outlines of certain counterproductive narcissistic messages, such as those that would deny another's separate identity.

Armbrester and Strause also remind readers of promising uses of Gerald Marwell and David R. Schmitt's list of sixteen compliance gaining strategies.[15] These are themes of family messages. Suggesting possible narcissistic dimension, any of the sixteen might be used in study of conversation or other informal interaction.

Compliance-Gaining Strategies With Examples from Family Situations

1. Promise	(If you comply, I will reward you.) "You offer to increase Dick's allowance if he increases his studying."
2. Threat	(If you do not comply, I will punish you.) "You threaten

to forbid Dick the use of the car if he does not increase his studying."

3. Expertise (Positive)

(If you comply, you will be rewarded because of "the nature of things.") "You point out to Dick that if he gets good grades he will be able to get into a good college and get a good job."

4. Expertise (Negative)

(If you do not comply, you will be punished because of "the nature of things.")
"You point out to Dick that if he does not get good grades he will not be able to get into a good college or get a good job."

5. Liking

(Actor is friendly and helpful to get target in "good frame of mind" so that he will comply with request.)
"You try to be as friendly and pleasant as possible to get Dick in the 'right frame of mind' before asking him to study."

6. Pre-Giving

(Actor rewards target before requesting compliance.)
"You raise Dick's allowance and tell him you now expect him to study."

7. Aversive Stimulation

(Actor continuously punishes target making cessation contingent on compliance.)
"You forbid Dick the use of the car and tell him he will not be allowed to drive until he studies more."

8. Debt

(You owe me compliance because of past favors.)
"You point out that you have sacrificed and saved to pay for Dick's education and that he owes it to you to get good enough grades to get into a good college."

9. Moral Appeal

(You are immoral if you do not comply.)
"You tell Dick that it is morally wrong for anyone not to get as good grades as he can and that he should study more."

10. Self-Feeling (Positive)

(You will feel better about yourself if you comply.)
"You tell Dick he will feel proud if he gets himself to study more."

11. Self-Feeling (Negative)

(You will feel worse about yourself if you do not comply.)
"You tell Dick he will feel ashamed of himself if he gets bad grades."

12. Altercasting (Positive)

(A person with "good" qualities would comply.)
"You tell Dick that since he is a mature and intelligent boy he naturally will want to study more and get good grades."

13. Altercasting (Negative)

(Only a person with "bad" qualities would not comply.)
"You tell Dick that only someone very childish does not study as he should."

14. Altruism

(I need your compliance very badly, so do it for me.)
"You tell Dick that you really want very badly for him

to get into a good college and that you wish he should study more as a personal favor to you."

15. Esteem   (People you value will think better of you if you comply.)
    (Positive)   "You tell Dick that the whole family will be very proud of him if he gets good grades."

16. Esteem   (People you value will think worse of you if you do not
    (Negative)   comply.)
                "You tell Dick that the whole family will be very disappointed in him if he gets poor grades."

Perceived Understanding

One more means of exploring the subject grows out of Dudley D. Cahn's writing on measuring perceived understanding.[16] The "feeling of being understood, or perceived understanding," he reports, "is inferred from cues in social interaction and refers to the communicators' feelings following their perceived successes and failures when attempting to communicate with one another." This research clarified and extended the idea of confirmation, finding that confirmation results from support of one's *preferred* self-concept. Application of this perspective to the study of rhetorical indisposition seems promising. Consult Cahn's *Letting Go.*

Creative investigators will devise designs and methods to suit their purposes. They should be ready to make adaptations as suggested by the work at hand.

In conclusion—the study of rhetorical indisposition is about failure in rhetorical interaction: human incapacitation in achievement of consubstantiality, the inefficacious and unhealthful pursuit of confirmation. Rhetoricians conducting these studies must be knowledgeable on human motivation and development, use of biographical data, and interdisciplinary supporting material. With that knowledge, and a sound understanding of unfavorable narcissism, researchers can discover possible subjects and appropriate methodologies, and then begin their work.

The studies of the following four chapters illustrate use of the case method of investigation.

5

The Peoples Temple:
A Rhetorical Study of Collusion[1]

WILLING PARTNERS

In the twenty-five years preceding the catastrophe at Jonestown in Guyana in 1978, hundreds of people in Indiana, California, and elsewhere came into close contact with Jim Jones, best known as the leader of the Peoples Temple.[2] For many, including most of the over 900 who died in that jungle community, the relationship was deep and lasting. Moreover, it was a relationship that can be studied rhetorically, as a study of people choosing association and seeking means of personal effectiveness. In contrast to other reports on this subject, this study centers on relevant dynamics of the *exchange* between leader and followers. The view here is that the people *chose* to involve themselves with the leader and, further, that he was as attracted to them as they to him. Without their messages on self-need and state of being, displayed cues that he perceived, they would have remained objects of insignificance to him. Inexorably, Jones was driven by a goal to build a cohesive community of adherents, and he interpreted their revealed readiness as invitation. He solicited and selected only those who signalled availability. Their very presence to him was an overture; Jones "saw them coming," to put it colloquially—but *they* were looking as well.

This, then, is a study, not of Jim Jones and his "victims," but of the relationship of willing partners.

THE PEOPLE

Who were the members of the Peoples Temple, that organization which sprang forth in Indiana in the late 1950s and which was officially dissolved in 1983, five years after the Jonestown tragedy? The characterization here is based primarily on the time of their zenith as a flourishing body in California in the 1960s and 1970s.

The most numerous of those who joined the Peoples Temple presented a background of faith and practice in fundamental Christian religion, lower

89

and lower-middle class status, and minimal formal education. The great majority were black, and a significant number were elderly. These were the people Jones wanted. In the early 1950s, before settling on a locale for his first church, Jones would spend time driving around Indianapolis looking for the right neighborhood, that which would offer a congregation responsive to his personal mission.

To Jones, the people projected more than ordinary vulnerability, personal insecurity, dependence, and loneliness. Having known fear and desperation, many were without a sure sense of their status in this life and were doubtful of their future. In exchange for support, they would offer devotion and loyalty. They were people ready to accept a helping hand and contribute gratefully in return. Limited in power, seeking greater certainty and regular benefit, they put themselves under Jones' protective care. They found these, along with social warmth, useful work, and other gratifying reasons to belong. Reportedly, they were good workers, committed and contentedly involved in Peoples Temple projects. The organization accommodated all behavioral characteristics of members, e.g., those persons with a tendency toward states of rage or violence were provided creative and constructive assignments such as body guard or doorkeeper. All had a niche.

Thus the greatest number came into the organization as seekers of a place, wanting and willing to be defined by benevolent, caring authority. In their choice, they were unaware of the compromise and ultimate cost of endowing another with omnipotence and ratifying his ethos of dominance. They were accustomed to deferring to power — and this seemed like a good bet.

A much smaller segment of Peoples Temple membership, possibly 10–20 percent of the whole, was younger, more idealistic, politically and socially liberal, and predominantly white. These members came as activists, with moral purpose and humanistic commitment. Their spirit was representative of zealous youth of the period, and though knowing social alienation, they had not given up on harmony among people and world improvement.

They, too, were good workers, prepared to dedicate themselves to building a successful, racially integrated socialistic community in an indifferent capitalistic America.

They, too, were willing to yield themselves to dominant authority. While filling positions of leadership in the Peoples Temple, they accepted the status of dependent and controlled persons, like the larger portion of the membership. Notwithstanding their superior education and higher social ranking, they seem to have been oblivious — in their preoccupation with immediate needs and goals — to the price of trading off independence for confirmation.

THE MAN AND HIS CHOICE

Of course, Jim Jones himself was the most prominent participant in the rhetorical interaction relevant to the growth, conduct, and decline of the Peoples Temple. He was born and reared in a small town in Indiana, the confused child of a brooding, forlorn, and generally ineffective father and a dominant, verbally strong, notably individualistic and assertive mother. The feisty Lynetta Jones, herself an "aggressively ambitious achiever," said that her ambition for her son "knew no bounds." She needed him to succeed. "Don't be a nothing like your dad. . . . You have to make something of your life and be somebody. Work at it. Nobody's gonna help you."[3] The stimulation of the father was nil; of the mother it was extremely intense and reflective of her unrelenting narcissistic requirements. The boy in that home missed out on enjoyments of a normal life, a fact that he was keenly aware of and felt deeply. Contrasting in form and force, the two kinds of parental narcissism influenced the quality of the child's experience in mirroring and exacted their toll.

Hurting with the perception of his family background as different and deficient, this intelligent, attractive, sensitive boy found himself alone and isolated — a subject of perverse confirmation. Nonetheless, he responded to this neglect and inadequacy — and the kinds of injury to self that such a beginning can yield — by developing a well-groomed, outwardly social, and charming presence.

The deprived and denied child, recouping his losses, in "relentless pursuit, above all to preserve the self," as Gregory Rochlin explains human motivation,[4] would win his way. Responsive to the powerful maternal model, he perfected strategies of advancement and winning favor. From abuse and inappropriate illusioning he became accomplished in playing all roles deemed necessary to his ends. At an early age, he could con the sweet neighbor lady with his innocence and then with equal artistry regale the men at the car garage downtown with a precocious performance of profane and foul language. As his longings for recognition and dominion grew, young Jim Jones would gather neighborhood children in the loft of the barn at home, there to present sermons and lessons on life, funeral services for dead animals or emulations of Hitler.[5] Signs of extraordinary verbal facility were increasingly evident. He created, structured, and controlled this backyard society, revealing behavioral patterns that remained fixed and characteristic. As played the boy, so the man.

Jim Jones' adult leadership was marked by a sense of uniqueness, entitlement, vacillation in belief, avoidance, use of idiosyncratic language, substance abuse, moodiness and changes from seeming kindness to extremes of brutality, rage, and self-pity. Too, Jones' sole occupation seems to have been as conductor of Peoples Temple affairs. Theatre, sports, art, fictional literature, secular music, and dance apparently played very little, if any, part in his life.

Early, and throughout his life, Jones' faith in ordinary modes of influence was weak; he was quick to resort to extrarhetorical strategies: untoward narcissistic behaviors such as a falsehood, deceit, hypochondria, tantrum, and violence. Once when a visiting school friend insisted that it was time for him to go home to do the chores, Jones threatened to kill him unless he stayed. As the boy walked away, Jones got the family revolver and fired it, hitting the tree that the boy had just passed.

Jones began his professional career as a young Methodist student preacher, identifying with the downtrodden while seeking credit and admiration for his efforts. Another role that he learned early was "healer." Unbothered by ethical restraints and truth while in pursuit of personal aggrandizement, he lured people to his meetings for "miracle cures." The trick was to call sick people forth, have them taken to a back room, and soon thereafter to display to the crowd intestinal parts of animals represented as cancerous human tissue removed by assistants. Hundreds attended these meetings and were convinced of Jones' great gift.

After leading a number of congregations, all in racially mixed areas of Indianapolis, Jones eventually established the Peoples Temple, and by dint of great energy and charismatic manipulation, he attracted a sizeable and devoted following. Then came ordination and affiliation with the well-respected Disciples of Christ Church.

But gradually he began to preach less on Christian gospel and more on communal commitment, elevating himself as the inspired leader and the people's protector. The sheltered ones loved Jones' pulpit arrogance. I am all the god you need, he shouted insolently, in one sermon of 1971: "I come in the power of God in religion," and "I will do all the miracles you said your God would do and never did." In reference to his personal appearance, he declared, "I *come* with the black hair of a raven! I come as God socialist!" That other God will be no match: "If you don't need a God, fine. But if you need a God, I'm going to nose out that God. He's a false god. I'll put the right concept in your life." Tell me, "What's your sky God ever done?" You must know that the "only happiness you've found is when you've come to this earth God!" Who has given you a bed, a home, and food? *"I, Your socialist worker God,* have given you *all* these things." Then, he threw down the Bible and stood on it, daring that other God to stop him. And in utter narcissistic audacity, he hollered, "I know where I am going. I know what I believe. And I know what I'm doing. . . . I am freedom. I am peace. I am justice. . . . I AM GOD!!!!"

The crowd went wild, cheering and cheering.[6]

Encapsulated, the thrust of his message was "Follow *me*; give to *me*; exalt *me*; depend on *me*; do as I your father, your God, instruct and you will be somebody, here in this temple, safe against those who would destroy us." The membership submitted, in trustful, admiring awe.

Thus was the gospel of Jones, sometimes socialistic and sometimes Christian but often irreverent. As time went on, an "us-against-them" view of life came to dominate in his messages. But whatever his theme of the moment, the ethos of the Peoples Temple was the forcibly imposed ethos of Jim Jones. He found his power in extremely individualistic leadership, freely adjusting the brand of religion, while driving and conniving for adulation and total control, masterfully clearing all ideological and human obstacles from his path. After the move from Indiana to Redwood Valley in Northern California, the Peoples Temple became more cohesive and central in members' lives. Jones had secured his family. From there, the group made forays on San Francisco and Los Angeles, gathering recruits and money. Through good works and use of the Peoples Temple's impressive voting membership and physical presence at public meetings, Jones and the Peoples Temple became an acknowledged political force in San Francisco in the 1970s.

Especially significant, if not astounding, was Jones' success in suppressing information on internal conditions and ideological orientations of the Peoples Temple: e.g., instances of physical abuse of members, unconventional sexual behaviors, socialistic doctrine, and various forms of coercion. While always apprehensive and defensive, Jones became intensely fearful of exposure in the summer of 1977 and undertook a mammoth move toward greater isolation and security. After the first major published exposé of Peoples Temple activity, an article by Marshall Kilduff and Phil Tracy,[7] he and hundreds of the family withdrew to Guyana, joining other members who were there settling the jungle acreage acquired earlier. In the following months, Jones' paranoia increased in severity. Fearing full exposure and imagining loss of everything as a consequence of Congressman Leo Ryan's visit and murder, he performed his last "creative" act, an evil and brilliantly conceived final step in the shaping of his masterpiece. On November 18, 1978, the people of Jonestown joined with him and died in a well-rehearsed act of mass murder and suicide. They who had lived in continual retreat would once more defend themselves, this time in total withdrawal.

Though the leader gave it his name, Jonestown must be taken as a cooperative effort, unless one comes to define community involvement there as slavery or view the members as captives without choice. More reasonably, it was part of their bargain with Jones, to supply him with the raw materials — malleable human substance — for casting a unique piece of institutional art — a working communal monument deserving of respect and acclaim, an object to have and show. In turn, members secured a home and place of self-investment, not to mention an identity as part of an admired social colossus.

EXTRARHETORICAL NARCISSISTIC STRATEGY

The project that was Peoples Temple required a kind of genius from the chief architect, first in locating the human material. As Tim Reiterman reports, Jones found religious people to be the best prospects, for "they were the most easily conditioned to self-sacrifice, devotion and discipline." He selected them from church rolls, particularly of black and other working class congregations; these people had toiled for their daily bread, knew suffering, and were responsive to messages of hope for a better life. He showed them the great, caring heart of a man who was earnest in feeding the hungry, reconciling differences among peoples, and healing the sick. To the larger membership, and young idealists as well, Jones presented the Peoples Temple as "an alternative to the established social order,"[8] an uncomplex, promised land.

Such effort would seem to call for use of powerful, sustained persuasion. And Jones — at school he always "ranked at the top of his class in public speaking"[9] — was a persuader. He who could assume the role of kindly humanitarian appeared to Marshall Kilduff and Ron Javers as a "warm soul with a soft baritone who called the old ladies 'dear' and nodded his head while he listened."[10] According to one former Peoples Temple member, "He was pleasant, well-spoken, appealing. He was dynamic in voice and gesture and imposing in appearance. He knew when to shout or lower his voice."[11]

Yet, these uncritical observances refer to traits and postures which, though useful to one who would control people, hardly explain main sources of his power. Reiterman gets closer to a convincing explanation, noting that "it was Jones's personal magic — above all the black magic, webs of ideas and disguised threats — that weaned people from their pasts and tied them to the Temple's future."[12] It was narcissistic evil in the extreme.

It is the view here that in trying to understand Jones' "weaning" of the people — especially in such radical acts as influencing long-standing Christians to exalt the preacher who rejected their Bible — it is an error to find him a rhetorical artist. The source of his strength in bringing together and holding those people lies mainly in the resort to extrarhetorical devises. Notwithstanding Jim Jones' craving for family and his presentation of himself as a "family man," he was an individual apart — and against. He was given to *handling* others, not to discovering means of reciprocity in adult exchange. His deep yearning for acceptance and confirmation found expression in effective domination of a collected stock of humanity. His methods were of guile and coercion, not respect and persuasion.

Among his strategies were lying and deception, "divide and conquer," sexual manipulation, brutality, feigned illness, and feigned attack. For Jones, concealment was a first-order and characteristic function of all activities of the Peoples Temple, both internally and in relations with outside persons and groups.

Jim Jones lied gracefully and effectively. In San Francisco, his false story that a rival black minister had seduced two white women helped him to steal away scores of the minister's congregation. On numerous occasions he boasted to Peoples Temple members that women of the organization were begging to have sexual relations with him. In an effort to clear his way for extramarital relationships, Jones once adopted a cruel program of reclassifying wife Marcelline's status in their household. Part of the plan in subordinating her was to convince her and her family that she was mentally ill, even suicidal. Despite that episode in their married life, Marcelline remained loyal and compliant to the end. These and other modes of dissembling gave him success in his many manipulations of people.

Jones was adept at effecting alienation among members of families who belonged to the Peoples Temple, thereby keeping them as individuals faithful to him only. Too, those who joined the Peoples Temple were pressured to cut off ties with outside family and dedicate themselves to Jones and the group. To maintain control, he created a rivalry system of members criticizing other members and informing on each other, seeking to outdo each other in showing their faith to Jones and the cause.

Jones used sex as another method of control. He himself had sexual relations with many Peoples Temple members, both men and women. Any woman who might have believed that she was his favorite had to accept eventually that "Father" was obliged to sexually service others as well. When it suited his ends to break old unions among the membership, he urged free exchange of partners in intimacy; at other times he ordered abstinence for all. He pressured heterosexual males publicly to admit repressed homosexuality, thereby attempting to form pliant members.

Methods of brutality were similar. Jones held "catharsis" sessions in which members were criticized and held up to public ridicule. Peers were urged to censure each other: to berate, intimidate, and break down strong egos. Certain defiant or exploitable members were publicly spanked, paddled, or flogged. Some deviators were made to engage in boxing matches with stronger persons, for "re-education." In Jonestown, a number were placed in primitive solitary confinement.

Occasionally, Jones, a hypochondriac, found his effectiveness in a collapse or fake heart attack, e.g., to gain sympathy for himself and anger against a recalcitrant member who defied "Father" and thereby caused his "illness." Again making his person the issue, Jones might stir up the community with claims of outside threats on his life or stage fake acts of violence against himself and threatening telephone calls.

GREAT COMPROMISERS

Reading reports on the history of the Peoples Temple, one often receives the impression that the organization was one mammoth and grand stage production, a theatrical contrivance with two kinds of business: one for insiders and another for the rest of the world. Those inside were trained to act not only for intracommunity satisfaction and success but also to put the best light on their community when facing people in the larger world. The maintenance of discipline among members and resulting concealment of aberrations, shifting inner ideologies, and unconventional conditions is truly amazing. Part of an explanation lies in adoption of successful means of handling news and information. Another part lies in recruitment of amenable people, and Jones' creation of fear to enforce personal omnipotence.

The dominant end as revealed in the above discussion of strategies was to condition the people, to bring them to compromise themselves. The consequences of making themselves accomplices were self-diminishment and corresponding loss of personal power. In accepting Jones' care and "love," his promise that the ends justify the means, his theology and name as Father, his sanctioned interpretation of all events at the Peoples Temple and members' behavior; in becoming Jones' informants, confidants, and sexual partners; in near-complete giving of self and personal property, including real estate and social security checks, etc.—in these ways members established their commitment and complicity. They got in too far to get out. They were had—kept and contented in *their* place.

Yet it is not that everyone remained blind to conditions. As one member said, in reference to Jones' sickness in Jonestown—in the last weeks, "We all knew he was mad, but we were compromised to the point that we could not question him."[13] Though crazy, Father knew best. Probably representative of many members' feelings is the confirming message of an old woman in Jonestown, as she attempted to soothe the anxious Jones: You are the "only father I have. I love you, Father. I have no family but you." Another female member, while acknowledging the repressive regime in Jonestown and admitting to feeling like a misfit there sometimes, kept the faith on ends justifying means: "I know I'll never leave. I love what we have too much. It's far more important than me or mine."[14] "You are the savior of the world," said another in a personal letter. "Dad, you are our God. I will never turn back. No matter what the cost, I am going all the way with you."[15] Thus did they reveal their narcissistic dependence, their self-defined lot as children. It was their family. They belonged there, together, and with Father. They had fused their being with that community and its head. The idea of making a change was unacceptable; relatively few defected.

COMPLEMENTARY NARCISSISM

Such was the members' narcissistic preoccupation with their own states, their ills and losses. They acquiesced, yielding in the challenge to their beliefs and values. They were people in regression — in retreat from individuation — unwittingly choosing to forego growth and self-determination in their surrender to authority. The reward was identification with — being an essential part of — an assumedly progressive mission: together with others in pride, safety, and comfort. Disastrously, they let themselves be named as children, knowing their way to the parental heart. They offered their attractive selves for seduction, conditioning, and compromise.

Narcissistically burdened persons attract others of like bent. Dependent for their supplies of self-confirmation on others who also are narcissistically encumbered, they are less successful with emotionally healthy, mature people. Thus Jones and those who turned to him were in a tragic sense "made for each other." They chose each other. Jones strategically played omnipotent father to their well-practiced and rewarding subordinate role. They complemented each other narcissistically. Psychoanalytic theorists like Jürg Willi would names Jones the narcissist and the people complementary narcissists. Using terms of his theory, we can understand how the people merged themselves with Jones, forfeiting themselves to the aggrandizement of the leader and the grand design. Their goal was to appropriate an idealized self from him.[16]

So the little tyke from Lynn, Indiana — a smart, imaginative, cute kid who was not provided with foundations of love and growth — learned how to take care of himself. He made a place for himself, and he became somebody, at incalculable cost. From childhood days, and on to the end, his career was a program of gathering and using people in self-serving, sequestered activity governed by his peculiar kinds of rules. Reiterman notes,

> It was outside the institutional framework in a vacuum of authority where Jim could make his own rules, that he first felt confidence and some power. Outside school, he could control the same playmates who intimidated him at school. He structured the environment to suit himself, using a certain knack that, when full-blown in adulthood, could rightly be called genius. He learned at a very early age how to attract playmates, keep them entertained and maintain a hold on them.[17]

One of Jones' former classmates corroborated: "If Jim wasn't going to be the leader, then Jim wasn't going to do it."[18] As a boy and as a man, Jones would be the director or he would be nothing. There was no in-between. He would be all powerful or powerless abjectly. His satisfaction was in being absolute father to the neglected, to people like himself.

In sweet collusion, the leader and members defied general social and civil norms and kept all others at a distance, not aware that their close community was a creation of people going backward: a return to barn loft lectures and rediscovery of a father to obey and please. The followers sought refuge; the leader sought control. His behavior can be explained with psychoanalytic theory on the narcissism of the cult leader. Such a leader is one whose "unwillingness to compromise" and fearlessness against his enemies is experienced as "solidarity and independence" by unquestioning disciples. He is seen as strong, a martyr or victim — their idol with whom they identify and for whom they will make extreme sacrifices. Thus does the sect form around him, as his supporters in idealization consider him to be an omnipotent but threatened leader or prophet. In "guiding humanity towards paradise," he will choose any available method of aggression. "He fights so mercilessly and cruelly that his followers tremble with fear at the thought of finding themselves in the enemy camp."[19] This was Jones!

His entire life and theirs were massive and sustained inventions in defense, strategic fabrications of selves against an alien, hostile world. From their conspiracy arose the pillar to social and rhetorical pathology known as Jonestown.

RHETORICAL INDISPOSITION

Equal to Quintilian's "Good Man" theory in representing rhetorical qualification is the "good audience," the rhetor in the role of active, useful respondent. (See Chapter nine for details on functioning of the good audience). The rhetorically deficient Peoples Temple members were not a good audience. Their willing capitulation in the quest of need-satisfaction and ill-fated confirmation disallowed exercise of mature rhetorical processes. Their consistent messages to Jones, in symbols of anomic resignation and deference, validated his narcissistic, antisocial individuality, i.e., "gave him his head." The people's unfavorable general narcissistic nature rendered them ineffective rhetors in answering Jones' narcissistic seduction. In their peculiar idealism and dependence, they neither initiated effective counteraction nor provided corrective feedback. As people with minds and ideas, they were potential senders of socially promising messages. But instead they validated with messages contributing to disaster. Desperately wanting to believe, they passed over uses of reality checking. They chose to be reactors, secondary figures in an anomalously symbiotic medium. The welding to Jones, with acceptance of his imposed definition of their being and reliance on his praise and ministrations, included relinquishment of roles of decisionmaker and rhetorical self-provider. In confirming Jones' guardianship and finding security in constraint, the people neutered themselves rhetorically. They were people who, while wanting to save themselves, gave up on themselves. They neglected their dignity and true independence, an essential part of which is actively observing and checking presentations of others. They "participated in creating the authoritarian structures in which they eventually became ensnared."[20] Thus, this is first a study of that participation and their rhetorical failure.

Jones, too, repudiated rhetorical processes as means of accomplishing goals. Unable to trust himself or others, he was drawn by intense narcissism to use pseudopersuasion: verbal legerdemain, coercion and violence, and fakery. He had phenomenal ability in selecting audiences, in pretending, and in meeting raw narcissistic need. His concealment and camouflage for appearances — his evil art — was a marvel. The rhetorical coward would not risk true argument, nor dare to present himself before an uncompromising audience, without gimmick or ruse to assure success. Jim Jones was a rhetorically indisposed human being.

AUDIENCES, GOOD AND BAD

In the twenty-five years of Jim Jones' professional involvement in people's lives, incidents of social interdiction were rare. Before Assemblyman Ryan's trip to Jonestown, the only major successful effort to put light on the activities of the Peoples Temple was the Kilduff and Tracy article that appeared in *New West* magazine in 1977. Reiterman reports very few instances of people attempting to check him. In one case, a colleague in the Christian ministry tried to help Jones face personal problems; another conducted a brief personal investigation of his activities. Occasionally a member dared to criticize Peoples Temple practices, and at least twice Jones' son Stephan publicly rebuked his father. Certain defectors applied pressure at times. In Guyana, a Catholic priest who had been duped into allowing Jones to use Sacred Heart for a healing service, published a printed message dissociating his church from Jones' organization.[21]

Notwithstanding such occasional promising gestures, Jones enjoyed unusual freedom from — and did not receive benefit of — the corrective behavior of good audiences. Indeed, it would seem that all significant individuals and organizations in Jones' life were negligent at one critical time or other in checking his behavior. In truth, he was a person neglected.

Mr. & Mrs. James Thurman Jones allowed son Jimmy to grow, run, and set his own course without good care. Jones' wife Marcelline, also a complementary narcissist — vulnerable, loyal, dependent, selfless — who both idolized and feared her husband, was aware of his excesses and defects but spared him again and again and often stood as his apologist. Behavior of other immediate family members followed a similar neglectful line.

Jones' ministerial assistants – perhaps bewildered at times, yet obedient and loyal – did not challenge his self-aggrandizing behavior, e.g., his self-deification.

Political figures, whether uniformed, unbalanced, or compromised, let him get away with it. Some were disarmed by invitations to an impressive Peoples Temple dinner or the surprise of a homemade Peoples Temple cake on their doorsteps. Many were lulled into trustfulness by well-publicized community improvement programs of the Peoples Temple; others were unable to pass up valuable political support that Jones offered.[22]

The Indiana Department of Revenue, the San Francisco District Attorney's office, legislators at all levels, a mayor of San Francisco, a California lieutenant governor, the wife of a United States president, were among those who either validated Jones and the Peoples Temple or missed important opportunity to bring them to account. The Guyanese government overlooked serious problems. Agencies of the United States government had reason to take action but did not, e.g., the FBI, CIA, and Federal Communications Commission. Certainly the most neglectful federal office was the Department of State whose interoffice communications on Jonestown and laxity in monitoring events and conditions there amounted to endorsement.[23]

Many other professional persons and groups – informed and uninformed, compromised, passive, or sympathetic – came into close contact with Jones and the Peoples Temple, only to sanction their questionable activities or not take effective corrective action. In the 1960s, one psychiatrist diagnosed Jones as seriously ill mentally, and two prominent attorneys retained by Jones seem to have had more than an inkling of dangerous conditions at Jonestown. In 1971, a medical doctor reported to the Indiana State Board of Psychology Examiners on his observations at a religious service in which Jones "healed" a sick person through removal of a "cancer." Jones managed to prevent a testing of the material, and the Board dropped the investigation. The Disciples of Christ allowed the Peoples Temple, a member organization, to continue with impunity even while the group ignored requirements of baptism and regular communion. Further, headquarters failed to conduct an adequate investigation of other member churches' questions and charges, e.g., on Jones' naming himself the reincarnation of Jesus Christ. When Jones villified Baptist minister George L. Bedford and lured away great numbers of his congregation, the latter took no action in response. Another San Francisco preacher, Cecil Williams, had direct experience with methods of the Peoples Temple yet seems to have been indulgent. Other church officials and church councils occasionally had reason to be suspicious of Peoples Temple activities, yet they conducted only limited investigations and took little action to check the group.[24]

Though ultimately the most responsible audience, representatives of the fourth estate failed at moments to tell the story well. Dr. Carlton B. Goodlett, publisher of the San Francisco *Sun Reporter*, ignored bad reports on the Peoples Temple and actively supported the organization. In 1972, the *San Francisco Examiner's* nationally known religious editor, Lester Kinsolving, looked into practices of the Peoples Temple and planned a series of several articles. But by the time the fourth installment appeared, Jones and the membership had mounted such great pressure that the cautious *Examiner* management killed the series. Reiterman reported that "Virtually nothing came of Kinsolving's stories." Reiterman also reported that a religious writer of the Fresno *Bee* discovered allegations similar to those learned by Kinsolving; possibly compromised, the paper did not publish them. Additionally, a 1978 *National Enquirer* article on the Peoples Temple that never made it to print may have been killed through efforts of Peoples Temple attorney Mark Lane using $7,500 of his clients' money. The *Guyana Chronicle* would not reprint accusations on happenings at Jonestown, reportedly influenced by national interest.[25]

Tough, professional journalists could have their heads turned momentarily by attractive features of the Peoples Temple. Arriving at Jonestown, Reiterman was impressed by people who seemed happy in a well-run camp. An unnamed reporter "was very excited by what they were doing at Peoples Temple" in San Francisco.[26] Even after an attempted knifing of Congressman Ryan and other questionable behavior observed at Jonestown, reporter Charles A. Krause of the *Washington Post* stated that he "rather admired" Jim Jones' goals and believed that the Peoples Temple was "more or less succeeding" in its "noble purpose."[27]

RHETORICAL FAILURE

Indeed, it was not unusual over the years for people to be impressed by what they were shown in brief, controlled visits to Peoples Temple facilities in Indiana, California, and Guyana. But must we accept the event in Jonestown as "a tragedy in which fates were assigned both by chance and by inevitable circumstance, beyond the control of any government agency or political party," as Krause insists?[28] Is it not more apt to say that many people ratified and encouraged activities of the Peoples Temple and in so doing unwittingly played a part in the continuation of their tragic enterprise? Many people failed as good audience — first of all those who chose membership and involvement in the Peoples Temple — and many others:

the physicians, ministers, teachers, psychologists, newspeople, attorneys, appointed and elected public officials, members of government agencies, etc. If a good audience is in reasonable measure an active, informed, self-respecting and uncompromised, independent, *and* effective agent, all persons and groups discussed in this study are culpable on one count or another. In inaction or in overt and *seeming* self-interest, many people allowed themselves to be violated. That is a principal finding here. People failed themselves in denying themselves, in not choosing to be as they might have been. Results of their behavior shocked the world.

6
Joseph McCarthy and the American People: A Rhetorical Interpretation of Their Relationship

In the catalog of American political villainy, no name is more prominent than "McCarthy" — unless it be "McCarthyism": a classification of behavior denoting inquisitorial investigative tactics and reckless, sensational accusation. As remembered, Joseph McCarthy was a man easy to hate — too easy perhaps. He was a powerful figure. And the source of his power was the American people, a fact less acknowledged than his more obvious personal character.

The principal purposes of this chapter are to review his rise to power and his strategies and, in particular, to come to an understanding of his primary motivation as revealed in audience response. The contention here is that McCarthy's political dominance — and the nation's failure to restrain him — is a story of *peculiar rhetorical interaction*: of the rhetorical immaturity and untoward narcissistic behavior of one individual who took advantage of the narcissistic tendencies and needs of a large segment of the American people. In the final analysis, this is a study of audience, and, as such, it may yield a clarifying perspective on relevant political dynamics of that unhappy half-decade in American history.

EARLY POLITICAL ACTIVITY

Joseph Raymond McCarthy graduated from Marquette University law school in 1935 and passed the bar soon thereafter. Following a year's experience as a small-town Wisconsin lawyer, he was elected president of the Seventh District's Young Democratic Clubs and ran unsuccessfully for district attorney. Switching to the Republican party, he ran in 1939 for circuit court judge and was elected. McCarthy had entered the race even while knowing that his law partner and benefactor — a prominent attorney who had taken him into his established practice and provided him with a position in the community — had had an interest in running for that same office. McCarthy betrayed his partner. He won the judgeship through great expenditure of energy, e.g., in going door-to-door and presenting himself as a good neighbor with genuine personal concerns about interests of the electorate, but also by playing untruthfully on his opponent's age. Though the incumbent was sixty-six, McCarthy often referred to him as a man of seventy-three years — and sometimes eighty-nine.[1]

McCarthy's record as judge is marked by unethical behavior. In one classic case of judicial misconduct, he destroyed trial notes that doubtless would have revealed his impropriety in excusing a dairy company from obeying marketing laws. "Swift justice" was a mark of McCarthy's style. Upon coming to the bench, he did not let stiff Wisconsin laws on marriage dissolution keep him from granting "quickie" divorces to political friends.[2] As Robert Griffith found, "McCarthy brought to the circuit court the same driving energy and the same casual disregard for established rules and precedents that by now characterized all his actions."[3] The law was his to ignore or use as he would. The McCarthy pattern was evident from the start.

IN THE MARINE CORPS

With the coming of World War II, McCarthy discovered another opportunity for self-advancement. Though members of the judiciary were exempt from military service, he volunteered and received a commission in the Marine Corps in 1942, while not resigning his judgeship. He served in the Pacific area, in a rather ordinary role: interviewing fighter pilots returning from missions. Yet he made his presence felt, becoming known among fellow officers as an "operator" and "promoter" who was active in centering attention on himself and inflating his contribution to the war effort. As a publicity stunt, he once fired 4,700 rounds of ammunition from the rear gun of a grounded dive bomber.[4] Though not a pilot or crew member, he occasionally was allowed to go along as a passenger on relatively safe missions and even to shoot the tail gun now and then.[5] In future political activity he would tell of his career as "tail gunner." He variously reported his number of "missions" as fourteen or seventeen or thirty, escalating the figure as years went on. He asked for and received the Distinguished Flying Cross, yet his Marine Corps record contains no justification for the award. In political speeches, McCarthy would refer to his unhappiest military duty: sitting in his island dugout writing great numbers of letters home to families of lost pilots. Thus he lied on three counts: writing such letters was not his duty; he never lived in a dugout; records show that in its entire existence his unit lost a total of five officers and two enlisted men. Not a participant in real heroics, McCarthy invented an impressive military record, including reference to several combat wounds. He even managed somehow to secure a purple heart for a leg injury received aboard ship outside a combat area when he fell down a set of steps while participating in the antics of a traditional equator-crossing ceremony.[6]

RUNNING FOR THE UNITED STATES SENATE

In 1944, while the war continued, McCarthy took a leave from the Marine Corps to seek Republican senatorial nomination in Wisconsin's primary election. Again, his campaign behavior was notable for industry, vigor, *and* impropriety. He flouted the military regulation forbidding service personnel from discussing political issues and ignored the state statute against judges holding any other political office during the term of their election. Though soundly defeated, he put his name in voters' minds, with attractive appeals and promises.[7]

Resolved to reach the Senate eventually—and incidentally sporting a "combat" limp for the first time, he ran for the circuit court bench in 1945 and was reelected.

Then, in 1946, with singular audacity, McCarthy campaigned for the Republican senatorial nomination on the slogan "Congress Needs a Tailgunner." His opponent was the venerable Robert M. LaFollette, Jr., who in contrast to the aggressive and indefatigable McCarthy campaigned hardly at all. With lies, innuendo, great energy—and benefiting from coincidental political alignments in Wisconsin—McCarthy was the victor, by a slim margin. LaFollette who in the 1940s had been named by journalists and political scientists as the best United States Senator was defeated by the man who in the 1950s was to be named the worst. In the general election, he was a Republican running in a Republican year, and he won by a landslide.[8]

SENATOR McCARTHY

What are attributes of a "worst" Senator? Partly it was a peculiar cynicism. "From the beginning," Allen J. Matusow relates, McCarthy "displayed only contempt for the traditions of the Senate, defied powerful colleagues, and indulged in debating tactics that other senators sometimes found irresponsible."[9] Griffith notes that what "was remarkable about McCarthy's Senate apprenticeship was not policy positions—liberal or conservative, internationalist or isolationist—but rather his continual violation of the rules, customs, and procedures under which the Senate operates."[10] McCarthy chose to be an institution unto himself, without respect for the one to which he had been elected.

On issues, his first three years in the Senate are noteworthy only for his support of special interests. A case in point is his standing on the side of sugar lobbyists who sought decontrol of prices at a time of great shortage. In this effort, the Senator let the sugar people know that they had a spirited and dedicated ally. His part in the debate on the sugar question featured blatant lying, gross manipulation of statistical data, and rancor. Coincident to his commitment to the cause of sugar was his financial need of the moment and a wealthy sugar lobbyist's endorsement of a $20,000 note for deposit into McCarthy's bank in Appleton, Wisconsin.[11]

McCarthy's next major commitment was to the private housing industry. Builders seeking government loans needed approval of the Reconstruction Finance Corporation whose operations were reviewed by the Senate Banking and Currency Committee. McCarthy was a member of that committee and a supporter of granting loans to the building industry. In this time of a critical housing shortage, he opposed public housing. The president of one construction company that received government loans gave the Senator $10,000, ostensibly as payment for a thirty-six page booklet on government aid to the housing industry that McCarthy had written.[12]

Without doubt, McCarthy did little to distinguish himself in his first three years in Washington, except reveal a dubious character, showing himself as one who in minutes would turn a "staid and dignified Senate debate into an angry brawl." But he must have begun to sense political deficits, and perhaps allies started to counsel him, e.g., on his uncertain status in the party. Moreover, charges on past behavior were bringing him close to disbarment in Wisconsin, and a state investigation was underway on the allegation that he violated election laws in running for senatorial election in 1946.[13] Clearly, it was time for Senator McCarthy to find a source of positive attention and power before election day drew much nearer.

"COMMUNISTS IN GOVERNMENT"

Joseph McCarthy solved his problem at Washington's Colony Restaurant on January 7, 1950, where he dined with Father Edmund A. Walsh, Dean of the Georgetown School of Foreign Service, Charles H. Kraus of the political science faculty at Georgetown University, and Washington attorney William A. Roberts. After dinner, the four took up the problem of discovering an appealing election issue for the Senator. Several issues were suggested, but it was Father Walsh's question that registered with McCarthy: "How about Communism as an issue?" That was it! "The government is full of Communists," said McCarthy. "The thing to do is hammer at them."[14] The rest of the world was soon to hear the first strike of McCarthy's hammer.

Of course, the threat of communism was not a new issue in American politics. It had appeared in the 1920s and 1930s. But during World War II, the United States enjoyed an alliance and friendship with the Soviet Union, and fears were allayed. Then with the USSR as postwar adversary, aggressive anti-communism became a central premise of government policy—as expressed in the Truman Doctrine—as well as a major theme of conservative politicians in their attack on the allegedly inconsistent Truman administration.[15] Richard M. Freeland writes that what served as origins of McCarthyism—the "essential energies of post-war anti-communism"—were developed deliberately by the Truman administration in 1947–48, to mobilize support for the Marshall Plan. Implanted in the public mind was the idea that the "United States was imminently threatened by a massive, ideologically based assault upon everything Americans valued." National fears grew, eventually providing McCarthy with an extraordinary political opportunity. Specific events used by him to illustrate the menace of communism to America were the Soviet Union's explosion of an atomic bomb in 1949, China's fall to communism, the Korean War, and Alger Hiss's associations with communism.[16] As messages of alarm began to provoke their latent insecurities—their narcissistic inclinations—more apprehensive Americans became uneasy and possessed of deep-seated fears over vague internal threat and subversions, loyalties of leaders, conspiracies, and related issues.

By 1950 when McCarthy joined in on communism, America's vulnerability to the message was at a peak; a responsive audience was ready. He found his adherents—and source of power—beyond the Senate and beyond the state of Wisconsin. He went to a national audience, to the people across the country. To launch his rhetorical rocket, he chose the Lincoln's Day meeting of the Women's Republican Club of Wheeling, West Virginia. While no authenticated and complete text of his speech is available, the Wheeling *Intelligencer* reported that he included the following statement in his tirade on the communist menace:

> While I cannot take the time to name all of the men in the State Department who have been named as members of the Communist Party and members of a spy ring, I have here in my hand a list of 205 that were known to the Secretary of State as being members of the Communist Party and who, nevertheless, are still working and shaping the policy in the State Department.[17]

Though later claimed by McCarthy to have been "fifty-seven," the "205" figure is corroborated by both the news editor and program director of radio station WWVA. On the next day he spoke in Salt Lake City and on the day after that in Reno, with substantially the same content as presented in Wheeling.[18]

These audiences, and others who gathered on different occasions over the next four years, did not see the contemptuously narcissistic, advantage-seeking United States Senator, but a true patriot who had discovered evil in government and was called to warn the people. He was received as a hero by menaced Americans. Jack Anderson and Ronald W. May describe his typical reception:

> Usually he would be preceded by a color guard, followed by a mass recitation of the Pledge of Allegiance to the Flag. Then Joe would walk on stage to the thunderous roar of the crowd. He would wave tolerantly or clasp his hands above his head in a gesture of bravado; then he would hold up his hands for quiet. Invariably, his first sentence would be: "Well, it's good to get away from Washington and back here in the United States."[19]

His message was shocking — and all so clear:[20] The nation was at war — and in the final battle. It was the Christian world vs. the communist world; God vs. communism's "religion of immoralism"; the antitotalitarian side vs. the Soviet orbit. Dismissed by Karl Marx, God became a "hoax." McCarthy's astounding statistics — impossible to check at the moment — showed fantastic increases in populations of people living under totalitarian regimes and great declines on "our side."[21] This once strong nation was "each day losing on every front." Why? Because of traitors in government, the worst of whom were in the State Department: "the bright young men who are born with silver spoons in their mouths." The State Department was "thoroughly infested with Communists" — "I have in my hand fifty-seven cases of individuals who would appear to be either card carrying members or certainly loyal to the Communist Party" and "helping to shape our foreign policy." McCarthy dwelled on the activities of the deposed Alger Hiss, Roosevelt's "chief adviser at Yalta" (a false statement). He took particular delight in ridiculing Secretary of State Dean Acheson: "this pompous diplomat in striped pants, with a phony British accent" who in blasphemy "proclaimed to the American people that Christ on the Mount endorsed communism, high treason, and betrayal of a sacred trust."

Thus he cut to the quick of American security and faith in government: godless agents — in huge numbers — had got inside the compound, and with full support of disloyal leaders were delivering the nation to the enemy. He had proof — in his hands! Worst suspicions were validated.

Overnight, McCarthy established himself as America's watchdog and guardian: a bold, intrepid man with power and guts — one to be acknowledged, to be feared and given room. He acquired an ardent following, the largest of any other demagogue in the history of the United States.[22] "The government's infested with Commies!" vouched millions, after hearing the nightly news commentary on McCarthy's latest harangue. Not long after the Wheeling speech, in the elections of 1950, he became the most sought-after of all Republican speakers. In September, he addressed rallies in Illinois, Wisconsin, Indiana, Tennessee, Maryland, Connecticut, California, and New York. Reportedly, he received 2,000 invitations to speak in campaigns that fall—more than those received by all other Senators combined.[23] McCarthy was confirmed in his role! Candidates needing to stir up enthusiasm among the electorate welcomed his appearances. The Red issue had its uses.

Speaking in Kansas in January of 1951,[24] he told how the left-wing press had accused him "of almost everything but murdering my great-great-grandmother." But he was determined to carry on for the good of the country; after all, somebody had to do it. As a kid on the farm, he said, he and his brothers had to "dig out and destroy" the skunks that threatened the chickens; it was a "dirty, foul, unpleasant, smelly job," but "the jobs that most badly need doing and are left undone are more often the most difficult and unpleasant jobs."

NARCISSISTIC TECHNIQUES OF THE DEMAGOGUE

In the Kansas speech and others that followed, he capitalized on the theme of Armageddon. America was losing the dirty war; traitors had infiltrated government; American citizens were selling out to atheistic communism.

With the Korean War underway, he had a fresh stock of pathetic materials with which to deepen the fears and heighten the perils faced by America. He opened and closed the Kansas speech—one in which George C. Marshall received blame for the loss of China to the communists—with graphic reference to American blood spilled in Korea. He told the heart-rending story of a "typical, young American boy" from Middleburg, Pennsylvania, Bob Smith, who was home now but whose "hands and legs are still in the hills beyond the Yalu River," the result of a foreign policy wrought by Americans who have led "us along the road to disaster . . . a road which will be strewn with Bob Smiths" and "watered with the tears of American wives and mothers . . . who are again being forced to travel deep into the valley of darkness and despair."

Everywhere he spoke, McCarthy sketched the communist problem as uncomplicated and terrifying, founding his case on "complete and unchallengeable documentation" of betrayal. His was a "pseudo-rational" appeal that created "the illusion of proof where there is no proof," as Barnet Baskerville demonstrated.[25] In Chicago, a week before the presidential election of 1952, McCarthy made special use of visual aids in documenting allegations.[26] At points in the speech, once while waving a daily newspaper and later a piece of plain paper and then a "photostat," he swore to his Palmer House audience of 1,150, "I hold in my hand" a document proving so and so's disloyalty. Democratic candidate Adlai Stevenson was the principal target. Another trick on that occasion was his asking a person identified as an FBI agent — "in the audience here tonight" — to stand up for all to see, by which he sought to make some obscure point regarding Adlai Stevenson's lying about the man's age. Then off on another inconclusive argument, he exhibited a photograph of a barn, presumably in Massachusetts, which he represented as a storage place for communist documents. He somehow connected that place to alleged subversion of Alger Hiss and then used that to indicate Stevenson's support of communists. Great numbers of insecure Americans did not question the specious reasoning of Joseph McCarthy.

This strategy of association, a technique of connecting his victim to persons or events given communist taint, was a principal weapon of McCarthy. In Chicago in 1952, he named candidate Stevenson as a friend of Archibald MacLeish (respected poet and once librarian of the Library of Congress) whom he defined as the man with "the longest record of affiliation with Communist fronts of any man that I have ever named in Washington." He did not elaborate, confident in America's acceptance of his word and meaning. A similar but even snappier gimmick involved linking his subject to a symbolic cluster of "Red" names to show immediate guilt by association. Stevenson was "part and parcel" of the "Acheson-Hiss-Lattimore group." In the same speech, McCarthy gave his connecting device an especially nasty, and childish, twist. He twice substituted the discredited Alger Hiss's first name for Stevenson's: " . . . Alger — I mean Adlai — Adlai in 1952 . . . ." and "I should like to ask Alger — I mean Adlai Stevenson . . . ."

It must be noted that while the Chicago speech, broadcast on national radio and television, was presumably in support of Dwight Eisenhower's campaign for the presidency, it became another event in the "McCarthy campaign." As always, he exploited the occasion for his own ends, making only brief reference to the election. When asking the people to vote the Republican ticket, he sought to advance *his* program: "if you want me to continue this job . . . give me a hand," he asked. *His* personal success was the first goal.

When not linking his enemies with communism, McCarthy got on by evasion, exaggeration, and distortion. "The man just talked in circles. Everything was by inference, allusion, never a concrete statement of fact. Most of it didn't make sense." Such was one Associated Press reporter's feeling of frustration.[27] Also, McCarthy lied freely and often. Richard H. Rovere named one of his techniques the "multiple untruth." Unlike Hitler's "big lie," the "multiple untruth" is not necessarily large, but instead is "a long series of loosely related untruths, or a single untruth with many facets." The package of lies has so many parts that it is not possible to keep all of them in mind at the same time. Trying to grasp the whole, one might "seize upon a few selected statements and show them to be false," which "may leave the impression that only the statements selected are false and the rest true." This strategy has an added and greater advantage: since no one is able to recall which statements have been disproved and which have not, the former can be used safely over and over again. In the mass of facts, or Orwellian "unfacts," McCarthy concealed the "unpremise" on which his structure rested.[28]

The liar was also a bully. With whatever scraps of evidence that were available, no matter how far-fetched or inconsequential, McCarthy would work up some semblance of a case against a foe. Then he would attack his victim viciously. He learned, he said, from an Indian called Charlie "to kick his opponents below the belt until they were helpless."[29]

As a boxer in college, McCarthy was known as a wild slugger, one who rained gloves on his opponent. His way was "rough and rampageous," like the "techniques that he brought later to the political ring." He had no skill — only "sheer guts" and "recklessness."[30] And such was a quality of his speechmaking. He was the furious battler riding roughshod, crudely and with no finesse. With seeming courage and readiness to fight, he offered himself as America's tough kid — uncouth, perhaps, but on the right side. His primitive bent and insensitivity had appeal in the 1950s.[31]

THE FALL

Joseph McCarthy's mission to seek out and destroy communists in government lasted just four years. In December of 1954, the Senate voted to censure (condemn) him, concluding that he had "failed to cooperate" with the committee investigating his conduct, "repeatedly abused" committee members and thereby obstructed "the constitutional process of the Senate," and that such conduct was "contrary to senatorial traditions."[32]

After the so-called Army-McCarthy hearings that were broadcast on television, millions of viewers across the land formed an answer to the question that Army counsel Joseph Welch put to McCarthy in a moment of great national drama: "Have you left no sense of decency?" Now the people knew, and many changed their attitude. They had seen his behavior "under the lights," and needing this man no longer, they withdrew his special commission. McCarthy was finished. Still a member of the Senate, though largely ignored by colleagues and the press, he died at the age of forty-eight in 1957, of a liver disease attributed to heavy drinking.[33]

BACK TO THE BEGINNING

While the McCarthy story has been retold often, certain questions on reasons for his success and failure remain unanswered. It is not enough to know that millions of Americans cheered him, which they did. Or that he enjoyed support and encouragement (or sometimes mere toleration) of powerful conservative figures, which he did. Or that fear of his power dampened efforts of Democrats to restrain him or that he was clever and unprincipled, etc. To understand McCarthy and his career, we must go back to the beginning.

His story starts at the hearth of Timothy and Bridget McCarthy, father and mother. Joseph was the fifth of nine children of that stolid Catholic family who tilled 142 marginally productive acres in the Grand Chute township in Wisconsin. Typifying habits of the region, the McCarthy family was not given to intellectual concerns or to interests beyond caring for their own and securing the daily bread. Like others of the "Irish Settlement," Timothy McCarthy was a provincial, suspicious man — a stern, strict, and demanding taskmaster whose life was spent in hard, physical work. Apparently, Joseph was bullied and teased by siblings and peers, but some relief from the oppressive and uninspiring environment was provided by mother Bridget who was generous with comfort and protection for her favorite. The boy was insecure, sensitive and awkward — the ugly duckling with a stubby physique. He clung to his mother, while facing the viscissitudes of early life, growing up with pain and frustration.[34]

We cannot know all that we would like to know about conditions in the McCarthy family, e.g., if that authoritarian father was sensitive in his treatment of Joseph and fair in handling one child's abuse against another. Nonetheless, we can raise questions related to influences and events in the home. For instance, was the mother with her velvet hand effective against the father's hand of iron? Studies show, as we discussed the topic in Chapter two, that mother and father do not impinge separately on their children but have a combined effect and that the presence of a third person — e.g., the other parent or another child — will change the interaction in the dyad. For one thing, touching is reduced. And what was the nature of the parental relationship? Babies do sense the quality and tone of parental interaction and are affected by it.[35] What we do know is that Joseph McCarthy spent his entire life in desperate effort to answer injury and deficiency — the origins of which seem to be located in his earliest years.

McCarthy received his first formal education in a one-room school. Terribly withdrawn and self-conscious, he was a reluctant participant in play and games. Former classmates report that his feelings were easily hurt and that "he never really learned how to play." Academically, he did well, and even managed to skip a grade. After graduation from elementary school at age fourteen, he helped his father on the farm. Then he tried raising chickens on his own, working twelve to fourteen hours a day, seven days a week. After that, he managed a grocery store. Nearing age twenty, he decided to attend high school and rushed through the curriculum in one year. And it was an eventful year. When not studying, which was seldom, he involved himself in school activities. He tried out for the basketball team but was unsuccessful. A schoolmate recalls that he was awkward and too rough; he "couldn't work with the team" or "learn the rules." He turned to boxing and enjoyed giving lessons to the younger boys and inviting them into the ring for five-minute rounds with him. Resenting being used as his punching bag, the boys stopped going to the gym.[36] As time went on, McCarthy became "a loud, amicable, and boisterously aggressive man." Now and then he may have shown signs of "the old fear and insecurity," but they "were now masked by the fierce intensity and energy which he brought to every undertaking." He faced every event or task with full force. Both "work and play were marked by a relentless though sometimes misdirected competitiveness. There was even a forced quality in his demanding conviviality."[37]

He entered Marquette University's school of engineering in 1930 but later switched to law. At the university, he held a variety of part-time jobs, tried boxing again and considered the ring as a career, learned to play poker, and joined the Franklin Club — a debating society. While yet a new member of the club, he had nerve enough to run — unsuccessfully — for its presidency. When the unwelcome vote count was announced, he angrily stabbed a knife into the floor of the meeting room and walked out.[38]

What conclusions on personality or character can be drawn from available information on McCarthy's years through college graduation? The following seem safe:

1. Experiences of childhood contributed to his development as an extremely insecure, shy boy.
2. He was socially maladjusted and not easy at play.
3. In early childhood, he learned and accepted the discipline of hard work.
4. As a child and in adolescence, he showed signs of possessing noteworthy intelligence, sensitivity, energy, and ambition.
5. At some point, probably around adolescence, a sullenness and cynicism began to appear, a view of the world as fiercely competitive and hostile.
6. From this view came acquisition of strategies for survival and control: rough and tough tactics for fighting his way through life.

Upon entering public life in his mid-twenties, Joseph McCarthy was a psychologically injured, smart, keenly industrious, enterprising and opportunistic, combative, and determined man. He was socially pragmatic, i.e., not genuinely sociable but a user of people whose nature initially might have appeared to others as social. His grim determination — all the more awesome, given his lack of ethical restraint — seemed connected to a deep and abiding commitment to making up monstrous deficits of self-esteem that had been accumulated in those formative years on the farm. Furiously driven by terrible lacks in self-esteem, he would be somebody – others be damned! – his behavior exhibiting graphically a kind of narcissistic motivation discussed profoundly by Gregory Rochlin in *Man's Aggression*.[39] He would proceed directly and purposefully, in a straight line one might say, charging through or over all obstacles.

NARCISSISTIC NEEDS AND RHETORICAL DISABILITY

McCarthy's aberrant narcissistic needs, some of which will be shown here as salient to his rhetorical peculiarities, were revealed in numerous behaviors: he drank heavily; he was subject to allergies and severe stomach ailments, which he occasionally used protectively; he was accident prone; he wore elevator shoes, though nearly six feet; he sought "mothering" from women; he was envious of the status of others. An intense poker player, he was known as a bluffer, a pretender without the cards – and he was clever at it. He never finished jobs, discontinuing an effort when personal interest or rewards diminished; he belched in public and used the foulest language when he chose – but then on other occasions could put on the cleanest, scrubbed-up "nice Catholic boy" image. Though obsessed with the idea of truthfulness, he lied continually and with ease; he was given to throwing public tantrums to meet his ends of the moment; he was oblivious to the injury that he inflicted on others, e.g., on their reputations. He was given to imagining the existence of conspiracies, looking for base motives in others, feeling persecuted, and experiencing delusions of grandeur. His quest for power and acclaim was brash, ruthless, and insatiable; he used gushes of goodwill to conceal inner doubts and untoward feelings; he found the topic of himself "endlessly interesting"; he never learned the art of genuine play; he placed himself above the law and constantly demonstrated a fundamental lack of integrity and principle. He had a genius for self-defense, e.g., in retreating from or evading a politically effective challenge to his behavior; he was given to attributing his own weakness or failings to others.[40]

In relating to people, McCarthy had a limited sense of the effect of his behavior on them. Like others narcissistically oppressed, he was numb to associates' sensations[41] and unable to "comprehend true outrage, true indignation, true anything." He could not understand why someone he had reviled on the Senate floor would later shrink from him. In the cloakroom during breaks in hot Senatorial debate, he expected all – even his targets – to be friendly toward him.[42]

McCarthy seemed to deny the reality of his involvement in those rancorous scenes of political interaction – or his sense of their meaning was distorted. To him, such encounters were events apart, put on for *public* confirmation, as he played his own appointed role on the political stage.

But off-stage he was a regular guy—or wanted to be so taken. "Why is Dean Acheson so cold toward me?" he doubtless pondered, somehow dissociating himself from the vilest of abuse he had heaped on the Secretary of State.[43] Now and then, in rather explicit splitting of his identity, he would adopt a public persona and refer to it in the third person, e.g., to "McCarthy" or "Senator McCarthy"—to that *other* person.[44] Metaphorically, one self was public, the other private. The private self, desperate for affection, likable and affable, was unable to understand why the deeds of the public McCarthy could direct such animosity toward the private.[45] His public self was tough, but the other was vulnerable and craved confirmation. As a narcissistically deprived, intensely defensive figure, he took "boos and jeers better than ridicule." When a University of Wisconsin audience laughed at him and thereby reached his private sensibilities, "he went completely to pieces."[46] He could handle disagreement and rebuttal—even welcome and use them—but not humiliation.

Assuming a patriotic posture, McCarthy put himself forward as "the exclusive Uncle Sam with a monopoly on loyalty." His was a self-granted charter of rights of inquisition and execution, and his "fight for America" was "little more than a fight for Joe McCarthy." In acting out the fantasy, assuming the "public figure he had conjured up from some bizarre notion of himself," he took the cause of self, a "servant of no one's purposes but his own." He was a man alone,[47] even while in the company of others; all functions were solitary and self-commissioned. Though he declared communism the issue in America's survival, he himself was his one and only issue; *his* survival was at risk. His driving force was self-perceived inadequacy and an unrelenting intent to prove otherwise. He was a self-doubting, injured man, seeking omnipotence, constantly in self-defense and personalizing every piece of apprehended information.

From all evidence, it seems clear that McCarthy was limited in substance—or he was unable to make effective social use of what he possessed. He appeared as an "empty" man, one with no direction and nowhere to go.[48] He had no plan or philosophy—no code, no values, no sound or steady premises. He jumped from moment to moment, from episode to episode. His "program" was entirely negative, built from deficiency. In arrogant thrusting forward of self, he moved by destroying, renouncing, ravaging, and persecuting. Morally maimed, McCarthy was a frighteningly individualistic politician who played fast and loose with a nation's fortunes. Without benefit of adequate social growth, he advanced through abuse and exploitation of others. With no moral doctrine to check his ambitions, he was a stranger to civil behavior and the generally accepted norms of public dialectic and argumentative give-and-take. He never reached rhetorical maturity. With bile in his soul, he found a measure of the same in America. *That substance became his capital.*

THE PEOPLE OF AMERICA

How is it possible in a great democratic nation for a crudely opportunistic, dishonest, violent man to enjoy political success for so long? An answer lies in the fact that biography treats only one side of any rhetorical story. His audience—the people—were at once McCarthy's source of personal gratification *and* his potential corrector. They were available for satisfying his need for grandiosity *or* for denying his appeal to *their* already-piqued narcissism. As confirmers, the people were central and necessary to his ends, but if a "good audience," they would provide control, i.e., check messages that threatened the community and offer the necessary disillusioning of socially detrimental advantage-seeking.[49] For four years they did gratify him, seeking the while to gratify themselves. Yet as will happen in a democracy that allows extended indulgence of gross individuality, the people ultimately came to their better senses; the "truth" was forced out. This time the enforcing event was the Army-McCarthy hearings, conducted by the Senate and broadcast over national television. At long last, the country had a full view of the Senator in action. Before the thirty-six day investigation ended, he had offered close-ups of just about all of his many characteristic verbal and nonverbal moves in both reckless accusation and anxious self-protection. While group insecurity motivates attachment to narcissistic leaders, it also makes for fickleness. Groups caught up by such a leader have a proclivity to withdraw allegiance rapidly. Such narcissistic relationships last only as long as the sustaining illusion lasts.[50] With the defrocking of McCarthy on television, an intense era ended. The people saw justice done.

Though the shorter part of this report, the behavior of fearful Americans at mid-Century may be as significant as one United States senator's. Both had essential parts to play. Together, theirs was a *folie a deux*, the collusion of two unhealthy forces: the interaction of McCarthy and his audience, both parties rhetorically indisposed. The political and social climate in America gave McCarthy the occasion. American opinion leaders' successful naming of the Soviet Union as the evil international enemy and communism as the subversive threat within, gave McCarthy fertile ground. Only recently at war with Germany and Japan, the country in the 1940s and 1950s engaged in a critical cold war with the Russians. Media reports told of spying. Politicans and journalists alluded to operations of foreign agents in business, government, education, and entertainment. The people heard cries that the nation's security was imperiled. With deceit and treachery, the Reds were out to pick this great plum that was America. Thus a highly defensive atmosphere developed. From felt insecurity and paranoia, grew specters of conspiracies at work, erosion of trust in democratic government, and suspicions about leaders and groups. Intellectuals became "eggheads" or communist sympathizers; liberals became visionaries soft on communism.

While many political figures of the country helped to create and profit from desperation of the period, McCarthy was the most effective. His awareness of human vulnerability and fallibility was the sharpest and most cynical. Knowing that his cause could be furthered only by going outside the Senate, given its restraints on individuality, he went to the wide-open national arena and addressed a large, general audience.

McCarthy's Appeal: At the Surface

On one level, McCarthy was a man acting on others with base appeals, now obvious to us. From the Wheeling speech in 1950 and on to his eventual condemnation in 1954, he made skillful use of print and broadcast media.[51] He knew how to keep his name on page one. Reports of his speeches, press conferences, and other statements excited journalists, and brought them running. Possessed by a vita of grief and sour affect, he knew of human discontent. Thus with uncanny craft in manipulation, he played on built-up anxieties and grudges of the people: on ignorance, confusion, suspicion, frustration, and passions of pride and hate. Fabricating and sensationalizing, — with both vulgarity and his peculiar sorcery, he offered a simple and dismal picture of America's falling back in the vital struggle. The problem was communism; the solution was equally simple and sure: eradication. Any means were justifiable.

He secured an audience and soon a following. With resulting party power came fear of his retaliation, as well as "nourishment for his strange ego, and money." His earlier followers were from the outermost fringes: "where grievances and anxieties were the strongest and least grounded in reason; where the passion for authoritarian leadership was greatest; where the will to hate and condemn and punish could most easily be transformed into political action." Hate groups and super patriots "fell into his lap." The rich and the poor came to him with allegiance and money.[52] The response of citizens in the Fort Atkinson, Wisconsin, town auditorium was typical. "When Joe McCarthy had finished Saturday night, there were few skeptics in the jammed auditorium. We were in a position to witness perhaps 400 of the 700 in the audience." Just two people kept their seats. All the others "rose as one person, clapping and cheering. Among them were four able Fort Atkinson industrialists, two competent Fort Atkinson labor leaders, and half a dozen loyal Democrats."[53]

It is true that the "haters rallied round him," and the "zanies and zombies," but large numbers of supporters were regular Republicans who fastened onto him as a means of defeating Democrats, so long in power.

Economic gain was envisioned by others. Religion was a factor as well, e.g., among Roman Catholics who found reason to come to him, particularly the Irish with memories of past humiliations. Certain rich Texas oilmen supported McCarthy, in their interests. He drew a number of notable intellectuals, too, e.g., William F. Buckley, Jr., who saw morality in McCarthyism. He attracted not only those to whom fascistic movements have always appealed but also those wary of internationalism, classlessness, and the welfare state. People with *resentments* became McCarthy people: those with gut-level fears of atheists, homosexuals, academicians, the "effete," and those with sundry insecurities and self-needs. He built "a coalition of the aggrieved" and persuaded many others that "he was speaking the essential truth."[54] Advantage-seeking and soreness in America—variously manifested—set up for McCarthy a large, diverse, responsive audience.

McCarthy in Affective Penetration

But let us go beyond the usual audience analysis, attempting to discover a more satisfying interpretation—perhaps a model—of a rhetorical relationship involving a narcissistically indisposed person and the people who had been stirred up by political forces and messages of the day. In one sense, the disquietude of McCarthy and his audience was uniform in motive: all sought what the speaker sought—validation of self. Rhetor and audience would serve each other. On the surface of rhetorical events was the behavior of one pragmatic mid-western politician acting on people, using words. Far below in the psyches of many Americans occurred a triggering of archaic deficiencies and antipathies—a pricking of wounds of long ago, of infancy. With his simplistic vision of destroy or be destroyed, he agitated insecurities. Carrying marks of *his* earliest human encounters, McCarthy reached *their* tender parts. The injured one became the injurer, operating below the conscious level of feeling and experience, motivating others' dolor. Rewounded—as all can be—many Americans regressed to *primary processes.*[55] Such is the first "law" in crisis: when menaced, the self responds with well-rooted protective strategy.

Basic to the human condition, narcissism is a universal force. No one is free from it. Though most people escape the kind of emotional stresses of childhood and exacting narcissism experienced by McCarthy, all people have known narcissistic injury.[56] Memories of early trauma are buried in the individual psyche, to be expressed when a certain level of threat is reached. Insecurity is the force behind the appearance of narcissism: felt inadequacy in the face of perceived attack on the self. Of course, McCarthy sensed this part of human nature, as he played on American's fears of annihilation, their frustrations, and their uncertainties regarding personal power. Contributing to the "sandbag" mentality of the time, he made use of vulnerability in the people of America. It is an interesting feature of human behavior that the narcissistic respond to the narcissistic.[57]

While it is sometimes difficult for people to accept the fact, they share with others the same behavioral tendencies when experiencing threat. One such tendency is to identify with the aggressor. When oppressed by sensed diminishment of self and personal anxiety, e.g., when caused to envision the menace of a strange and sinister alien force that seeks world domination — and when subjected to incessant and strident claims of treason within — humans will turn to aggressive, seemingly stronger and more powerful figures. "Identifying oneself with an aggressor . . . becomes a means of overcoming the feeling of being helpless, weak and dependent by assuming the stature of strength." The role of passive victim is intolerable. Ignominy must be relieved; self-esteem must be restored. Such is the common goal in recovering from narcissistic injury. Thus are demagogues allowed to persecute heretics and bigots allowed to create scapegoats: addressing the insecurity of the masses — exploiting their narcissism by whipping up fierce expressions of fear. In such wise did McCarthy use the people — and in a manner not unlike that of leaders of the Third Reich.[58]

McCarthy's audience, then, came to feel something of what he felt — he the hurt man with sure swift "access to the dark places of the American mind"[59] — he the artist in affective penetration whose grief over earliest personal losses made available kindred reference in the American psyche — he the tyrant who in unyielding, uncaring search for dominion discovered and quickened the narcissistic tyranny that is characteristically human[60] and particularly virulent in an audience coached on its fear as Americans had been since 1947. He pushed through, irresponsibly cathecting the people, disturbing their psychic vitals, and awakening ancient forces that sought objects.

Americans heard McCarthy and a notable number confirmed him in his behavior. In their distress — their weakness of the moment, they yielded: in their fear of him and of his power over them, in their need of him to take their cause and act for them and defend them. In this way did they answer their exigence. The people in *their* indisposition, knew analogous substance, and they defensively backed this unhealthy soul in mounting and sustaining his short and tragic career. Ready, lured into accepting parts he seductively assigned, they endorsed and supported his operations, for their survival was at stake. A large segment of the American audience in the 1950s thus failed the test of adequate citizenship. In rhetorical terms, they — we — were not a "good audience." Not disposed to check McCarthy's message — behaving as poor listeners, incapacitated by crisis — we went along. It can — and did — happen in America (as it had during witch trials and the Know-Nothing movement). A significant feature of behavior in the early 1950s was defensiveness—the prime indicator of aroused narcissism. How else to explain the felt impotence and suspension of general belief in decency, equity, and justice? Like bedeviled mortals incited to join a mob, Americans temporarily gave up on democracy. Under unusual pressure, we found self-preservation the issue and consequently suffered loss of faith in civility and fair play, the right of free speech, and presumption of innocence. Unconcerned with protecting civil rights of citizens accused of disloyalty, we sanctioned extreme measures to smash the Red threat. Perhaps Maslow's theory on the hierarchy of needs has application here: while caught up in meeting basic needs, a people may not be disposed to attend to upper-level needs. Preoccupied with self-defense, they may deny their "better" impulses, e.g., to be an unselfish neighbor or a brother's keeper or a citizen willing to be counted and to risk consequences of permitting free exchange of ideas—*to be a good audience.* As Edward R. Morrow in 1954 had said, after Shakespeare, "the fault, dear Brutus, is . . . in ourselves."

And such is the condition that promotes rhetorical indisposition.

Thus Joseph McCarthy in his time took advantage of others for his aggrandizement. And thus those others—we cannot call them victims—returned messages of assent. They affirmed his aim, sustaining his illusion of omnipotence, in quest of their own; they fostered continuation of mutual hallucination. Rhetorically, roots of McCarthyism are to be found in audience inadequacy—in people aberrantly moved to revisit their old, old insecurities and dependencies, those lying beneath surface suffering. In this sense, McCarthyism is narcissistic weakness, reflecting "an ailment within us."[61] American rhetorical health in the 1950s reached a low level; the audience was incapacitated, "not good enough," as Winnicott might have been willing to judge it.[62]

On a level with Jefferson's admonition on maintenance of eternal vigilance in a democracy, is maintenance of rhetorical health and stability, particularly as characterized by intelligent, confident, and unimpeded discovery of sound policy, along with courageous questioning and effective challenging of forces opposed to the public good.

7
The Rhetorical Crippling of Paul Morel

Well-written fictional literature is a rich source of material for the study of human interaction. One such piece of literature is D. H. Lawrence's novel *Sons and Lovers.*[1] It provides a superb model for learning about unfavorable narcissistic influence on the rhetoric of people in relationships.

As suggested in the chapter title, the analysis here centers on one figure. But no one's rhetorical story can be told without reference to the manifest imperatives of other rhetors. Paul Morel made his way with numerous others who contributed significantly to events of his life. While his impairment dominates that of others', he is one with many; all play narcissistically against one another.

THE STORY

The novel is set in the midlands of England, where lived the Morel family in their humble thatched cottage, the ordinary dwelling of the poor in their coal-mining town. As miner Walter Morel — earthy, and once effective with his natural charm — weakened in roles as husband and father, Gertrude Morel, intellectually and socially above her husband, assumed family leadership. Losing one son and no longer feeling love for her husband, she turned to the younger boy and built her life around him. Mother and son became dependent upon each other's presence, creating a symbiotic relationship.

Gertrude had not wanted her new baby. But Paul, as she named him, soon warmed her heart and found a favored place in her life. As she held him, she felt "as if the naval string that had connected its frail little body to hers had not been broken." And "With all her force, with all her soul she would make up to it for having brought it into the world unloved." In serving him, she would answer her regrets.

Though lacking in education and refinement, Walter Morel was a man of basic goodness: honest, direct, and not without compassion. But after a long hard day down in the mine, the tired father would frequently stop off at the public house. Coming home drunk, he banged around the

kitchen, ranting and pulling drawers out of cabinets, etc. Morel's rash behavior upset everyone, certainly young Paul. Jolted on one occasion in infancy, he gave a "little convulsed start." During another violent episode
when the mother was injured by a flying object, the baby cried plaintively.

Paul was delicate and quiet as a child — often sick. In fact, Gertrude
never expected him to live. In early years, he sometimes had fits of depression. Once, at age three or four, when he was crying, the father shouted
to the mother, "If he doesn't stop, I'll smack him till he does." At times
he cried himself to sleep. Perhaps it is no wonder that Mrs. Morel came
to give him special treatment, "different from that of the other children."
His needs *and hers* were strong and insistent, intersecting intimately. While
reading of the soothing that Gertrude Morel gave her son, one remembers
Bridget McCarthy of Wisconsin who favored Joseph: how alike were the
motivations of these two burdened mothers with their disadvantaged sons!

Paul came to hate his father, and when the man made endearing and
quite sincere gestures, Paul rejected them. At a point in his boyhood, he
would pray every night: "Lord, let my father die" or "Make him stop drinking." He gave his love to the mother and became exceedingly mindful of
her well-being. He suffered with her, and not only when the father was
abusive. "When she fretted he understood, and could have no peace. His
soul seemed always attentive to her." It hurt young Paul that "she never
had her life's fulfillment: and his own incapability to make up to her hurt
him with a sense of impotence, yet made him patiently dogged inside.
It was his childish aim." Paul "loved to sleep with his mother," even well
into childhood. He "lay against her and slept, and got better; whilst she,
always a bad sleeper, fell later on into a profound sleep that seemed to
give her faith." As respective needs of consolation were met, collusion was
established.

The hardy but unfulfilled mother and the injured, shy and sensitive
son had each other. And thus they fell into a tacit agreement: they would
provide for each other and act in accord with the wish and will of each
other. Their relationship came to be the union of two people — each special
for the other — who set up for themselves a private space apart, to live their
lives through and for each other, fused as one.

As time went on, it became clear that Paul was a clever boy. He did
well in school, making admirable accomplishments in mathematics and
languages. His talents in writing and painting were especially notable. Then
in his early teens when it was time to go to work, his skills stood him in
good stead as clerk for a small manufacturing firm.

"I'm the man in the house now," fourteen-year-old Paul told his mother,
when the father was hospitalized after a mine accident. And "Everything
he did was for her." In subsequent years when Paul would come home

from work in the late evening and relate events of the day to Gertrude, "It was almost as if it were her own life" on which he reported. And she "unburdened herself of all she had pondered, or of all that had occurred to her during the day. . . . The two shared lives." Thus mother and son, intimate in all ways save as husband and wife, built their snug, tight world of interpersonal self-sufficiency.

The first threat to the mother-son relationship arose as Paul, in his teens, became interested in beautiful and spiritual Miriam Leivers who lived with her family on a farm nearby. Though considering herself Paul's inferior, he who painted and knew algebra, French, and German, the diffident and sterling lass could imagine herself loving him, if she were stronger than he: "If she could be mistress of him in his weakness, take care of him [he had been ill recently], if he could depend on her. . . . " Thus another woman of unmet narcissistic need was drawn to Paul Morel. The first woman — jealous Gertrude — was cool and aloof with Miriam, having her say through veiled and subtle expressions. Though bitter, she "was too wise to have any open rupture."

Seemingly selfless Miriam, who generally had "scorned the male sex," awakened Paul's masculine purpose, and, while occasioning in him great ambivalence, eventually provided him with opportunity to become free of the confining mother-son bond. Through Miriam's "sacrificing" of herself in physical love, Paul achieved symbolic manhood. Yet she, too, would possess him, and Paul then had to reckon with two great opposing forces: maternal commitment and "lad-and-girl" love. Caught and confused, Paul denied Miriam's offer of self; he could not be other than boy-lover to her; he would release no more of himself than that.

Paul's second romantic relationship was with Clara who was married but estranged from her husband. She was thirty, five years Paul's senior. Less threatened by Clara — perhaps more sure of Paul now — Gertrude did not attempt to disturb her son's new relationship. And, while not complete, Paul's satisfaction with Clara was greater than it was with Miriam. Clara's worldliness and physical appeal were more rewarding than Miriam's unselfish devotion and dreamy spirituality.

Clara fell in love with Paul, but he did not respond in equal measure. Physical passion — on his schedule — was his limit. Revealing narcissistic incapacitation — his rhetorical indisposition — he innocently told his mother, "I think there must be something the matter with me, that I *can't* love." I love Clara "better than Miriam. But *why* don't they hold me?" He added, "I never shall meet the right woman while you live." She answered calmly, with a kind of settled wisdom, "We'll see, my son." What better case than Paul's is to be found to fit the theory on oppressive narcissism annulling the ability to love.[2]

When Gertrude died, Paul was completely adrift, "crumpled up and lonely. His mother had really supported his life. He had loved her; they two had, in fact, faced the world together." Now "his own hold on life was so unsure, because nobody held him." He felt "unsubstantial, shadowy, as if he did not count for much. . . . " He was utterly alone in the world, having "no place in it! Whatever spot he stood on, there he stood alone." Yet, though his mother "was gone abroad into the night, . . . he was with her still. They were together."

A RHETORICAL ANALYSIS AND INTERPRETATION

Most "speeches"—rhetorical acts—of fictional rhetors are conversations. In this novel, written by a master in dialogue development, key exchanges occur between Paul and Gertrude, Miriam, and Clara. Of course, there are others, including some involving more than two people. It is from analysis of the content of these interactions that most rhetorical data are derived for this study. Also very useful are the novelist's necessary interpretations, e.g., on intrapersonal events and nonverbal behaviors.

Possessed of great narcissistic need, mother and son complemented and fed off each other in their little province removed. Thus they created their own rhetorical deprivation, in denying themselves independence and the power of healthful correction. In symbiotic relation to mother Gertrude, son Paul was contained, his growth at an end.

Shunning horrors of separation from her, he made a tradeoff of manhood for security, thereby founding his own rhetorical impotence. He accepted domestic soothing and serenity, while straining against the situation and his ineffectualness in putting up a fight for personal individuation. But the odds did not favor him.

Let us look into Paul's rhetorical development, using categories of analysis introduced in Chapter three: general behavior and affective states; spirit and processes of discovery; perceptions; beliefs, values, and ideals; and relationships.

General Behavior and Affective States

Episodes from Paul's life after infancy show him to have been rather self-conscious but "finely-made," and bright. He loved nature and enjoyed playing in the fields, picking berries, and looking at the flowers. His school essay on famous women won a prize in a competition sponsored by a children's newspaper, and later, two of his paintings won first prizes. Another prize painting sold for twenty guineas. When he sold some designs, a career in art appeared possible; he was confident in his work, despite "fits of depression, shrinking, everything." But an artist he was not to be, for as inner struggles consumed him, the flame died.

Paul participated in certain "public performances," e.g., the friendly debates at family gatherings in Miriam's home. Once in a "hard, ironical mood," he entertained Miriam's family with a derisive, mocking description of behavior at Methodist church services. The orthodox family loved his "take-off," as it was put, but Miriam found it too clever and cruel. She saw hate in his eyes and felt "he would spare neither himself nor anybody else" (how clear are the signs in retrospect). He joined in at the public house, too, but he was not a "favorite debater" there, "being too quick and overbearing. He irritated the older men by his assertive manner, and his cocksureness. They listened in silence, and were not sorry when he finished." Thus did indicators of Paul's nature and wounding in infancy appear as unattractive personality characteristics and rhetorical liability.

As Paul became involved with Miriam and correspondingly felt his mother's disdain and heartache, he had times of terrible anxiety, and his eyes grew dark with pain. People saw the sunshine go out of him and noted the habitual appearance of knitted brows. Resentments and manipulations of an insecure mother resulted in feelings of grief, guilt, and shame for Paul. His behavior now was marked by highs and lows. Caught up in the great conflict of his life, he was alternately melancholic and hostile. Yet in the broadest sense, he was inert: withdrawn and out of action, while given to intermittent outbursts of acerbity, evidence of his misery. Though resolving to break off with Miriam, he realized he "could neither break free nor go the whole length of engagement. And this indecision seemed to have bled him of his energy" and exacerbated his rhetorical maladaptation.

But under the spell of the physically desirable Clara, he revived; his "brow cleared, and he was gay again." The days of discovering and experiencing Clara were a high period, a time of self-confidence and fascination. Clara evoked from him a certain worldly tone, and in one of their earliest conversations, she unwittingly encouraged him to test Miriam's interest in adding physical intimacy to their relationship. Paul determinedly went to Miriam, cut through his reserve and with her abandoned his virginity in a seige of intense lovemaking. Though not receiving pleasure, Miriam "lay to be sacrificed for him," for his need. Finally initiated, Paul felt "a youth no longer" and spent a week with Miriam, wearing "her out with his passion before it was gone." But the glow of masculine success left almost immediately, for to make love he had to "put her out of count, and act from the brute strength of his own feelings." Depression came over him and as the "sense of failure" grew stronger, he wanted "to run, to go abroad, anything," to withdraw.

After years of being together as boy-girl friends and then as lovers, Miriam and Paul had come to an understanding on "belonging together." Yet, their definitions of that idea were not entirely mutual, for the irresolute Paul did not — could not — belong to Miriam. But where lay his hope for self-satisfaction? What young woman would fill the void in his soul? The voluptuous Clara, perhaps? In any event, one late afternoon as Paul and Miriam sat on the bank of a stream, he — the infant who when it "has drunk its fill, throws away and smashes the cup" — let Miriam know his mind — as well as he was able to know it.

"I have been thinking," he said; "we ought to break off."

"Why?" she cried in surprise.

"Because it's no good going on."

"Why is it no good?"

"It isn't. I don't want to marry. I don't want ever to marry. And if we're not going to marry, it's no good going on."

"But why do you say this now?"

"Because I've made up my mind."

"And what about these last months, and the things you told me then?"

"I can't help it! I don't want to go on."

"You don't want any more of me?"

"I want us to break off — you be free of me, I free of you."

"And what about these last months?"

The unprepared and injured Miriam could but take the blows. The decision, arbitrary and unilateral, was out of her hands. Helpless, she cried, "I have said you were only fourteen — you are only *four*!" And then in anger, "You are a child of four."

Paul did not answer but said to himself, "All right; if I'm a child of four, what do you want me for? *I* don't want another mother." There it is. One mother is enough. He would be free — somewhat.

"What do you want to do?" Miriam asked.

"Nothing," answered the rhetorically indisposed Paul Morel — "only to be free."

When the man who would be free arrived home, his mother — who knew of his intent to talk with Miriam — rose anxiously. She had been waiting to hear about it. "I told her," Paul said.

"I'm glad," Gertrude replied — with great relief — "Now have some supper," she said very gently.

Paul had taken — and given — to the limit of his confining narcissism, but he could not love Miriam. He could not give himself permission; indeed, he was not free.

When he turned from Miriam to Clara, it was with passionate purpose. Making love with Clara, on wet leaves in the woods by the river, after a long, muddy search for the right place, Paul was "tumultuously happy." And, fascinatingly, it was in that rapturous moment that he fell into brief use of the midlands dialect of his father, ordinarily vulgar to him and unwarranted by his mother: "But tha shouldna worrit," he tenderly assured Clara: "Dunna thee worrit." Though his intent was to convince his lover that their act was right, more compelling is the thought that in a singular and fleeting five-second lapse in his ruled life, he forgot his training and self-repressing compromise, knew true freedom of soul, and dared to make a genuine, tender offering of a caring self. While the only evidence is four short lines out of 420 pages, we can imagine the kind of personal power and rhetorical success that might have been his had he been able to allow himself more of his father's simple social liberty. In near-complete denial of his paternal roots, Paul gave up a valuable part of self that would have been convertible to useful rhetorical currency.

Paul was intensely enamored of Clara. His thoughts often centered on features of her body: her stature like "Juno dethroned," the arch of her neck; creamy arms and throat, breasts and shoulders — beauty that sent "his blood . . . sweeping up in great white-hot waves." Walking with her, his pride "went up," for he felt, narcissistically, that people who knew her eyed him "with awe and admiration." Yet, given Paul's indisposition and fears, it could not last, and against the thought of possession by Clara, Paul came to holding himself back and assuming a solitary posture apart from her. Moreover, his mother had cancer. Unsatisfied with Clara and seeing his mother's terminal illness progress, Paul faced terrifying loneliness:

> He felt as if his life were being destroyed, piece by piece, within him. Often the tears came suddenly. He ran to the station, the tear-drops falling on the pavement. Often he could not go on with his work. The pen stopped writing. He sat staring, quite unconscious. And when he came round again he felt sick, and trembled in his limbs. He never questioned what it was. His mind did not try to analyse or understand. He merely submitted, and kept his eyes shut; let the thing go over him.

His one major consistent act was to give his mother primary status among all others, to oblige her without deviation.

Paul found himself rhetorically ineffective, fixed in his condition, and indifferent toward opportunity to meet it. Bewildered, unstable, alienated, and without sure gauge of social realities, Paul wavered in addressing most critical situations and challenges. Whether passive or in action, he was defeated. He could not manage his life adequately or take self-benefiting steps. The rhetorical starch was out of him.

Spirit and Processes of Discovery

One of Paul's fundamental impairments was in inventing means of engaging others. His acquired passivity yielded a low level of rhetorical ambition and disallowed his realizing a state of liveliness and channeling of energy that are necessary to interpersonal success. His entire being was dampened in his plight. Clearly, he protected himself carefully in explorations with Miriam and Clara, guarding against being swallowed up by them. Though stepping outside of home, he did not go far — and he looked back, always. Uncertainty and dependence coming out of simultaneous dissatisfaction and contentment underlay his enervation.

Thus Paul's once-keen and active mind remained dull, underutilized. From a cognitive perspective, his is a story of wasted intelligence, neglected mental resources, of emptiness and stagnation. Distracted and dispirited, he operated without the full power required in discovery of mature roles and strategies needed to conduct a daily life with others, with effect and mutual reward.

Perceptions

As a child among his brothers and sister, and in later years, Paul appeared responsive, observant, broad in outlook, ready for experience and growth. But as he in his need yielded to exigent maternal need and allowed the establishment of their predicament, his compass narrowed. Simply put, he grew to a point and stopped. In judging most others' states and behaviors, his norms were subjective, of a self-centered child constrained by personal circumstance. His confined, wizened perspective led him to limit the range of sanctioned behavior in others, imposing perceptions which resulted in unreliable views of other's intent, e.g., Clara's, and reduction of his rhetorical effectiveness.

Paul's outlook on life and society did not develop fully and therefore was an untrustworthy guide for him in deciding and in evaluating options. The major distortion came from his inability at any moment to free himself from his bondage and, thereby give himself a chance to define himself as a mature, independent, self-reliant person. The condition of fusion with the mother influenced all impressions and blurred all perceptions of objects to come into this field. Consequently, he misvalued Miriam and Clara — particularly Clara — except as palliatives or objects of trial experience. Self-interest and personal conflict reduced his appreciation of distinction in their being. His rhetorical effort and gain were circumscribed accordingly.

Beliefs, Values, Ideals

Though a regular attendant at chapel, Paul began to question the orthodox creed and to move toward agnosticism. Simplistically, "He had shovelled away all the beliefs that would hamper him, and cleared the ground, and come more or less to the bedrock of belief that one should feel inside oneself for right and wrong, and should have the patience to gradually realize one's God." More apparent as a source of meaning and comfort were natural phenomena, immediately available: flowers, birds, fields, trees, moon and stars, clouds and sky. These objects of deep appreciation and innocence in the play of nature contrasted sharply with his own wretchedness and subjection. In simple religious and natural values may have lain one hope for Paul. Or were they only a child's inventions — small and bright windows to his dark chamber of self-confinement — yet insufficient? Very likely so, for the prevailing structures of Paul's mind came from the warping in infancy and the code composed by mother and son. Domestic bliss, sharing, protection, loyalty and constancy were prime desiderata. "She was the chief thing to him, the only supreme thing." Such was the major premise of his being.

It was in Paul's regression to primary process thinking — his childlike mental activity — that the character of his narcissism and acceptance of the maternal injunction were typified.[3] He worked from "dream" premises, finding enthymemes in his own unrefreshed reservoir. They reflected his provincial beliefs, those of his world with Mother — in the "pretty house" that he would acquire for the two of them — and the patently false idea of mother and son together forever. He would "have a cottage with his mother, paint and go out as he liked, and live happy ever after." Expressed at age fourteen, that image persisted and recurred throughout the years, in one shape or other. Miriam's counter idea, the open offer of her gift of self, paled in contrast to Gertrude's. Other lines of argument on which he built his being are the superiority of personal over social authority and sexual baptism as fundamental to manhood. Incidentally, his conviction that a person's worth is not to be determined by class is, perhaps, one small observable indicator of paternal influence on invention. Contributing to most conflicts in his life, and regressive in motivation, was the premise of natural freedom: that the good life precludes interpersonal restraint and woe. The bulk of Paul's premises and enthymemes were infantile and incestuous in spirit, largely out of intimate and childish maternal connection or defensive reaction to it. They were intrapersonally mandated, his alone and his fused with Gertrude's.

Caught between two demanding idols — freedom and security — Paul brooded, agonized, cried in despair, and declined in cognitive strength. Torn and indecisive, without constant will, he vacillated and drifted. Yet, though he held fast in faithfulness to Mother, e.g., assuring her that he only *liked* Miriam — "I tell you I *don't* love her" — he otherwise "had no fixity of purpose, no anchor of righteousness that held him." His ideal of freedom — the rationale that backed his resistance to being possessed and absorbed by Miriam and Clara — did not carry over to Mother. It did not operate when needed to help him to act on undoing the maternal tie. Childlike fantasies conflicted with the thought structures of a man who would be. And "to be" — to assume manliness and gain benefits therefrom — would seem to have required both denial of the childish principle and acceptance of values and burdens of adulthood. Paul's archaic cognitive twists were fundamental to his rhetorical disability.

Relationships

The master relationship was mother-son, dictating dynamics of all others. It was based on the power of domination, of mother over son — and then of son over mother, as agreement and mutual dependency were established. Each was the other's strength and only steady source of narcissistic supplies. Each was driven by personal requirements of association and fear of loss: the desperate urgency to have somebody, to hold and be held. Given the terms of their compact and coercive character of their resulting existence, individual choices in behavior would have required tremendous will, great courage and suffering. Paul made some movement toward independence, took small steps, but he did not stride. And always "he came back to her. And in his soul was a feeling of the satisfaction of self-sacrifice because he was faithful to her. She loved him first; he loved her first."

The mother-son relationship worked. Roles were contracted and neatly implemented. Reciprocity, compatibility, and generosity characterize interaction of participants. Mathematically, things balanced; benefits were equal. But qualitatively, the equation was false — and doomed, for the son remained as child. Continuation of the relationship required his regression. He stayed with the partnership as set and thereby denied himself a future as a man and effective rhetorical person. The compact was Paul's one grand choice, made in his interest, as he immaturely perceived it. Though in youthful ache and anguish his soul cried out for release, his behavior provided no evidence of ability to have chosen differently, given competing personal constraints.

His decision for mother fixed a condition and norm, making adequacy in other relationships unlikely, particularly with women. After meeting the maternal offer of federation with "yes" — or making the offer himself —

Paul never came close to abrogation; all of his restlessness and hopeful countermovements failed against that fast bond.

Of course, Paul did not love Miriam; he could not. She was available, responsive to the point of his immediate need. But he only used her, "seeking his own way and his own pleasure," accepting her unselfish bequest of self. At times, he was cold and cruel with her. As he viciously criticized and scolded, Paul revealed his own narcissistic suffering, but Miriam absorbed the abuse and remained ready for him, even in rejection. And he, while resenting her possessiveness, kept in touch, as though expecting favorable outcome, hoping for appearance of some *deus ex machina*, much as a child envisions a magical act bringing resolution and relief. Enforcing his unadjustable design on their relationship, Paul denied her individuality and difference, "almost unaware of her as a person."

Though Miriam did strike back — just once, when she forthrightly called him a four-year-old child, she soon dropped the indictment, hopeful of soothing him and having him in time. Indeed, if Miriam's narcissism were the main topic here, the discussion would include her using *him*. Unhappy, co-dependent Miriam is no more victim than Paul, but, in fact, Paul was "not there" for her — ever. She looked but "could not find him," for he kept "fighting away" from her. Fearful and stiff, Paul would not be held by her. When toted up, Paul's personal expenditure of self in their relationship — in all those hours and days of walking, talking, and loving — adds up to a meager sum.

He took from Clara as well, using her passion to find his own. In their playing and loving together, Clara temporarily awakened in Paul not only pleasure but also an exciting dimension of physical identity, at once of child *and* man. In one scene at Clara's home, Paul the child, in frenzied anticipation of making love, had to forego gratification while waiting — and waiting — for Clara's mother to go to bed. It seemed *hours* for poor Paul, alone in the bedroom, standing by, "wide awake and writhing in torment." Thus suffered a child blocked from receiving a man's gratification.

The relationship of Paul and Clara was founded on their respective needs: his for a woman with passionate presence to name him a man and free; hers for a man to name her a woman needed and esteemed. Knowing "how stark and alone" he was, she consoled him and gave him access to her warm, responsive body. Initially, needs were met, but when Clara expressed interest in ordinary daytime relations as well — and "something permanent," Paul resisted and declared that in the daytime "I want to be by myself." He would not be had. Threatened and disenchanted, he complained, "love should give a sense of freedom, not of prison."

As Paul and Clara began to lose their grace, "mechanical effort spoilt their loving." Clara came to true insight and told Paul, " . . . you've never come near to me. You can't come out of yourself. You can't. . . . you've never given me yourself." Miriam had had a similar revelation, but Clara, perhaps the most rhetorically disposed major figure of the novel, would not endure it. Coming to realize her status with Paul, she reported feeling "as if it weren't *me* you were taking," something "just for yourself." She found herself a woman participating in her own exploitation. Paul, too, wondered about *her* significance to *him*. Once on the beach, he saw her at a distance and assessed silently: "Not much more than a big white pebble" and "almost nothing among the morning." He asked himself, "What is she, after all?" — "there is she, fretting, always unsatisfied, and temporary as a bubble of foam. What does she mean to me . . . ?" — "It's not her I care for."

Unlike Miriam, the more self-regarding Clara untied herself from the one "who was not there with her," the "make-believe lover" whom she could not "soothe into forgetfulness."

One last time, Miriam came to Paul, not to "relieve him of the responsibilities of himself" — no, that could not be *her* choice; hers was to "sacrifice herself to him." That is all. She could not have him, but she would comfort him. Paul rejected the offer, unwilling to deny himself for her, as he imagined the proposal and its consequences. Though alone, an alien in his own town and world, he had his dead mother; "he was with her still. They were together." The master relationship endured, for as Jürg Willi wrote, the difficulties in separating from an "omnipotent and omnipresent" narcissistic mother are great. An oppressively narcissistic child, in collusion with the mother as complementary narcissist (or vice versa), "can never be rid of her, even if she has long been dead."[4]

In his situation, the rhetorically indisposed Paul operated with limited means: with behavior hindered by defensive fear, passivity, depression, self-confinement, and fury; with diminished inventional spirit and power, unreliable perception, and regressive thinking.

Closeness and concession to his mother dramatically and antithetically paralleled the distance and self-protectiveness that dominated in relationships with Miriam and Clara. The man who professed love of freedom, kept it from himself. In unfavorable narcissism that developed early in infancy, the compact with his mother as well as his disinclination to nullify it, and resulting personal and social incapability, lie the origins of the rhetorical crippling of Paul Morel.

8
Disillusioning Too Late: The Rhetorical Backsliding of Tiberius Gracchus

GREAT ORATOR?

Among orators of the Roman Republic, Tiberius Sempronius Gracchus, who lived from 161 to 133 B.C., has been ranked as one of the greatest. But in their work, critics have not undertaken full analyses of his rhetorical activity, choosing instead to make generalized comment, such as references to his oratorical "power."[1] Among all commentators, Cicero is the most willing to point up defects, e.g., in style. He does recognize that Tiberius "was a man of uncommon genius" but adds, charitably, that he "had but a short time to improve and display it."[2] More than qualified praise, Cicero's is faint. His overall assessment may be the most accurate available.

Cicero was an astute rhetorician, and if we were to find him among us today and active as a critic, perhaps he would conclude that Tiberius' story is not about rhetorical success; that mainly it is about unfavorable narcissism and rhetorical indisposition. If he were to make such an assertion he would have to give some background and argue his case, perhaps along lines such as the following.

QUESTIONS ON TIBERIUS' ORATORY

One reason that few scholars have looked critically at Tiberius' oratorical career is that only fragments and paraphrases of his speeches exist. What does it mean to say that Tiberius was a powerful orator? Does such judgment suggest consistent effectiveness and success? What were sources of his power, i.e., in which of the parts of oratory or particular strategies lay his strength? Further, to what extent are evaluators influenced by Tiberius' indisputable political significance in the late Republic? To what extent by admiration of his stance as a courageous young reformer who dared to challenge the enemies of the people? To what extent by his family status? To what extent by the oratorical *promise* of this young man who while bred and trained for statesmanship did not achieve it and died at twenty-eight? Is his standing as a major historical figure in any way attributable to rhetorical ability?

Such are the kinds of questions that arise insistently as one reads history of the period. Indeed, a rhetorical examination of Tiberius Gracchus' participation in events of his day forces denial of most traditional positive judgment on his speaking: his story as orator is not of unqualified success, certainly not of triumph — nor of sound judgment, nor possibly of ultimate good intentions. Nor is it of "greatness," arguably. Indeed, his public behavior, marked by extreme individuality and defensiveness, evoked intense hostility among leaders in Rome and contributed to tragedy in his life and nation.

Tiberius Gracchus became a rhetorically indisposed public figure — unable or disinclined to call up rhetorical resources in facing pressing political problems.

ILLUSIONMENT

Though the known period of Tiberius' activity as orator comprised but three seasons — the winter, spring, and summer of 133 B.C., very important influences on this Roman nobleman's career were established generations back. They must be acknowledged. First is of family. Born into an illustrious and aristocratic family, and into a culture that placed high value on ancestry, Tiberius was handed a sterling legacy — and an extraordinary burden. Both his great-grandfather and great-uncle had brilliant records in military leadership. Moreover, both served as consul, the highest elective office of the Republic. His father went higher, recording two military triumphs and serving twice as consul, and then as censor. "Yet," as Plutarch writes, the father "was more renowned and esteemed for his virtue than his honours,"[3] if that is conceivable. When he died, his statue was erected in the Forum, there to remind citizens and family of exemplary Roman citizenship. It was up to Tiberius to equal or better his father's contributions.[4] Another of the father's remarkable accomplishments was his marriage to Cornelia, daughter of the distinguished patrician Scipio Africanus.

With a matchless background — of two noble families supplying exceptional prestige and station — Tiberius was trained to assume an exalted place. Certain features of his education were characteristic, e.g., emphasis on building sound Roman character through emulation of esteemed models of the past and contemporary figures such as eminent orators of the Senate.[5] But the unique and most telling factor in Tiberius' education was the mother, Cornelia, who dedicated herself entirely to her sons (brother Gaius received similar attention). It was she who controlled the rearing and finishing, especially after the father died when Tiberius was nine or ten.

Noteworthy in Ciciero's view was her nurturing "in the elegance and purity of language." For more formal lessons, Cornelia secured outstanding tutoring to enrich Tiberius' mind "with all the stores of Grecian literature." Tiberius was "constantly attended by the ablest masters from Greece." Diophanes, teacher of oratory and "the most eloquent Grecian of his age," seems to have been chief among these.[6] Excellent training was assured, including oratorical. Blossius, the Greek philosopher who was to become friend and supporter of Tiberius, may have been one of his teachers employed by Cornelia.

Clearly, Cornelia's interest in her son's perfection was intense. Tiberius, Alvin H. Bernstein concludes, was "raised by a fiercely ambitious woman who in the eyes of many exemplified Roman motherhood."[7] The mother's investment was personal and unrestrained. Included in her maternal strategy was the use of coercive power. Plutarch, reports, for example, on her unmerciful upbraiding of her sons "that the Romans as yet called her the daughter of Scipio, than the mother of the Gracchi."[8] Cornelia, daughter of the conqueror of Hannibal and herself possessed of an abiding desire for glory, needed — for herself — aggrandizement of her sons.

Prescriptions of the Roman culture were definite and severe as well. It was demanded of a young man in his *cursus honorum* that he make nearly complete yielding of self to state requirements and discipline. His life was not his own. All accommodation was from his side; the state remained rigid and unyielding. Thus, from early childhood, the aspiring male, obliged to live up to precise expectations, invested in an idealized "false self," as Donald W. Winnicott would explain it.[9] In this, he denied — and lost — himself.

The result of Tiberius' ancestral, educational, cultural, and parental crafting was a youth with an unmistakable mandate. His was to be a lofty role in Roman leadership. More than commissioned, he was *ordained* with grand destiny. All forces in his molding worked from that warrant. Thus was he illusioned — and without limit. Young Tiberius was to be great; he could know no obstacle.

It was not surprising then, with his *cursus honorum* well-nigh certified, that upon receiving the toga of boyhood he was admitted into the college of augers, an unusual and high honor,[10] and that as a teen-age army officer he distinguished himself, e.g., in being the first to climb enemy walls at Carthage.[11] His public career began quite as promised.

DISILLUSIONMENT

But then came disaster. It was in another military engagement that Tiberius' days of glory would end and adversity begin. As far as historical data tell, it was the first setback of his life — the first disconfirmation of his thoroughly illusioned self. The event occurred after his election as quaestor for the year 137, while he served in that capacity with an army in Spain, under Gaius Mancinus. As fate would have it, the entire Roman force was captured, and the Numantine victors, remembering Tiberius' father as friend, insisted that Tiberius be named to represent the Roman army in negotiations. Thus favored with the advantage of enviable paternal patronage, Tiberius stepped in to work out a settlement. A major result was release of all troops, with the Numantines keeping all Roman property. On the long journey home, he doubtless felt gratified, convinced that he had saved the lives of 20,000 soldiers. The father's legacy had provided special office which the son had used for Rome. Surely he would receive praise.[12]

But he was in for an immense surprise: the Senate did not share his perception of accomplishment. Upon arriving in Rome, the legion was jolted by senatorial outrage and formal repudiation of the "base and scandalous" settlement with the enemy. As leader, Mancinus was convicted and subjected to complete dishonor. Tiberius was spared regular punishment, owing to his popularity and perhaps the intervention of a politically powerful ally.[13] Yet, he felt the sting. The young man of destiny, who *knew* he "was doing all things right,"[14] who had never been judged wrong, took rejection of his treaty as a painful personal rebuke.[15] History provides no better illustration of severe narcissistic injury and cataclysmic consequences thereof.

POLITICIAN WITH A MISSION

Yet, Tiberius' adversity was not without sweet uses, for in it he received convincing evidence of his popularity among the people. While the rich and noble, including senators, suffered from a degrading defeat in Spain, friends and relatives of the returning soldier found good reason to rejoice. To them, Tiberius was the "preserver of so many citizens," and they flocked to him.[16] Put down by the Senate but lifted by the people, Tiberius was elected their tribune for the year 133, giving him the position from which to effect recoupment of his injured self. He would have his day.

Upon assuming office, he took a bold step, the first of a remarkable series. The result would be his death within a few months and a severely shaken Republic. Plutarch has it that as he passed through Etruria on his way to Spain, Tiberius had been troubled by the sight of so many slaves working the land. Once, free farmers had worked the public allotments, but over the years most of the free acreages had come into possession of the nobility who put slaves to the tilling. Cheap slave labor displacing freeholders was one of the many problems plaguing Rome in the 130s. Moreover, with the need of troops to fight foreign wars and quell uprisings of slaves, the pool of men for military conscription was diminishing.

Since slaves did not serve in the army, the responsibility of filling their ranks fell upon small farmers and peasantry, who, after their years with the legions, had only the city as home. Other serious conditions stemmed from unemployment in the city, policies favoring upper classes, and general exploitation of the masses.[17]

Depressed by the unsympathetic ruling oligarchy, the people sensed sympathy in Tiberius and saw in him a source of hope, and doubtless he came to discover his hope in them—as it related to personal as well as political ends. In any event, he listened to their appeals and read their writings "upon porches, walls, and monuments," calling upon him to reinstate them "in their former possessions"—they who had been forced off the land. The people "excited his zeal and determination" to act.[18] Tiberius found a cause and an opportunity to balance accounts.

Thus, the newly elected tribune did not delay in bringing forth a major reform proposal. Drafted with the assistance of certain political leaders but sure to arouse opposition of the gentry holding the land, it was intended to put small farmers back on the land in large numbers. Essentially, the measure called for enforcement of the old laws limiting acreage of public land that one man could hold and for removal of persons illegally possessing it.[19] Tiberius assumed the role as leader of reform.

MOTIVATION

From one historical perspective, Tiberius' motivation related to awareness of Rome's problems and complaints of the people. Other factors may have contributed to his controversial, if not daring, attempt to enact corrective legislation. Cornelia, never a disinterested party in her sons' fortunes, may have urged him to take the step. Diophanes the rhetorician and the liberal philosopher Blossius are possible sources of influence,[20] they with their democratic "Hellenic ideas."[21]

But the proud young Roman did have pressing personal reasons for taking action. Among them, as noted by Plutarch, was his rivalry in public speaking with Spurius Postumius, a young and aspiring man of his acquaintance. Back from the war, Tiberius felt himself losing ground in the race for "fame and influence." Absolutely unwilling to occupy an inferior position—determined to outdo Spurius—he jumped into controversy defiantly and thrust forward a radical proposal that would surely set off the people—and secure their favor.[22] The young man needing a project to advance himself—to redeem himself—found his chance.[23] That is one explanation; we shall find another that extends it.

Consistent with his individualistic turn, Tiberius made an extraordinary—and fateful—decision on advancement of his proposal. Departing from the long-standing procedure of consulting the Senate on proposed legislation, he took the bill directly to the popular assembly for debate and decision. So doing, he deliberately flouted the *dignitas* of the Senate.[24] Though sure to anger the aristocracy, reforms were needed and Tiberius' measure did have intrinsic merit. Appian thought it a "most excellent design," if it could be carried out.[25] Certainly, his plan may be taken as constructive and for the general good. Yet in his manner of securing enactment, he put himself *against* the order, ultimately defeating self—if not cause. In this light, he appears as an ambitious, vindictive noble, one who had been sure of praise but was shamed by the fathers and who now would hurt others as he himself had been hurt by them. Cicero's opinion is convincing: Tiberius entered on the political scene with memories of injury, "with a heart full of resentment against the great and good,"[26] i.e., the Roman establishment.

Tiberius' move to bypass the Senate doubtless provided him certain personal satisfactions, but it does not seem to have been intelligent. True, many in the Senate stood to suffer financially by Tiberius' measure and therefore did oppose it, but he did have friends and supporters in the Senate. A full hearing was possible, had he honored convention and rules of political courtesy[27] and tried with senators the arts of persuasion in which he had been well-trained.

Tiberius Gracchus and the Roman Senate, that political body representative of his own station in life, became fierce adversaries. From the moment that he chose to ignore the Senate, he and they—the powerful and rich, the ruling authority of Rome—were in opposition. On nearly all occasions of his speaking and proposing, his overbearing manner and the consequential senatorial rigidity dominate the scene. Theirs were continued positions of self-defense, with one side rancorously countering the other. Heavy in narcissistic investment, both sides were constrained to dominate, furiously. But the conflict became a no-win situation.

STRATEGY AND COUNTERSTRATEGY

Though only fragments and paraphrasings are available, we have evidence that Tiberius made a number of speeches on the land problem and his proposed remedy. Appian records that the "illustrious man, eager for glory," delivered "an eloquent discourse," first extolling the valiant Italian people, who were now becoming paupers and declining in numbers. Continuing, he inveighed against the multitude of slaves in agriculture: faithless people and useless in war.[28] Plutarch's interpretation of Tiberius' main arguments differs somewhat, if indeed he and Appian are reporting on the same occasion.[29] One passage, purportedly in verbatim phrasing, gives indication of Tiberius' passion:

the savage beasts . . . in Italy, have their particular dens, they have their places of repose and refuge; but the men who bear arms, and expose their lives for the safety of their country, enjoy in the meantime nothing more in it but the air and light; and, having no houses or settlements of their own, are constrained to wander from place to place with their wives and children.

The ordinary Roman soldier fights and is killed to maintain the wealth and luxury of the rich. He has not one foot of land to call his own.[30]

From available accounts, it is clear that Tiberius' aim in speaking was more to arouse the people than to convince conservative magistrates of his plan's feasibility. As Plutarch observed, he directed his harangue to "an enthusiastic and sympathising audience,"[31] effecting a great display of popular sentiment and thus infuriating the Senate. Those whose interests he supported knew not—nor cared not—about the peculiar private motivation of his mission. And so it has been through history. How many causes— good and bad—have been promoted by the rhetoric of intense, individualistic and narcissistic demand—by justice for others found coincident to personal justice?

Frustrated and embittered,[32] the Senate chose indirect strategy. They enlisted tribune Marcus Octavius to serve as their surrogate, to do their bidding. He was to work in the assembly to obstruct Tiberius in his effort to secure passage of the bill. The angry Tiberius reacted by changing his bill to be even more severe against the wealthy and kinder to the peasantry. The result was much debating in the assembly between the opposed tribunes, Tiberius and Octavius: "a fine battle of words and tempers."[33] Following a number of extrarhetorical power plays by Tiberius, e.g., sealing the treasury and thereby stopping all use of state monies, "the rich proprietors" allegedly developed plans to murder him. He then, against conventions of civility, took to wearing a short sword.[34]

At voting time in the assembly, Tiberius delivered a long speech in which he urged justice for the common people. He argued the worth of citizens over slaves as contributors to the public interset and for the necessity of having a large body of brave men ready to fight for retention of possessions taken in conquest. Give the people this land on which to raise children—so Rome can hold its acquired territory and occupy "the rest of the habitable world." Thus he exaggerated "the glory and riches on the one side and the danger and fear on the other"—admonishing the rich and exciting the poor—"as well as others who were moved by reason rather than the desire for gain." Following the lengthy speech that included appeals to ordinary citizens, landholders, and all Romans, Tiberius ordered the scribe to read the proposed law.[35]

Thereupon, Octavius, acting as instructed by the Senate, vetoed the procedure, exercising his tribunician right to intercede against an act of a colleague. At the next meeting of the assembly he repeated his action, which, according to Appian, led to certain leading citizens beseeching Tiberius to consult with the Senate on the proposal. Tiberius yielded and went to the Senate, but upon receiving an upbraiding from the senators in that curious and adversarial consultation, he returned resolutely to the assembly to continue his fight. After failing in passionate plea to persuade Octavius to step aside, the disconsolate Tiberius, unwilling "to retreat ignominiously, to suffer a second public defeat and humiliation,"[36] took "a course neither legal nor fair" and secured a vote of the assembly to depose Octavius.[37] With that bumptious act, the suffering heir to glory crossed the Rubicon; never before had a tribune used his extraordinary power to remove a colleague from office.[38] With all opposition in the assembly now stilled, the bill passed and became law, and Tiberius saw to it that he, his brother Gaius, and father-in-law Claudius were elected as commissioners to oversee implementation of the reform program.[39]

ESCALATION OF CONFLICT

Defeated in its purpose to stop passage of the bill, the vengeful and obstinate Senate refused to provide sufficient funds for the commission to do its work. But as fortune would have it, a source of funds became known to Tiberius, and once more he acted in petulance against the order. It happened that the King of Pergamum had died, bequeathing his kingdom to Rome. Unimpeded by the tradition assigning management of bequests and acquired territories to the Senate, Tiberius put forward an assembly bill earmarking the king's money for use by his commission; moreover, he announced plans to see to it that the *assembly* administer the deceased king's entire kingdom. Thus Tiberius, in "wild escalation of the conflict," revealed obvious demagoguery.[40]

It was at this point that Tiberius, when bested in an exchange in an assembly meeting, may have realized that sentiment was turning against him. Embarrassingly unable to answer a hard question put to him on the issue of deposing a tribune, he seems to have sensed that his irregular treatment of Octavius offended Romans generally. Consequently, he delivered a lengthy apologia, striving to warrant his act of deposition. In the speech of defense, built from democratic theory that he made sacrosanct, sacred history of the Roman Republic, and a law of religion—and perhaps prepared with the help of liberal friend Blossius, Tiberius reminded Romans of the duties and obligations of tribunes to support the people's interests. Yes, a tribune is inviolable, he acknowledged—but only as long as he guards and protects the people. Turning to analogy, in oblique reference to his deposing Octavius, Tiberius argued to justify his drastic act. Recall, he asked, how Romans removed the kingly Tarquin when he acted wrongly. Even one of the venerated and influential vestal virgins would face execution should she transgress, he reminded. Likewise, a tribune who offended against the people should be removed. As a "sacred present," the people have "lawful power to transfer the tribuneship from one man's hands to another's." In this way, Tiberius sought to validate his behavior, by identifying it with extreme measures — and hallowed events and rules — that related to politics and religion and which were sanctioned and given precedence by the people. If it helped him get through a critical moment, the speech succeeded more by invention of affective appeal than logical comparisons of events.[41]

Continuing in his cause, Tiberius took a major — and final — contemptuous step: he announced candidacy for election as tribune for 132. If not actually unlawful, immediate reelection violated the spirit of the constitution, which in itself had the force of law to Romans.[42] Against the wall, fearful of future prosecution as a private citizen, Tiberius sought "refuge in the very tribunician sacrosanctity of which he had deprived his colleague."[43] The brash Tiberius would not be stopped by "sacred" law, regardless of reverence that Romans attached to it. A thing is not sacred if in opposition to consuming narcissistic purpose.

The meeting of the assembly called at election time to confirm his eligibility prompted an emergency meeting of the Senate. As angry senators deliberated means of curbing Tiberius, a number broke for the assembly with clubs in their hands and parts of benches. Tiberius' life is near its end. Attempting to flee, he and 300 of his followers were killed.

It is important to note that up to this time, the Republic of Rome had endured without an instance of bloodshedding in public affairs. For those nearly 400 years "the sword was never carried into the assembly."[44] The violence of that day and events leading up to it marked the beginning of 100 years of disorder, lasting to the end of the Republic. The turbulent and brief political career of Tiberius Sempronius Gracchus constitutes a major turning point in Roman history, if not a legacy. His narcissistic adamancy and the Senate's intractability provide a monumental negative model on failure in resolving conflict.

RHETORICAL SUCCESS AND FAILURE

What were Tiberius' rhetorical skills and accomplishments?

Something of an answer can be found through a standard analysis. He doubtless knew rhetorical success early in his career. One example, in his eyes, was negotiation of the treaty after the military defeat in Spain. Too, his apologia seemed to serve adequately in a critical moment. And near the end, when canvassing the people in his campaign for reelection, he was very effective. But most significant, and probably the provenance of this reputation as orator, are those pathetic speeches on the land question soon after his election as tribune. This vigorous figure of unquestioned prominence attracted and excited the people, raising their hopes for new opportunity. His strengths were in projecting a cry of outrage over conditions and then offering an appealing solution. In fervent acknowledgment of the human misery, injustice, and other circumstances depressing the people, he evoked popular sentiment and thereby structured a base of power which, he had determined, was not accomplishable by working through the Senate. At every turn he was able to bring about a large turnout of the people. Specifically effective were his fiery style, as reported, though Cicero did criticize his style; extant fragments and paraphrases of his speeches do suggest high energy and intensity in expression. Certain usages, e.g., comparison and contrast, lamentation, and admonishment of the rich were compelling, quite obviously. Jamie L. Kauffman,[45] wanting to report on Tiberius' invention of argument while finding scant materials available, adds knowledge on Tiberius' ideas and lines of argument by isolating and naming his *assumed rhetorical roles* and conceiving of them as strategies. For example, Tiberius found success in stirring the people through inventions of humanitarian and imperialist roles. With knowledge on rhetorical requirements in fulfillment of roles, an investigator can extrapolate relevant lines of argument. For example, as imperialist, Tiberius answered the nation's economic and social needs through development of premises extolling use of national power in expansion and glorifying conquest.

Notwithstanding instances of art and achievement, Tiberius' rhetorical errors and failures predominate. For example, he was deficient in the arts of political action, as historians generally conclude. He lacked the political wisdom and skill required in handling the large task that he chose;[46] he made serious errors in judgment and acted hastily;[47] he took "little heed of the past or the future" or of consequences of his actions;[48] his constitutional innovations were "ill-considered and impracticable";[49] he was an idealist and unable to countenance compromise; he was not "a clear-sighted and practical statesman";[50] he "simply did not know what he was doing."[51] These evaluations by modern historians are harsh, yet even Appian, generally uncritical and liking Tiberius' plan, finds fault, e.g., with his "too violent manner."[52]

Starting with his decision to bypass the Senate, Tiberius revealed a disinclination to rely on rhetorical processes. His behavior was characterized more by fierce individualism than good leadership and sensible accommodation. Tiberius' continuing insolence yielded a return in kind. Insulted and threatened, the haughty Senate would not soften or make any effort to come to terms, and with Tiberius' every new rash act or popular appeal, fears of senators grew, and positions intensified. His ruinous narcissism evoked theirs. The major critical events were Tiberius' unsuccessful try at dissuading Octavius from interceding with the veto and the subsequent deposition of Octavius. He had a chance then to turn back and wait for a better opportunity. Though Octavius' veto, if left unchallenged, would have meant defeat of his bill, Tiberius could have allowed the matter to rest for the moment. But unable to envision the disastrous consequences of his obduracy,[53] he persevered.

Tiberius was not one to wait; he desperately needed satisfaction. And so he became a legislative "scrambler," trying this and then that in vain effort to force down a law and finally to keep himself alive, politically *and* physically, to fight another day. His were feverish defensive moves: snubbing the powerful, rousing the rabble, manipulating, apologizing, and imploring. From election to death, he was a man rhetorically on the run.

ORIGINS OF RHETORICAL INDISPOSITION

But, if we would understand Tiberius' rhetorical failing, we must go beyond standard analysis and get closer to the man, for, patently, *he himself* became the prime issue in those last calamitous months of 133 B.C. As Henry C. Boren observes,

> Since it was Tiberius who was adding vast powers to the tribunician office, thrusting aside the opposition of Senate, magistrates, and even other Tribunes, obviously it was the person of Tiberius Gracchus himself—the individual, not a mass movement based on a particular philosophy—who threatened the existing order. His enemies saw that clearly enough.[54]

His purpose was to prevail over *them*; theirs was to stop *him*. Such was the essential feature of that grave political interaction in 133.

Without full awareness of the several constraints that impinged upon the life of the agitated Tiberius Gracchus, one cannot come to a satisfactory explanation of his troubled political and rhetorical career. Few significant figures in history have been forced to carry burdens like those placed upon that man. Their weight contributed to his failures, and together they account for origins of his rhetorical indisposition. First to recall are ancestry and family, with the extraordinary requirements of performance that were imposed. The lore of forebears' deeds impressed on him since infancy became a fixed part of his identity and was internalized as standard and value against which he would measure his own behavior. The child who was "named" and confirmed by his ancestry developed in a world of progenatorial tyranny. He had no other perspective. Further, his environment was extremely competitive. In a Roman world so given to rivalry and factional struggle and questing for advancement and honor, aspirants took very seriously any challenge to purpose or dignity. Like his contemporaries, this young man felt incredible pressure. Pride was a mighty motivator, as was avoidance of shame.

And to act and compete with expected brilliance, Tiberius was groomed and finished under the family administration of Cornelia. She provided everything.

But *everything* was too much. As Heinz Kohut writes, the development of a "consolidation of the self" — essential to effective functioning in the adult world — requires "optimal frustration of the child's narcissistic needs."[55] Winnicott calls this vital process *disillusionment*. The adequately functioning parent (the so-called "good enough mother") "starts off with an almost complete adaptation" to the "infant's needs and as time proceeds . . . adapts less and less completely, gradually, according to the infants growing ability to deal with failure." In this way, "the infant can actually come to gain from the experience of frustration, since incomplete adaptation to need makes objects real." Close adaptation to need that is continued too long "resembles magic" and is "no better than hallucination."[56] Decreasing adaptation allows for gradual abrogation of omnipotence. But Cornelia could not let go to allow a building of strength for the future. She used her son as a "narcissistic extension of herself," as Sophie Loewenstein states it in reference to ambitious parents who exploit their special offspring. The child of a Cornelia seeks to achieve an ego-ideal through "driven strivings for fame and glory." If frustrated in execution, the child "may resort to defensive grandiosity" and ultimately become "severely depressed, paranoid, and enraged."[57] Such was Tiberius' pattern. He was reared on magic; hallucination carried him through early life — and was apparent in his mood as he made that journey home from Spain. Biographer Charles Oman writes that Tiberius Gracchus was one of those "unfortunate persons who are from their earliest years held up as models . . . till they are led on to entertain the strongest views as to their impeccability and infallibility."[58] Fallibility was not allowed a place in the lexicon on Tiberius' identity.

Young Tiberius *was* "led on" and thus was he responsive to the close adaptation of his obsessive mother. Pressures of conformity were too powerful to resist. In Winnicott's terms, it can be said that he yielded to environmental demands and grew in strict, undisturbed emulation of illustrious ancestry and other great Romans. In compliance, he was forced into a "false existence." And the moment of tragic letdown came, when, as Winnicott would have put it, Tiberius could not bear "the full blast of disillusionment."[59] Cornelia did not provide her son with capability to meet adversity, and when faced by it, he was not prepared. Experience in disillusionment came too late, not when a child at home or in early training but in the field of battle — first military, then political. Prepared only for success, he was not equipped to meet denial or the consequences of error.

The First Challenge to Omnipotence

Rejection of his Numantine treaty introduced the first challenge to perfection in his protected, unreal life. Set down hard, he received an injury to self that abruptly changed everything. Traumatized, his diminished self sought only for restoration. As "prisoner of his own *dignitas*,"[60] he found his exigence in his pain. Responsive to demands of culture and family, he had forced upon him a false self, but he could not stay with it. He regressed, *seeking to take back his life.* The soldier broke rank, and in Rome, that was unacceptable. Distraught and insolent, increasingly defensive, he gave up on irksome and uncertain rhetorical processes that he had studied, reverting to use of more direct — primitive and basic — personal forces. Such are the workings of coercive narcissism.

Success became urgent. But in Rome of 133, success was yet by way of law and convention. The state "functioned in a kind of precarious balance 'by the senate proposing, the people resolving, and the magistrates executing.' This was the accepted order to things in the Republic and surprisingly it worked reasonably well for several centuries," John M. Riddle notes.[61] It would not permit violation. Unhappy Tiberius violated rule after rule, and with each new infraction, he "further tempted his opponents to do the same in their search for a means of dealing with the threat he presented."[62] The greater the personal demand, the greater was his departure from the code of Rome — and by the man whose forebears had never swerved.

Losing rhetorical consciousness, Tiberius came to operate as an individual apart and against. In regression and rage, rendered rhetorically indisposed, he resorted to unsanctioned behavior, thereby alienating significant audiences: first the Roman fathers and eventually most others. His was the tragedy of a self formulated in perfection — put "above history or experience and too noble to bear opposition."[63] If arts of invention — of competence in choosing argument and behavior for rhetorical occasion — constitute a necessary measurement of excellence, Tiberius must be judged a failure. His story is not of a great orator but of a young man persistently assured of personal omnipotence, who after severe and unexpected narcissistic wounding, lost his rhetorical sense, flew off the course of glory, and led his Republic closer to its death.

9
Rhetoric and Civility

THE IDEA OF CIVILITY

It is said in medicine that health cannot be understood and appreciated fully without knowledge of pathology. So, too, in rhetoric. The chapters on the Peoples Temple, Joseph McCarthy and the American people, the Morels, and Tiberius Gracchus, are case studies in rhetorical pathology that illustrate origins, behaviors, and consequences of rhetorical dysfunction. Products of unsatisfactory environments, the subjects came to suffer impairment in rhetorical interaction. Theirs was unfavorable narcissism, the force of self giving *misdirection* to the rhetorical imperative of which all humans, seeking confirmation of self, are possessed. Their lives reveal behaviors *against* or *from* others — or *with* others in disastrous fusion. The four cases are large writ examples of despairing, threatened, inadequately confirmed people who powerfully — and futilely — were constrained to find solace, security, and assurance of self-worth. Theirs were hopeless quests — always the fate of those who remain indisposed. These are cases of incivility. But before making that connection, we need to come to a concept of civility and its constituent elements that will provide a measuring device for assessing relevant behavior. Actually, our prior discussion of the rhetorical disposition and its development have prepared us for this next step, for origins of civility are traceable to infancy.

Civility is a social virtue and an old idea. Sophrosyne, a name for self-control and moderation valued by the ancient Greeks, may be close in meaning. Opposed was hubris: excessive pride, insolence, and arrogance. Inherent in the Greek idea of arete, the exercise of civility involved adherence to the four cardinal virtues: courage, temperance, justice, and wisdom. Contrasted to the Greek ideal is the realism of Sigmund Freud's vision. To him, civility arose as an expedient accommodation from the human struggle between individuality and claims of the group.[1] Yes, said Erich Fromm, the human struggle is constant, but it is between forces of regression — a return to animal existence — and progression, arrival at human existence.[2]

146

Many have expressed themselves on the topic. Martin Buber, for example, held that "actual humanity" — civility, we might say — exists only where unfolds the capacity to confirm others appropriately.[3] The definition of Burton Zwiebach reflects beliefs of the ancient Greeks. He views civility as a dimesion of the "common life" and characterized by replacement of "intemperate self-interest with concern for our fellows and with traditions of restraint, forbearance, grace, tolerance, compassion."[4] Lawrence Rosenfield and his colleagues construct three general critieria of "man at his best." Such a one is first of all *thoughtful* — about self and others. This criterion includes reflectiveness, e.g., thoughtfulness in choosing and using language symbols. It also includes receptivity — giving "the world a chance to explain itself" — and personal responsibility. Second, the individual at best is *careful*. A part of caring is respecting others, appreciating ranges of human behavior, responding and empathizing. The third criterion is *good humor*. The person of good humor recognizes, relishes, and seeks the incongruous. Basic here is flexibility and a certain abandon, e.g., as found in the absence of constant need in life for symmetry, congruity, normality, and perfection.[5]

All these views on the topic have relevance to our study, but in the position of political scientist Heinz Eulau, we find full and clear recognition of the necessary connection to *human interaction* — of *rhetorical process as a function of civility*. Eulau contrasts civil behavior with self-centeredness and the personalizing of life's frustrations, e.g., in blaming, resenting, attributing wrongness or unfairness, resorting to temper tantrums, etc. We would categorize these as modes of distracting narcissism: defensive acts. A person inclined in the extreme to behave in these ways, with "no conception of being an integral part of society whose proper operation depends significantly on his behavior or of having responsibilities to others," is not a civil being. The civil person enjoys a maturity which chiefly consists "in the habitually exercised capacity to respond to others and events without the demands of self constituting the sole criterion according to which to behave or to make judgments." The civil person recognizes that situations outside the self and the demands of self are distinct and separable. Common patterns of civil behavior are acts of "persuading, soliciting, consulting, advising, bargaining, compromising, coalition building, and so on" — as opposed to "such forms of behavior as coercing, confronting, deceiving, manipulating," etc.[6]

Incivility, as unsocial or antisocial behavior — or omission — is broad in expression. It is reflective of rhetorical indisposition and narcissistic imaturity. Civility, too, is broad in scope. Typifying a rhetorical disposition, it issues from favorable narcissism. At the heart of rhetorical maturity, civility is a social good — an ethical value — and a rich source of ethos.[7] It is expressed in the symbolic behavior of one with another, i.e., it is effected rhetorically. And that is why rhetorical indisposition precludes the capacity for civility. Incivility, on the other hand, prevents all but temporary rhetorical success with mature, rhetorically disposed others; the very being of the mature individual rejects uncivil acts and will withhold credit.

Perhaps we now have a base for setting down some components of civility. Interpreting and drawing from sources like the respected Greek tradition, the realism of Freud and Fromm, the optimism of Buber, the existentially framed ideas of Rosenfield, et al, the rhetorically informed wisdom of Eulau, etc., we come to eight fundamental elements.

ELEMENTS OF CIVILITY

Knowledge and Awareness

Clarence Day once said that "the test of a civilized person is first self-awareness."[8] We should include in that a knowledge of one's personal interest and intent in relating. Then we must add others' needs, positions, and interests, along with a sense of right and wrong as pertaining to choice making in given interactions — and awareness of consequences thereof. Important, too, is knowing that caring about others is basic to achieving one's ends: that values of reciprocity, mutual satisfaction, equity, accommodation, and social sensitivity[9] are to be acknowledged.

Will

A willingness to engage with others, making a willing presence as an active, cooperative, and motivated player in social interaction is essential to community welfare: the will to help shape public order.[10] Passivity reduces benefits and alters the character of an exchange, and withdrawal by one party ends it. To speak up, to speak out — indeed to speak to any indicated chosen end, may be an act of civility, for as Thomas Mann said, "Speech is civilization itself. The word, even the most contradictious word, preserves contact — it is silence which isolates."[11] The participation of one individual is dependent on the participation — stimulation — of another. But whether to involve oneself is a first choice, one as critical as any other. And, we must admit that the decision not to participate may be the more civil, upon occasion, e.g., in not confirming the uncivil behavior of another. That, too, is an act of will.

Respect

A self-respecting person is not only advantageously prepared for rhetorical success but also prepared to respect others in any exchange. It might be said that in respectfully affirming others, one affirms oneself. Security and self-esteem are basic to the kind of resilience that marks civil interaction, e.g., when one is secure enough to resist the impulse to answer narcissistic petulance with a self-demeaning defensive outburst. Indeed, civility is directly opposite to maladaptive self-protection. A respecting self need not plea for deference. Also to be noted are tolerance and respect for chosen roles of others and community rules that facilitate functioning, among them being the rule favoring persuasion over violence.

Courage

Rhetorical grit must be acknowledged: making a personal disclosure when it seems needed, risking self — "putting it on the line," e.g., when in a try at resolving a conflict, one dares to give what should be given or say what should be said. Too, it may take a certain kind of courage to listen to a message that threatens one's status, to hear another person out and offer useful feedback. One person's act of courage may result in increased well-being in a group or entire community.

Ability

The topic here is rhetorical acumen and strength, mainly. *The facilitation of civility is a rhetorical function*; it is achieved through symbol and strategy — by decisions to say this instead of that and in that way instead of this. It is not something that "just happens." Perceiving reality, predicting outcome and adapting to it, discovering fitting argument, balancing self-interest and community welfare, and all other representations of rhetorical competence are among the valued abilities of members of a functional community. As Cicero knew, it is rhetorical art that gives effectiveness to knowledge — as well as helping to discover it.

Independence

Though certainly related to self-respect and courage — and at times understandably conflicting with cooperation, the act of a person standing apart may constitute the highest order of civility. It is an autonomy of being that marks personal individuality. A memorable example is the independence of the main character (played by Henry Fonda) in the excellent film *Twelve Angry Men*. The story is about jury members of a murder trial deciding on the defendant's guilt or innocence. Although the only member who at the outset discerns inadequacy in the prosecution's case, the principal character stands fast. Eventually all others join him, largely as a result of his independent strength and persuasive powers. Independence is opposite to fusion, e.g., the fusion of Manny and Madeleine, the couple referred to in prior chapters who trapped themselves in collusive co-dependence. When not individuated, i.e., not in enjoyment of mature individuality and independence, one does not have a real choice whether to relate to another, whether to commit oneself or not. Not able to be one's own person, one *forces* the relationship or becomes selfless. That is not the behavior of an independent — and self-respecting — person.

Freedom

Freedom and independence, though bound together in spirit, can be considered separately. Included in the idea of freedom are values related specificially to civil liberties, the exercise of prerogative, issues bearing on response to restraint, challenge to unacceptable policy, appreciating the democratic process, etc.

Responsibility

Taking responsibility for one's actions reflects social regard — good treatment of others. It is admitting and accepting obligation. It is showing trustworthiness, being accountable and in other such ways making a civil presence.

Civility, with these several components, is grounded in the first months of life. Each new child, in association with others, must start from the beginning in learning how to live and relate. With each, the story of civilization starts again.[12]

INCIVILITY OF THE FOUR RHETORS

The case studies of the foregoing chapters do not reveal contribution to civilization. At birth, each of the principal figures doubtless was a potential civil being. But circumstances changed all that. Let us pinpoint features of their incivility.

Jim Jones' withdrawal from the larger society, disrespect for self and others, irresponsibility, brutality, and violence are a few indicators of his deficiency in civility. Though less obviously operant, certain forms of incivility in behaviors of the Peoples Temple membership also stand out. Giving their lives over to Jones, they rejected freedom. They lacked the spark of independence for maintaining a viable community. Yes, they brought themselves together but not as self-respecting, autonomous persons. Their retreat from life — their self-imposed isolation — was not courageous, not a commendable act. And they did not stand up to Jones in his maltreatment. Such was their bent, their failing in civility.

Joseph McCarthy was a man against the world, a person who projected self-loathing. Surely, he is one of the most blatantly and tragically uncivil prominent figures in this nation's history. His lacks were in knowledge and awareness of the better parts of the human soul; respect for self, others, and the idea of community; courage to involve self in genuine dialogue; and personal responsibility. A captive of overwhelming noxious narcissism, he was not a free man. And what is the expected response of a politically free people subjected to a political leader's abuse? To the extent that Americans confirmed McCarthy in his chosen role as their defender and gave him license to proceed in his uncivil way — intimidating and morally maltreating them, they too acted uncivilly. America's score on civil performance as measured by the eight components was lower in the early 1950s than in any other period in the twentieth century. Where was the good citizen's knowledge and awareness of wrong treatment received, the will and ability to make refutation, the respect for self, courage, independence, the granting to others of freedom of expression, and a sense of responsibility? Now, apologists may consider this to be harsh judgment, even unfair. Perhaps so, but in that era we did experience a loss of faith in fairness, propriety, and democratic process — and the results of our actions and inactions are clear.

Tiberius Gracchus, subject of terribly burdensome cultural, ancestral, and parental constraints — minor forms of which we see occasionally today, particularly parental — was groomed to be a model of Roman citizenship. But he fell hard when disconfirmed at a critical moment, receiving a psychically penetrating blow that eventually led to irresponsible and unrhetorical behavior — sometimes disrespectful activity against himself and others — and to violent deaths. Tiberius could not keep together the carefully constructed pieces of self. His answer to great injury, his ill-conceived and frenzied attempt to recoup — his personal revolt against a false self — was an event in Roman history that contributed to the downfall of an entire political system.

Paul and Gertrude Morel's incivility was to each other. In confirming themselves — narrowing their community to the smallest size, they denied themselves opportunity to grow. Theirs was a social offense, a form of disrespect. Their perverted responsibility to each other and ignorance of consequences indicate irresponsibility. In their constancy, they were in fact indifferent to each other's real needs. Too, Gertrude's prejudicial rejection of her husband's graceless social manner and her inability or unwillingness to console him constitute incivility. Perhaps more apparent is Paul's self-exploratory use of Miriam and Clara.

All of these uncivil people caught up others in the web of their miseries. The narcissistically infirm are never unaccompanied. Whether acting from regression or inadequate growth, they always find others to be with — others who come to them. Together they display qualities of incivility.

INDIVIDUALISM vs. THE COMMUNITY

Apparent in certain of the four cases discussed above were cultural forces that played a part in occurrences, e.g., the demanding behavioral standard by which Tiberius' performance was measured and which produced great conflict.

In America today, the strongest cultural force conflicting with civility is *individualism*: the extreme of self-interest. To be sure, various manifestations of individualism have been in evidence in the nation for a long time. Recall that during his visit in the early 1800s Alexis de Tocqueville became concerned about its negative effect on social relations in America. But, before proceeding, let's remind ourselves that individualism is not individuality. The latter, a quality distinguishing one person from another, is socially useful — even a mark of civility, e.g., as representing strength of will, courage, responsibility, independence, and a spirit of freedom. No, individualism is something different: a doctrine or personal aberration enforcing the assumption that the individual and not society is the dominant consideration or end. In a philosophic sense, it is solipsistic, the self being the gauge of existence. In terms of social philosophy, individualism is narcissistic dogmatism: my principle myself — a premise of indifference to public sensibility or altruism. For example, public debate often bears on issues of individualism versus community interest. Holding to historic economic principle and rights of ownership, an advocate may strive to justify a radical change in the physical environment, e.g., cutting down a stand of three-hundred-year-old redwood trees that others of the community may want to preserve for general enjoyment. One side argues individual prerogative, and the other argues maintenance of a place of beauty and pleasure for all.

Current views on care for the nation's mentally ill give us another example. It is a complex question, but issues of individual rights are at the center. Should the state provide hospitalization for the mentally ill? From a perspective of individualism, the answer is no. It is not right to use the money of individuals for this purpose; an individual's responsibility is to his or her own. Too, it is affirmed that placing people in hospitals is a violation of their liberty as individuals. As a result of such rationales, severely incapacitated, psychotic persons, e.g., the schizophrenic, are now out on the city streets attempting to fend for themselves — individually. Is provision of care a community obligation? Is hospitalization an infringement on individual rights? Relatedly, is crime a community problem? Or drug use? Or education needs of the nation's children? Among others, these questions on individualism and the general welfare remain unresolved. One result of our neglect in facing them is continued unsocial behavior in the land: incivility.

Gone are the days of powerful and individualistic industrialists who operated without limitation on their conduct. Antitrust laws now exist; rights of workers are protected; activities restraining trade are outlawed. And yet, individualism is not gone. It is a way of being that is known to every school board member, county commissioner, state legislator, or other official who has had to deal with the clamor for special benefit. As an extreme of self-privilege, it is used to argue personal favor and exemption from obligation. Individualism is a manifestation of unfavorable narcissism: a principle or plea to justify particular materialism, to rationalize a peculiar "hands-off" policy, or to condone imperious actions of one powerful business seeking to eliminate a weaker. In some forms, the individualism of persons and organizations is an expression of social Darwinism, e.g., natural selection and survival of the fittest—the so-called "dog-eat-dog" mentality.

Other forms of individualism are ordinary incivilities, facts of our daily lives: the behaviors of "difficult" people,[13] inane and deleterious television programming,[14] monopolistic pursuit of attention,[15] inauthenticity,[16] and interpersonal insensitivity.[17] Willard Gaylin is one of a number of social critics now on the scene who are deeply disturbed about decreases in levels of civility in this culture. This is an "age of rampant individualism," Gaylin declares. Antisocial acts of individuals threaten community interest. Our culture has become dangerously violent, stamped with desperation and cynicism. Witness the hostility around us, the deep anger and explosive rage. We seem to be a hypersensitive people, keen in detection of signs that "raise doubts about our strength, reliability or stature, diminish self-respect or self-confidence"; any criticism is a threat. The response is fear and wrath. Regretfully, control measures of this culture have not been adequate in handling these "destructive self-serving impulses." How are we to temper this fierce individualism?[18]

In the past two weeks—as I write—four major writers of large metropolitan newspapers in New York and Washington, D.C., have devoted their columns to the problem of violent and individualistic behavior in America and the destruction of neighborhood peace. As it flourishes in this society, individualism is a reflection of both the pernicious narcissism that individuals acquire in inadequate environments in infancy *and* the cultural exacerbation of it. The culture supports and confirms unfavorable narcissistic patterns[19] that are set in the first months of life. The result is obvious and widespread incivility.

Robert Coles voices related cultural concerns, particularly in regard to the current overriding individualistic requirement "that each person follow his or her emotional dictates" and other irrepressible personal initiatives. His hope is for reestablishment of civility so as to spare ourselves "thousands, indeed millions, of breast-beating, fist-clenching, constantly jabbering and self-scrutinizing I's, with their haunting, unsettling refrain of recent years: *I* am all right; *I* have figured myself out; *I* know what *I* want—and that's all that counts. The sad paradox of a collective egoism."[20] Such is one trusted observer's deep concern.

Many of this culture's most potent enthymemes, e.g., those of advertisers and others who would influence the masses with appeals to dominant self-interest, would have shocked listeners in the Athenian Agora of Socrates' day. They would have shocked our grandparents! We are not shocked today — not enough. Ready and needy audiences are available to respond to messages that address their insufficiencies in self-gratification and that license their uniqueness, freeing them from arbitrary prohibition. Not appearing in these popular enthymemes are major premises suggesting responsibilities, regulations, and commitment. Our culture frees us from accepting moral reminders and guilt motivators that may appear in rhetors' enthymemes.

While individual autonomy is a valued and necessary condition in the conduct of a good life, social interests demand limits on behavior. The self cannot be held as a transcendent entity; enduring satisfactions in living are realized only with and through others; individualism abets individual and community fragmentation, putting the public welfare as well as prosperity of individuals at risk. As attitude and behavior, individualism annuls use of the rhetorical resources required in effecting healthful unions of persons or essential social cohesion. In exalting narcissistic singularity for its own sake, individualism is an enemy of effort toward consubstantiality. It is the parent of incivility.

A RHETORICAL CORRECTIVE: THE GOOD AUDIENCE

Given conclusions on the loss of rhetorical effectiveness stemming from narcissistic self-absorption and individualism, how might conditions be met? Is there a rhetorical corrective to this rhetorical problem?

Where can we turn but to the audience, the available and necessary source of correction to any unrhetorical behavior. Indeed, the audience shares the problem, for narcissism as rhetorical pathology is sender-receiver pathology. When in support of unsocial behavior of others, audiences seek satisfaction of their own narcissistic needs. Many who confirm unwarranted narcissistic entitlement were themselves "trained" to respond faithfully to narcissistically demanding mothers and fathers. Their life of service continues. In rhetorical terms, people use others by permission. The audience is the granter of special status or exemption from social sanction. Audiences let themselves be preyed upon; tyrants are made and sustained by others, through validation and tolerance. Aaron Stern's position, at once compassionate and hard, sets the tone for discussion of the role of audience in fostering narcissism. People who permit narcissistic persons to prosper with impunity are "loving patsies," he declares, "volunteers available to pick up the narcissist's dues for living."[21]

First, to know the function of an audience, we must see that agent as more than mere receiver, not a listener only. Maurice Merleau-Ponty was correct in contending, "I am not passive while I am listening; rather I speak according to what the other is saying."²² Truly, *audiences are speakers too, people of influence.* And the *good audience* is one of *good influence.* Favored is the person who has been blessed with good audiences in life: strong and loving parents, teachers, mates, friends, therapists, colleagues, and other rhetors who have been there. A good audience is a rhetor in its own right, rhetorically disposed and civil. The best prospect for reduction of rhetorical impairment lies in the good audience.

What are attributes of the good audience? Lest you worry about my going overboard in idealism here, the first feature to mention is the good audience's basic purposefulness. As a rhetorical entity, it wants something, of course. It seeks power, control, effectiveness, acknowledgment, etc. Let us accept that, for only in serving its own purpose can an audience be *real* to others — as opposed to mere hallucination. False mirrors lie. What good can we do if others know not what we are about?

For its own benefit, the good audience risks making itself available for interaction, openly presenting itself and its ideas or arguments, exposing the self and chancing losses, for rhetorical gain requires occupation of self with others and meeting the hazards that go with it. The opposite, occupation of self with self-distancing and protection from social intimacy, precludes rhetorical effectiveness.

Another mark of the good audience is self-respect, the sine qua non of true objectivity: an appreciation of one's separateness from other persons and objects — freedom from fusion and dependency. In this sense of being one's own person — an unkept choicemaker, objectivity relates to maturity.

Social awareness is another characteristic of the good audience. Included is perception of relevant constraints: evident values, cultural norms, prevalent feelings and attitudes; others' needs and how needs of all persons relate; exigencies motivating participants and their relation to respective purposes.

Rhetorical art in a given situation is also basic: discernment on personal needs, powers, capabilities and shortcomings, as they relate to others directly involved; cognizance of relevant issues, of role options available — where and when to accept, acknowledge, support, confront, counter, deny, argue, etc.; acceptance of the fact that one is indeed an influential being. The good audience is responsible for its own behavior; in owning up to its judgments, it gives promise of greater effectiveness with others. It is able to make advantageous decisions on utilization of resources, e.g., ideas, evidence, behaviors, methods; to predict outcomes and consequences of its own behavior; to assess probable risks and rewards; to perceive the importance of timing in rhetorical interaction and to know when an exigence is no longer viable, e.g., when to "let go" of an issue or topic.

Vigilant and perceptive, realistic and humane, the good audience listens to understand but will not deny self by giving unlimited license to others' behavior. Though any audience is a human agency and consequently is "good" relatively — to some relevant degree and in relevant ways, this "goodness" must be honored and given a place of trust in the rhetorical enterprise, for no acceptable alternative exists. Surely, we know enough about the disastrous intervention of other forms of power. Only good audiences can be relied upon to remind us of our indisposition or unpromising behavior — of messages threatening the community. Only the good audience can provide the necessary disillusioning of socially detrimental individualism or advantage-seeking and promote rhetorical consciousness.

A good audience recognizes the existence in this life of powerful, clashing forces: the personal vs. the social. The force exerted by unsocial narcissism as impelled toward grandiosity and omnipotent idealization — individualism — works to challenge the force imposed by general interests, community need, and rhetorical rule — society. In its practical wisdom and essential role, the good audience values certain postulates on the human condition: that altruism may have no natural advantage over negative narcissism; that social behavior is no more to be anticipated than individualistic behavior; that anyone's rhetorical awareness is less well-established than primary self-interest. Knowledgeable and aware, self-respecting, courageous, able, independent, responsible, free, and willing to engage, the good audience assumes its role civilly.

Roles to Meet a Need: Confirming and Disconfirming

Good audiences — those whose rhetorical presence increases chances for realization of effectiveness and civility in others — are our best hope. Remember the lesson of George Herbert Mead and Charles Horton Cooley, that it is only through others that we learn of ourselves and our behaviors. To become a person, to build a solid identity and develop an effective personality, are goals achievable only in realtionships. Self-evaluation is structured in the rhetorical environment. Ironically, it is others whom the alienated or self-estranged person — the narcissistically handicapped — really needs. But that must be someone who is psychologically healthier, e.g., a friend or paid counselor.[23]

In a different, more critical sense, a good audience is a social requirement. Narcissistic balance is impossible without assertion of rhetorical force. Further, good audiences advance social values. Wanting favor and dispensation, severe narcissism will persevere until positively affected by strength and stability in others who respond only to good treatment. Socially acceptable behavior can be evoked in many otherwise self-absorbed persons. Gregory Rochlin notes many times in his writings that only *other people* can temper narcissistic behavior. "It is the company of others which civilizes us." The need of relationships — to value and be valued by others — "is probably the strongest civilizing influence of all." Again, in testimony to the potential force in others: "Only the coercive necessity of a relationship profoundly affects the 'self.' The foundation for our regulatory devices is a social one"; self-seeking "must yield to social demands. Otherwise, we risk an intolerable isolation."[24]

A general function of the good audience is through the suasory character of its behavior to remind others of agreed-upon customs, conventions, and rules — the way the game is played[25] — and upon occasion to act as a *counter*cultural force, e.g., against individualistic expression. It is confirming and/or disconfirming — promoting standards or expectations and asking for adherence. The rhetorically indisposed will probably remain so until taught or caused to be civil. It is wisely said that silence gives assent: to ignore is to confirm. Another relevant thought is that unless the response is clear and telling, e.g., the disavowal definite, incivility will continue. Unfavorable narcissism eventually becomes a rhetorical problem. And, of course, the solution must be rhetorical, for behavior of the audience is always a significant variable.

Checking. One prime function of the good audience is to help the problem narcissist to come to his or her rhetorical senses. A way to accomplish this is to *check* the uncivility. To check is to return information to the person on results of the inappropriate behavior. It is to say, in effect, "I cannot accept your behavior" or "I must let you know how you're affecting me." A stronger tone may be indicated, requiring one to respond, in so many words and/or nonverbal symbols, with, "I sense what you're doing, and I can't let you get away with it, not with me." Checking reminds people, in their self-occupation, of rhetorical necessity, of the need to change strategy, if they would be effective with others. It is to say, "I'm here, and you must deal with me," or it may be the more drastic recourse of figuratively "sounding the horn" when people rhetorically "run a red light." Depending on purpose and situation, etc., checking may range from simple disclosure to withholding validation or absolute denial. The goal of checking in any interaction or relationship is to achieve understanding on acceptability of behavior and perhaps, incidentally, to support a cumulative effect of rhetorical conditioning. Checking is rhetorical mirroring but not counteraggression. "*Look at your rhetorical self,*" is the message; "Is that how you want to be?" To check is to excite or arouse rhetorical sensibilities, to make fitting request for a fitting rhetorical response. It is the unwisely tolerant who give effect to tyranny, abuse, and disruptive avoidance. It is they who complete the narcissistic enthymeme and by so doing validate the immature role. The good audience will not participate in that enthymeme.

In checking, the good audience shows genuine concern for others, refusing to confirm the demeaning attributes of dependency and childishness. Author Collette Dowling confesses her gratitude in being checked by two strong and caring good audiences, her psychiatrist and her friend, the first and second persons in her life who, as she reports, "did not support my dependency."[26] They dared to disconfirm.

But checking is risky strategy, for arousal of obstructive defenses is a possible result. After all, checking is a rhetorical move, with success dependent upon identification of interacting parties. Will the checked person accept — identify with — the disconfirmation? That's a fundamental question. If the subject is able to acknowledge a challenge as fair and essentially accurate, at the moment or eventually, his or her audience has been successful — and good. Good audiences are hopeful of discovering a base of shared value and bringing others to perceive and appreciate it — or to recognize that the *shared* value is higher than that anticipated by narcissistically holding out.

Simultaneous Confirmation and Disconfirmation. Another strategy, one with high rhetorical value, is a combination of confirming and disconfirming. In this instance, the competent responding rhetor checks the unacceptable behavior while balancing it with acknowledgment of acceptable behavior. It is more dialectical and less unilateral than checking alone — in spirit more "give-and-take" than "take-it-or-leave-it."

An example of near perfection in rhetorical practice is seen in the good audience that is thirteen-year-old Billy in the motion picture *On Golden Pond*, as he relates to the crotchety and unpleasantly narcissistic octogenarian Norman Thayer. One evening at the lodge, Norman "assigned" the recalcitrant Billy to read Stevenson's *Treasure Island* but apparently had no knowledge of Billy's acceptance of the assignment until one day when the two were fishing in the boat. As they fished, Norman, behaving typically, criticizes Billy harshly for letting his line go slack in the water. But in answer, Billy neither accepts the criticism nor becomes defensive. He is the good audience, speaking back directly, yet with respect: "All right! You don't have to yell at me. Who do you think you are, Long John Silver?" The old man's unhealthful narcissism is met, as acknowledgment of the gift of a good story provides positive validation. Norman recognizes the error of his hostility and answers humbly, but without loss of self-respect, "I'm sorry." Billy responds in kind, "That's all right." The exchange is a model of balanced rhetorical response, acceptance of a person's goodness while rejecting unacceptable conduct.

Another case is application of acceptance-rejection in a family setting. Mrs. K., a mother who is married to a verbally abusive narcissistic person has learned to advise her two adolescent children, "When he hurts you, *you have to tell him*, for if you don't, he'll keep on doing it. Do it lovingly." Risks exist for her and her family, and yet, as she reported, her instruction on being a loving good audience has yielded benefit to all parties. One more example of mutual satisfaction resulting from sensitive audience action involves a California couple on a camping trip. "Where's my soap," he asked accusingly. "You lost it," she answered in factual tone, "but you're welcome to use mine." Nice touch, lady.

Confirming. A third strategy for meeting difficult narcissistic behaviors is mainly confirmative. It is chosen out of awareness that in a particular instance, someone's ill-humored—even threatening—message was invented from a kind of narcissistic wounding that needs nursing, e.g., wounding from slight or unfair put-down. Thus, a therapeutic response may be indicated, rather than some sort of hard checking. The purpose is to evoke latent maturity. As good audience, one says something like "I understand how you feel" or "Tell me why you're upset" or "It's OK." Certain occasions call for therapeutic rhetoric—for consoling or soothing; others do not. We know that choices in audience invention can be critical, and often they require the best that a rhetorically disposed person has to give. Possibly one would not think of the ordinary interaction of employer-employee or drill sergeant-recruit as indicating therapeutic strategy, and yet that may not always be so. The double question faced by the respondent is something like this: "Will an illusioning presence be suitable in this case? Or will it backfire, i.e., validate the person's maladaptive mode?" But one experience of failure in bringing out another's strength does not mean that the strategy to confirm was wrong. Remember that the good audience is one that does not lose sight of personal purpose and need. Therefore, it may willingly and securely choose to "go the second mile"—and without loss of dignity, if there is a chance of mutual, intrinsic benefit.

It should be noted regarding all three strategic aproaches discussed here that often the best that one can expect in these challenging dealings is a moment of stability. But a *moment* is something to be enjoyed. Few are the opportunities for bringing about a radical or permanent change in the chronically self-absorbed, but we can be effective in helping to create happy moments of civility for all concerned—even days! Moreover, moments, if appreciated and remembered, may in some relationships appear more and more often. That is the cumulative rhetorical effect again, of the constant caring influence of a good audience: the rhetorical power that may eventually help to relieve the insecure person of that all-consuming need to continue in those self-protective, individualistic ways of being. Yes, one can evoke from another a show of dormant civility. In some cases, now and again. No, we cannot expect to change the Jim Jones's, but as a good audience, our personal model may positively affect an indisposed coworker or friend. It happens.

The good audience functions in any rhetorical situation: in the home, school, and elsewhere in life.

Home

The first good audience are good enough parents whose goals and behaviors allow for development of independence, a healthful sense of self and social awareness, leading to confident, effective interaction with others. They are the child's partners in beneficial mirroring experience, in attunement activity — caregivers who seek to reach appropriate levels of stimulation. They avoid pitfalls in rearing that may lead to unfavorable narcissism and rhetorical indisposition. As Rochlin observes, excessive gratification or overindulgence of wishes intensify narcissistic needs. "A child's narcissism . . . is not merely to be satisfied. It is something to be changed. The more narcissism is fulfilled and remains unmodified, the more absolutely its demands become an entrenched resistance to social adaptation."[27] Jean Piaget stresses the need for active parental participation: "For the individual left to himself, remains egocentric" and subject to anomie which will yield "only through contact with the judgments and evaluations of others."[28] Of others! Neglect is one sure cause of incivility. Jurgen Ruesch affirms, putting the topic in rhetorical terms, "The way the infant's early expressions are acknowledged will to a great extent determine his future ways of communication. . . . if children adopt certain reactions in emotionally important, usually familial, situations, they are later on likely to adopt similar reactions in structurally analogous situations." There must be encounters with reliable others to test thinking and develop methods of adaptation.[29] This is rhetorical training.

How is the child to get this needed training? Heinz Kohut's prescription is simple and reasonable. It is not "perfect emphatic responses" or "unrealistic admiration" that the child needs, he believes, but "proper mirroring at least some of the time." Kohut calls for "optimal frustration of the child's narcissistic needs," to promote "consolidation of the self" and provide the "storehouse of self-confidence and basic self-esteem that sustains a person throughout life."[30] Relating to confirmation of useful behavior and disconfirmation of the maladaptive, Kohut's strategy is rhetorical and relevant to this study; the parent as good audience will neither withhold all narcissistic supplies nor attempt to satisfy every request. Not all demands of a child are to be acknowledged. Stern is of a similar mind in this instance: "In the absence of adequate amounts of frustration, the child retains his narcissistic commitment, which will seriously undermine his potential to love as an adult."[31] Rochlin adds, "What narcissism a child may give up with the discovery that he is neither omnipotent nor in command of magic is compensated for by the conviction that he is valued."[32] The loving presence of a good audience helps the child build civility and moral strength for the future.

A postscript might be added. Should it not be advised, given the pluralistic society in which we live, that parents help their children to have experience in relating to people of varied cultural, ethnic, and social backgrounds, or who are different in other ways, e.g., mentally or physically handicapped? Such diverse interactions quite likely would further rhetorical growth, e.g., in providing valuable lessons on achieving consubstantiality with others, many of whom represent very contrasting behaviors, customs, and needs. Reusch expressed it in this way: A child should be reared in a situation in which he can assume roles for different ends, i.e., have a chance to "practice communication with a variety of people." Children who have "opportunity to check their views and beliefs" with people outside their circle "are faced with the necessity of integrating contradictory opinions and of finding some way of reaching agreements with others."[33] Given the multiplex character of our society, the need of sound rhetorical education is absolute. People different from ourselves can be good audiences for our children, and for us as well.

School

A school is a complex of rhetorical relationships, involving interaction of administrators, pupils, staff, and faculty. Let us put the focus on the schoolroom. Walking into a typical American classroom, at almost any level of instruction, one is struck by the rhetorical dynamics displayed. Verbal and nonverbal messages fly with such great rapidity all over the room — from here to there, back and forth and around — that it is impossible to catch the intent and nature of most. But one knows that all persons there have purposes in mind, and with their many strategies, they act upon one another. It is a fascinating rhetorical scene.

Everyone in the room is an audience of everyone else. What a splendid opportunity the teacher has to develop good audiences: right there, everyday in that small classroom society, introducing and inculcating rhetorical principles on purposes, identification, and roles of confirmation/disconfirmation, etc. Through practical rhetorical process and the model and guidance of the teacher, learners can get the needed theory and supervised experience: adding to rhetorical effectiveness, learning moral lessons, and consequently growing in civility.

What specific rhetorical learning goals are achievable in the classroom? Criteria developed by Gerald M. Phillips in treatment of reticent persons seem applicable to children generally and subjects of this study in particular, as they may be influenced by teachers — not to mention administrators, counselors, and other school personnel. Condensed, and converted from interrogative to prescriptive form, these points suggest rhetorical desiderata as well as functions of the good audience at school. The good audience, e.g., teacher, helps children:

1. to perceive situations in which their "talk would make a difference," to understand rhetorical "urgencies" and others' sources of effectiveness,

2. to discover people around them who might be influenced favorably, if approached on an exchange basis — as opposed to an egocentric basis; to understand the need to adapt to the situation and others,

3. to learn to specify goals in acts of communication and kinds of feedback needed in assessment of outcome,

4. to develop a repertoire of roles to use in adapting readily to needs of listeners,

5. to conceptualize and purposefully order ideas for oral presentation to others,

6. to develop a practical command of language,

7. to sustain discourse with others, in active reciprocity and not as monologists, faithful to theme and with appropriate vocal and other nonverbal contribution; to understand and be responsive listeners to messages of others, and

8. to assess responses accurately and to readjust with new goals and strategies when indicated.[34]

Implementation of such rhetorical behaviors will involve both formal and informal confirmation and disconfirmation. The end is rhetorical success and civility, through correction of counter-productive narcissistic activity. The good audience at school will invite — often insist on — use of rhetorical behaviors, and it will persist in influencing their development. In the process, the good audience at school helps to prepare children for *their* role as good audiences in life ahead. Thus one good audience produces another. And the benefit will accrue not only to others but also to oneself indirectly, as one learns to *listen to oneself.* That is, a person can create an *intrapersonal* good audience for personal use, an internalized and active sounding board to provide reliable guidance in thinking and doing.

Now to the largest realm of the good audiences, anywhere outside the home and school.

Elsewhere

Diversity of interaction in scenes of work, play, and all others is great, and accordingly the strategies for success are many. Think of the extensive variety of situations that we face with every person encountered. Each occasion in addressing any one calls for different ways to be, e.g., with bosses, employees, elected officials, neighbors, shopkeepers, former classmates, police officers, bus drivers, stock brokers, tour guides, homeless persons, lawyers, mechanics, soldiers, flight attendants, etc., etc.—people of varied cultures and personal histories.

The good audience must assume many roles, some requiring checking, some requiring the balancing of confirmation. With roles of checking, we question, confront, counter, deny, evaluate, and the like. With roles of confirming linked to disconfirming, we compromise, accept/reject, overlook/correct, and loosen/limit. With roles of confirmation, we embrace, support, acknowledge, praise, and sponsor.

Recall from Chapter one that the primary function of an audience in any rhetorical setting is to pursue its chosen purpose. When audiences do that, they send forth a basic message of rhetorical reality. Acting from their values, goals, immediate interests, etc., audiences present conditions—including opportunities and obstacles—to which others respond and may adapt. But behaviors of the rhetorically indisposed are maladaptive, often highly defensive. In not deferring to individualistic coercion and thus giving back a realistic view of his or her own individual needs and specific purposes, etc., the good audience remains a self-respectful model, one that may contribute incidentally to the narcissistic person's self-respect—or, at least, prevent dependency.

While based on a kind of Aristotelian logic and realism—not to mention human compassion, this position enjoys the essential agreement of Piaget, particularly on the concept of cooperation. Aristotle's audience, free to function in the rhetorical market place and constrained by awareness of social good and constituents of happiness, finds company with Piaget's self-disciplined citizen, possessed of a "consciousness of good," and responsive to "norms of reciprocity."[35] This compatibility of ancient and modern philosophy allows for a blend of reality and optimism, proportioned in accord with rhetorical/ethical requirements in given instances.

David Rapaport extends Piaget's view that social influence is necessary to meet narcissistic limitations. His prescription calls for perspectives of a variety of good audiences. His terms have rhetorical meaning: "Only the implicit reactions and explicit communications of a variety of other 'me's' can free the 'me' from its solipsism (autism) by providing mirrors to reflect various sides of the 'me'."[36] The good audience, then, is good rhetor, perceptive and responsive as it acts upon others, incidentally offering mirrors that guide others in perceiving the realistic interpersonal dynamics of the moment. The good audience offers vital information, to the end of disarming intrusive narcissism and promoting civility.

But in what manner is information to be conveyed? How are we to "let others know"? That would seem to be a main issue. One approach is suggested by the theory of transactional analysis: for example, the Adult ego state of one is presented to discover and arouse the Adult state of another, who, though less mature, potentially is able — as constrained by a good audience — to perform adequately. A related rhetorical strategy involves sending messages back that directly reflect the received effect of the other's behavior. Sometimes called making "I" statements or "owned evaluations,"[37] this is a procedure that can provide self-absorbed persons with valuable perceptions on their presence of the moment. Such information — explicit, unforced, and relatively free of bias — may come as a signal to the other to reconsider unproductive, regressive behavior, e.g., abuse of one sort or another. Instead of saying, "Why don't you calm down!," the good audience might say, candidly, "When you shout at me, I feel threatened." Instead of asking, "Don't you ever think of anyone but yourself?," the good audience may say, "I, too, have worthwhile feelings and opinions." Straightforward in approach, nonthreatening, and promising the ethos value of openness, this technique can work to reduce narcissistic game-playing and possibly put a relationship on a rational and adult basis, when indicated. To discountenance intrusive narcissism is to foster civility.

Thus works the good audience.

OUR RHETORICAL BEST

If we in this shrinking world are to raise the level of individual happiness in relating to one another, we must be prepared to give our rhetorical best — from the earliest moment of our influence. For parents and other caregivers, that means *from the moment the baby arrives.* Being there at the outset, with deeply felt and sustained messages of confirmation: "We want you!" — "We'll be here for you and with you!" — "Trust *us*!" That's *the way* to nourish and foster narcissism of the best kind, in all its vigor and strength. Through offerings of love and care, mature parents will come to experience the greatest of possible gratifications: THE DEVELOPMENT IN THEIR CHILD OF A DURABLE SENSE OF SECURITY AND SELF-WORTH.

With their continuation of that large and necessary activity, it will be easier for the child to handle the ever-present cultural narcissism that, through messages of the media and other sources, works against a healthful and realistic perspective, e.g., by reinforcing attitudes of individualism. As good audiences from the beginning, parents can affect the orientation and thrust of the child's rhetorical imperative helping to create calibrations that favor positive and productive strategies in relating.

What if . . .

What if parents were to devote an hour of each week during the last six months of pregnancy to work on their rhetorical awareness and ability? Call it a part of planning for parenthood. The first step would be to come to grips with an absolute truth: *that they are to be the most vital audience ever to be encountered by their offspring.* And *that what they feel and do in the first eighteen to twenty-four months of the child's life—what they say to the child verbally and physically—will have more impact on the child's growth than influences of all future teachers, mate, friends, etc.,—combined.* It *is* that critical! Parents *are* that powerful!

No award for scholarly or artistic achievement, no promotion to top executive, no league championship, no Wall Street coup, no Woman of the Year trophy, no Mr. Terrific Guy nomination, no victory of any kind — no performance! — can come close to equalling in merit the ordinary success of good enough parents. What they bring about no one else can. From them, the child gets an edge, making possible all of the other good things in life.

After the first years of home-based rhetorical concern and effectiveness, the schools must carry on. Every classroom can be a place where in doing their work of learning the children are guided in development of rhetorical appreciation — in discovering and refining roles for engaging willingly and freely with others and coming to accept that adaptation is necessary, yes, but that knowledge and respect of self and others are paramount. Further, young rhetors must build on lessons in courage, independence, and responsibility. Thus, their rhetorical disposition will be secured. And with their participation in it, ours will be a better, healthier society.

But all of us — not only parents and teachers — have rhetorical power and responsibility. Knowing the benefits, is it too much to ask of ourselves that we function as good audiences at all times when together with others? Only our rhetorical best can meet the scourge of narcissism that would coerce to its own special ends and restrict our movement and growth. We are the ones — when able to realize and maintain our maturity — who can generate reasonable, clear, and humanizing messages that confirm expressions of others' maturity while not confirming the regressive. We can be effective agents in lowering the level of costly unrhetorical interference, in promoting adequacy in rhetorical conduct and a consequent increase in the quality of life.

Every rhetorical moment is an opportunity for achieving civility.

Notes

CHAPTER ONE

1. Aristotle, *Rhetoric*, trans. W. Rhys Roberts (New York: Random House, 1954), 24.

2. *Institutes of Oratory*, 2 vols., trans. John Selby Watson (London: George Bell and Sons, 1910), BK. XII, 391-92.

3. John F. Kennedy, *Profiles in Courage* (New York: Harper and Brothers, 1956).

4. See *A Rhetoric of Motives* (New York: George Braziller, 1955) and *Permanence and Change*, 3rd ed. (Berkeley: U of California P, 1984).

5. See Kenneth N. Leone Cissna and Evelyn Sieburg, "Patterns of Interactional Confirmation and Disconfirmation," *Rigor and Imagination: Essays from the Legacy of Gregory Bateson,* ed. C. Wilder-Mott and John H. Weakland (New York: Praeger, 1981), 253-82.

6. Heinz Kohut died in 1981. For a brief biography and clear explanation of his theory, its origins and significance, see Susan Quinn, "Oedipus vs. Narcissus," *New York Times Magazine* 9 Nov. 1980, 120-26, 128-31.

7. Lynne Layton and Barbara Schapiro, *Narcissism and the Text: Studies in Literature and the Psychology of Self* (New York: New York U P, 1986), 27.

8. Heinz Kohut, *The Restoration of the Self* (New York: International Universities Press, 1977), 68, 132-33, 243, 268.

9. Andrew P. Morrison, "Shame and the Psychology of the Self," *Kohut's Legacy: Contributions to Self Psychology,* ed. Paul E. Stepansky and Arnold Goldberg (Hillsdale: The Analytic Press, 1984), 71, 72, 85.

10. Morrison, "Shame and the Psychology of the Self," 72-74, 86, 87.

11. Kohut, *Restoration*; Morrison, 85-86.

12. Morrison, 86, 88; Kohut, *Self Psychology and the Humanities: Reflections on a New Psychoanalytic Approach*, ed. Charles B. Strozier (New York: Norton, 1985); Kurt A. Schlesinger, "The Self and the Creative Process," *Kohut's Legacy: Contributions to Self Psychology*, ed. Paul E. Stepansky and Arnold Goldberg (Hillsdale: The Analytic Press, 1984).

13. Kohut, *The Analysis of the Self* (London: Hogarth Press, 1971), 108–09; *Self Psychology,* 12–13, 110, 198–99.

14. *See* Sonja K. Foss, Karen A. Foss and Robert A. Trapp, *Contemporary Perspectives on Rhetoric* (Prospect Heights: Waveland Press, 1985), 178–82.

15. *See* David Payne, *Coping with Failure: the Therapeutic Uses of Rhetoric* (Columbia: U of South Carolina P, 1989).

16. Kenneth Burke, "The Rhetoric of Hitler's 'Battle,'" *The Southern Review* 5 (1939–40): 1–21.

17. Gail Sheehy, "The Road to Bimini," *Vanity Fair* (Sept. 1987): 130–39, 188, 192–94.

18. Kenneth N. Leone Cissna and Sr. Suzanne Keating, "Speech Communication Antecedents of Perceived Confirmation," *Western Journal of Speech Communication* 43 (1979): 59.

CHAPTER TWO

1. Most ideas of Chapter two were first published in "Rhetorical Interaction in Infancy and Development of a Rhetorical Disposition," *Rhetorical Studies Honoring James L. Golden,* ed. Lawrence W. Hugenberg. Copyright © 1986 by Kendall/Hunt Publishing Co. With permission.

2. Quintilian, *Institutes of Oratory,* trans. John Selby Watson (London: George Bell and Sons, 1910), BK I, 3.

3. Joy D. Osofsky and Karen Connors, "Mother-Infant Interaction: An Integrative View of a Complex System," *Handbook of Infant Development,* ed. Joy D. Osofsky (New York: John Wiley and Sons, 1979), 519–48.

4. John Newson and Elizabeth Newson, "Intersubjectivity and the Transmission of Culture," *Early Cognitive Development,* ed. John Oates (New York: John Wiley and Sons, 1979), 271–86; Daniel N. Stern, *The Interpersonal World of the Infant* (New York: Basic Books, 1985).

5. H. R. Schaffer, "Early Interactive Development," *Studies in Mother-Infant Interaction,* ed. H. R. Schaffer (London: Academic Press, 1977), 14–15.

6. H. R. Schaffer, *The Child's Entry Into a Social World* (London: Academic Press, 1984), 14–17.

7. Stern, *Interpersonal World,* 5, 10, 11, 46–47, 67–68, 170–71, *passim.*

8. Schaffer, *Child's Entry,* 7.

9. Kenneth Kaye, "Toward the Origin of Dialogue," *Studies in Mother-Infant Interaction,* ed. H. R. Schaffer (London: Academic Press, 1977), 89–117.

10. John Newson, "An Intersubjective Approach to the Systematic Description of Mother-Infant Interaction," *Studies in Mother-Infant Interaction,* ed. H. R. Schaffer (London: Academic Press, 1977), 49–50.

11. Daniel Stern, *The First Relationship: Mother and Infant* (Cambridge: Harvard U P, 1977), 45–48; *Interpersonal World.*

12. Leon Yarrow, "Historical Perspectives and Future Directions in Infant Development," *Handbook of Infant Development,* ed. Joy D. Osofsky (New York: John Wiley and Sons, 1979), 897–917.

13. "Mother-Infant Interaction," 523–34.

14. Kaye, "Origin of Dialogue," 89–117.

15. Newson and Newson, "Intersubjectivity and Culture," 278–79.

16. John Newson, "Intersubjective Approach," 60.

17. *First Relationship*, 49.

18. *Interpersonal World*, 75.

19. Carol Gibb Harding, "Development of the Intention to Communicate," *Human Development* 25 (1982): 140–51.

20. Schaffer, *Child's Entry*, 119; "Early Interactive Development," 10, 11.

21. John Newson, "Intentional Behavior in the Young Infant," *The Psychological and Medical Implications of Early Experience*, eds. David Schaffer and Judy Dunn (Chichester: John Wiley and Sons, 1979) 94; Elizabeth Bates, *The Emergence of Symbols: Cognition and Communication in Infancy* (New York: Academic Press, 1979); Schaffer, *Child's Entry*, 130.

22. Joan E. Sieber, "A Social Learning Theory Approach to Morality," *Moral Development and Socialization*, ed. Myra Windmiller, Nadine Lambert, and Elliot Turiel (Boston: Allyn and Bacon, 1980), 138–44.

23. Lawrence Kohlberg, "A Cognitive-Developmental Approach to Moral Education," *The Humanist*, Nov.-Dec. 1972: 13–16.

24. Donald W. Winnicott, *The Child and the Family: First Relationships*, ed. Janet Hardenberg (London: Tavistock Publications, 1957), 62–63.

25. Donald W. Winnicott, "Transitional Objects and Transitional Phenomena," *Playing and Reality* (New York: Basic Books, 1971), 10.

26. Pietro Castelnuovo-Tedesco, "Reality Concept in Psychoanalysis," *International Encyclopedia of Psychiatry, Psychology, Psychoanalysis, & Neurology*, 9, ed. Benjamin B. Wolman (New York: Van Nostrand, Reinhold, 1977), 390.

27. Alice Miller, *The Drama of the Gifted Child*, trans. Ruth Ward (New York: Basic Books, 1981), 32.

28. Heinz Kohut, *The Restoration of the Self* (New York: International Universities Press, 1977), 187–88, 237, 87; *The Search for the Self: Selected Writings of Heinz Kohut, 1950–1978*, ed. Paul H. Ornstein (New York: International Universities Press, 1978), 368–70.

29. *Restoration*, 123; see also 188, 87, 237, *passim*.

30. Winnicott, "Transitional Objects," 1–25.

31. Charles Horton Cooley, *Human Nature and the Social Order* (New York: Charles Scribner's Sons, 1902); George Herbert Mead, *Mind, Self and Society*, ed. Charles W. Morris (Chicago: U of Chicago P, 1934).

32. Arnold H. Modell, "Comments on the Rise of Narcissism," *The Future of Psychoanalysis*, ed. Arnold Goldberg (New York: International Universities Press, 1983), 114.

33. Heinz Lichtenstein, "The Role of Narcissism in the Emergence and Maintenance of a Primary Identity," *International Journal of Psychoanalysis* 45 (1964): 53–54.

34. "Role of Narcissism," 53–55.

35. *Child's Entry*, 199–203.

36. *Interpersonal World*, 140.

37. *Interpersonal World*, 139–42, 148, 150, 157.

38. *Interpersonal World*, 207–11.

39. *Child's Entry*, 26.

40. *Child's Entry*, 42.

41. See Kenneth N. Leone Cissna and Evelyn Sieburg, "Patterns of Interactional Confirmation and Disconfirmation," *Rigor and Imagination: Essays from the Legacy of Gregory Bateson,* ed. C. Wilder-Mott and John H. Weakland (New York: Praeger, 1981), 253–82.

42. Colwyn Trevarthen, "Conversations with a Two-Month-Old," *New Scientist,* 2 May 1974: 235.

43. Stern, *First Relationship* and *Interpersonal World*; Newson, "Intersubjective Approach"; Yarrow, "Historical Perspectives"; Jerome Kagan, "Overview: Perspectives on Human Infancy," *Handbook of Infant Development,* ed. Joy D. Osofsky (New York: John Wiley and Sons, 1979), 1–25.

44. David W. Allen, "Psychoanalysis and Visual Conflicts," *Communication and Social Interaction: Clinical and Therapeutic Aspects of Human Behavior,* ed. Peter Ostwald (New York: Grune and Stratton, 1977), 243.

45. "Historical Perspectives," 899, 913.

46. Kohut, *Restoration, passim*; John and Elizabeth Newson, "Intersubjectivity and Culture," 281; Stern, *Interpersonal World,* 125–26.

47. Stern, *Interpersonal World, passim.*

48. Kohut, *Restoration, passim.*

49. Kaye, "Origin of Dialogue"; Nathan Schwartz-Salant, *Narcissism and Character Transformation: The Psychology of Narcissistic Character Disorders* (Toronto: Inner City Books, 1982); Osofsky and Connors, "Mother-Infant Interaction"; Yarrow, "Historical Perspectives."

50. Sheldon Bach, *Narcissistic States and the Therapeutic Process* (New York: Jason Aronson, 1985), 9; see also Evelyn Sieburg, *Family Communication: An Integrated Systems Approach* (New York: Gardner Press, 1985), 181–82.

51. Colwyn Trevarthen, "Descriptive Analysis of Infant Communicative Behavior," *Studies in Mother-Infant Interaction,* ed. H. R. Schaffer (London: Academic Press, 1977), 238–47; Hanŭs and Mechthild Papoušek, "Mothering and the Cognitive Head-Start: Psychological-Biological Considerations," *Studies in Mother-Infant Interaction,* ed. H. R. Schaffer (London: Academic Press, 1977), 63–85; John and Elizabeth Newson, "Intersubjectivity and Culture," 271–85; Lichtenstein, "Role of Narcissism," 49–56; Kaye, "Origins of Dialogue," 89–117; Stern, *First Relationship* and *Interpersonal World.*

52. Allen, "Visual Conflicts"; John and Elizabeth Newson, "Intersubjectivity and Culture," 272–76; Osofsky and Connors "Mother-Infant Interaction"; Schwartz-Salant, *Narcissism and Character,* 43–44.

53. Kohut, *Restoration,* 93f; Schwartz-Salant, *Narcissism and Character,* 43–44.

54. Schwartz-Salant, *Narcissism and Character.*

55. Kohut, *Restoration*; Schwartz-Salant, *Narcissism and Character*; Winnicott, "Transitional Objects," 11; Schaffer, *Child's Entry,* 168–95.

56. Kaye, "Origin of Dialogue."

57. John and Elizabeth Newson, "Intersubjectivity and Culture," 271–85; John Newson, "Intersubjective Approach," 57; Stern, *First Relationship.*

58. John and Elizabeth Newson, "Intersubjectivity and Culture"; Kaye, "Origin of Dialogue"; Bates, *Emergence of Symbols,* 34–39.

59. Kaye, "Origin of Dialogue."

60. *Speech Monographs,* 39 (1972): 75–91.

61. See, e.g., Victoria Hamilton, *Narcissus and Oedipus* (London: Routledge & Kegan Paul, 1982), 65–69; Gregory Rochlin, *Griefs and Discontents* (Boston: Little, Brown, 1965).

62. Stern, *Interpersonal World,* 6.

63. Stern, *Interpersonal World,* 124–25, 203.

64. Kenneth Burke, *A Rhetoric of Motives* (New York: George Braziller, 1955), 55.

65. Harold Barrett, "The Critic of Rhetoric as GOOD AUDIENCE," *Conference in Rhetorical Criticism,* ed. Susan L. Brock (Hayward: California State U, 1985), 1–9.

66. *Interpersonal World,* 92–94, 117.

CHAPTER THREE

1. Some of the material in this chapter first appeared in "Narcissism and Rhetorical Maturity," *Western Journal of Speech Communication* 50 (1986), 254–68.

2. Heinz Kohut, *The Restoration of the Self* (New York: International Universities Press, 1977); Gregory Rochlin, *Man's Aggression: The Defense of the Self* (Boston: Gambit, 1973).

3. Gregory Rochlin, *Griefs and Discontents: The Forces of Change* (Boston: Little, Brown, 1965), 283.

4. Sydney E. Pulver, "Narcissism: The Term and the Concept," *Journal of the American Psychoanalytic Association* 18 (1970): 319–41; Rochlin, *Griefs,* 96, passim.

5. Joan Vondra and Jay Belsky, "Infant Play at One Year: Characteristics and Early Antecedents," *Action in Social Context: Perspectives on Early Development,* ed. Jeffrey J. Lockman and Nancy L. Hazen (New York: Plenum Press, 1989), 173–206; Nancy L. Hazen and Jeffrey J. Lockman, "Skill and Context," *Action in Social Context,* 12.

6. Daniel N. Stern, *The First Relationship: Mother and Infant* (Cambridge: Harvard U P, 1977), 119–22.

7. Stern, *First Relationship,* 115–19.

8. Sheldon Bach, *Narcissistic States and the Therapeutic Process* (New York: Jason Aronson, 1985), 32–40.

9. Kohut, *Restoration*; Margaret S. Mahler, *On Human Symbiosis and the Viscissitudes of Individuation* (New York: International Universities Press, 1968); Arnold H. Modell, "Comments on the Rise of Narcissism," *The Future of Psychoanalysis,* ed. Arnold Goldberg (New York: International Universities Press, 1983); H. R. Schaffer, *The Child's Entry into a Social World* (London: Academic Press,

1984); Daniel N. Stern, *The Interpersonal World of the Infant* (New York: Basic Books, 1985).

10. Donald W. Winnicott, "Ego Distortion in Terms of True and False Self," *The Maturational Process and the Facilitating Environment* (London: Hogarth, 1965).

11. Winnicott, "True and False Self."

12. Stephen M. Johnson, *Humanizing the Narcissistic Style* (New York: Norton, 1987), 41–44.

13. Otto F. Kernberg, "Why Some People Can't Love," *Psychology Today* June 1978: 55–59; Heinz Kohut, *The Analysis of the Self* (London: Hogarth Press, 1971); Rochlin, *Griefs*; Nathan Schwartz-Salant, *Narcissism and Character Transformation: The Psychology of Narcissistic Character Disorders* (Toronto: Inner City Books, 1981); Jürg Willi, *Couples in Collusion* (New York: Jason Aronson, 1982).

14. Janet Karsten Larson, "The Rhetoric of Narcissism: Language and Survival in American Culture," *Christian Century* 9 Sept. 1981: 861.

15. Jurgen Reusch, *Disturbed Communication: The Clinical Assessment of Normal and Pathological Communicative Behavior* (New York: Norton, 1957), 117.

16. Bach, *Narcissistic States*; Joyce McDougall, "Primitive Communication and the use of Countertransference," *Countertransference: The Therapist's Contribution to Therapy*, ed. Lawrence Epstein and Arthur H. Feiner (New York: Jason Aronson, 1979), 267–303; Marie Coleman Nelson, ed., *The Narcissistic Condition* (New York: Human Science Press, 1977); Rochlin, *Griefs*.

17. Bach, *Narcissistic States*; Carl Goldberg, *In Defense of Narcissism* (New York: Gardner Press, 1980); McDougall, "Primitive Communication"; Nelson, *The Narcissistic Condition*; Rochlin, *Griefs*.

18. *Griefs*, 36.

19. Richard Sennett, *The Fall of Public Man* (New York: Knopf, 1977), 4.

20. Mark E. Stern, "Narcissism and the Defiance of Time," *The Narcissistic Condition*, ed. Marie Coleman Nelson, (New York: Human Science Press, 1977), 179–212.

21. Alexander Lowen, *Narcissism: Denial of the True Self* (New York: Macmillan, 1983), 64f.

22. Frank E. X. Dance and Carl E. Larson, *Functions of Human Communication* (New York: Holt, Rinehart and Winston, 1976), 55.

23. *Griefs*, 72, 74.

24. McDougall, "Primitive Communication," 296, 291.

25. *Griefs*, 101.

26. Bach, *Narcissistic States*, 124.

27. Richard M. Restak, *The Self Seekers* (New York: Doubleday, 1982), 359.

28. "Primitive Communication," 295.

29. See Jack Gibb, "Defensive Communication," *Journal of Communication* 11 (1961): 141–48.

30. Goldberg, *Defense of Narcissism*, 27.

31. *Defense of Narcissism*, 12–13.

32. Rochlin, *Man's Aggression*, 41.

33. Charles M. Rossiter, Jr. and W. Barnet Pearce, *Communicating Personally: A Theory of Interpersonal Communication and Human Relationships* (Indianapolis: Bobbs-Merrill, 1975), 160.
34. *Disturbed Communication*, 94.
35. See Sennett, *The Fall*.
36. Bach, *Narcissistic States*, 118.
37. McDougall, "Primitive Communication," 292–93.
38. Rochlin, *Man's Aggression*, 230–34.
39. "Primitive Communication," 297–98.
40. "The New Narcissism," *Harper's* Oct. 1975: 46.
41. *Narcissistic States*, 3–47.
42. "Primitive Communication," 295.
43. Johnson, *Humanizing the Narcissistic Style*, 48.
44. Carl L. Becker, "Everyman His Own Historian," *Everyman His Own Historian: Essays on History and Politics* (New York: Appleton-Century-Crofts, 1935), 242.
45. *Fall*, 220.
46. "Primitive Communication," 295.
47. Herbert McCloskey and John H. Schaar, "Psychological Dimensions of Anomie," *American Sociological Review* 30 (1965): 14–40; See also Richard D. Chessick, *Psychology of the Self and the Treatment of Narcissism* (Northvale: Jason Aronson, 1985), 22–23; Elwin H. Powell, *The Design of Discord: Studies of Anomie*, 2nd ed. (New Brunswick: Transaction Books, 1988).
48. "The Reticent Syndrome: Some Theoretical Considerations about Etiology and Treatment," *Speech Monographs* 40 (1973): 225.
49. "Anomie," 139.
50. *Narcissistic States*, 24.
51. Arnold Goldberg, "Narcissism and the Readiness for Psychotherapy Termination," *Archives of General Psychiatry* 32 (1975): 697.
52. *Man's Aggression*, 230–34.
53. *Griefs*, 234.
54. *Narcissistic States*, 29.
55. Maggie Scarf, *Unfinished Business: Pressure Points in the Lives of Women* (Garden City: Doubleday, 1980), 81.
56. Kohut, *Restoration*, 188.
57. *Narcissistic States*, 118.
58. "Some forms of Emotional Disturbances and Their Relationship to Schizophrenia," *Neuroses and Character Types* (New York: International Universities Press, 1965), 262–81.
59. Gerald M. Phillips and Nancy J. Metzger, *Intimate Communication* (Boston: Allyn and Bacon, 1976).
60. Restak, *Self Seekers*, 27–34.
61. Rochlin, *Griefs*, 333–34.
62. *Griefs*, 338.
63. "Narcissism," 335.

64. *Defense*, 82.

65. *Borderline Conditions and Pathological Narcissism* (New York: Jason Aronson, 1975), 234–36.

66. "Primitive Communication," 292, 297, 298.

67. For an intriguing application to terrorism of Heinz Kohut's psychoanalytic theories on narcissism, see John W. Crayton, "Terrorism and the Psychology of the Self," *Perspectives on Terrorism,* ed. Lawrence Zelic Freedman and Yonah Alexander (Wilmington: Scholarly Resources, 1983), 33–41.

68. "Can't Love."

69. "Narcissistic Object Choice in Women," *Annie Reich: Psychoanalytic Contributions* (New York: International Universities Press, 1973), 192.

70. Kernberg, "Can't Love"; *Borderline*, 228–31.

71. Aaron Stern, *Me: The Narcissistic American* (New York: Ballantine, 1979), 27.

72. *Disturbed Communication*, 9.

73. See also Roderick P. Hart and Don M. Burks, "Rhetorical Sensitivity and Social Interaction," *Speech Monographs* 39 (1972): 75–91.

74. *Me*, 183.

75. "The Later Manifestations of Mental Disorder: Matters Paranoid and Paranoiac," *The Interpersonal Theory of Psychiatry,* ed. Helen Swick Perry and Mary Ladd Gawell (New York: Norton, 1953), 351–52.

76. Anita Marie Stenz, *Edward Albee: The Poet of Loss* (The Hague: Mouton, 1978), 40–42.

77. Colette Dowling, *The Cinderella Complex: Women's Hidden Fear of Independence* (New York: Simon and Schuster, 1981), 146–58.

78. Charles L. Whitfield, *Healing the Child Within* (Pompano Beach: Health Communications, 1987), 28–29.

79. See Sharon Wegscheider-Cruse, *Choice-Making: For Co-Dependents, Adult Children, and Spirituality Seekers* (Pompano Beach: Health Communications, 1985).

80. Willi, *Couples in Collusion*, 63–64.

81. Harry Guntrip, *Schizoid Phenomena, Object Relations and the Self* (New York: International Universities Press, 1968), 175.

82. Arnold H. Modell, "Self Preservation and the Preservation of the Self: An Overview of More Recent Knowledge of the Narcissistic Personality," *Narcissism, Masochism, and the Sense of Guilt in Relation to the Therapeutic Process*, Bulletin #6, the Psychotherapy Research Group, Department of Psychiatry (San Francisco: Mount Zion Hospital and Medical Center, June, 1983).

83. Modell, "Self Preservation," 2.

84. Abraham H. Maslow, *Motivation and Personality*, 2nd ed. (New York: Harper and Row, 1970).

85. Merle A. Fossum and Marilyn J. Mason, *Facing Shame: Families in Recovery* (New York: Norton, 1986), 5.

86. Qtd., Fossum and Mason, *Facing Shame*, xi.

87. See Fossum and Mason, *Facing Shame*.

88. *Analysis*.

89. *Borderline.*

90. "Defensive Communication," 141–42.

91. *Disturbed Communication,* 212.

92. Scarf, *Unfinished Business,* 544.

93. "Primitive Communication," 297; see Bach, *Narcissistic States* and Salman Akhtar and J. Anderson Thomson, Jr., "Overview: Narcissistic Personality Disorder," *American Journal of Psychiatry* 139 (1982): 12–20.

94. H. R. Schaffer, *The Child's Entry into a Social World* (London: Academic Press, 1984), 1.

95. See Kernberg, *Borderline,* 229–30.

96. Aaron Stern, *Me.*

97. Willi, *Couples in Collusion.*

98. *Analysis,* 72.

99. "Some Forms of Emotional Disturbances." See also Reich, "Narcissistic Object Choice" and Nathaniel Ross, "The 'As If' Concept," *Journal of American Psychoanalytic Association* 15 (1967): 59–82.

CHAPTER FOUR

1. See Gerald M. Phillips and Nancy J. Metzger, *Intimate Communication* (Boston: Allyn and Bacon, 1976).

2. (New York: W. W. Norton, 1987).

3. *Eloquence in an Electronic Age: The Transformation of Political Speech-making* (New York: Oxford UP, 1988), 41. Jamieson develops the thesis on Bryan's self-victimizing in "The Rhetorical Imprint of the Past: Bryan vs. Darrow," *Conference in Rhetorical Criticism,* ed. Jamie Kauffman (Hayward: California State U, 1983), 1–8.

4. *Interpersonal Communication: Where Minds Meet* (Belmont: Wadsworth, 1987), 97–123.

5. *The Pursuit of Attention: Power and Individualism in Everyday Life* (New York: Oxford UP, 1979), 24–35.

6. Cushman, "The Rules Perspective as a Theoretical Basis for the Study of Human Communication," *Communication Quarterly* 25 (1977): 30–45; Shimanoff, *Communication Rules: Theory and Research* (Beverly Hills: Sage, 1980).

7. See Walter R. Fisher, "Narration as a Human Communication Paradigm: The Case of Public Moral Argument," *Communication Monographs* 51 (1984): 1–22.

8. Walter R. Fisher, "The Narrative Paradigm: An Elaboration," *Communication Monographs* 52 (1985): 347–67.

9. On self-conception, see Fisher, "Narration as a Human Communication Paradigm," 14, 16.

10. *Theories of Human Communication,* 3rd ed. (Belmont: Wadsworth, 1989), 131.

11. *Participant Observation* (New York: Holt, Rinehart and Winston, 1980), 28–35.

12. In addition to Spradley's *Participant Observation* are his *The Ethnographic*

Interview (New York: Holt, Rinehart and Winston, 1979) and, with coauthor David W. McCurdy, *The Cultural Experience: Ethnography in Complex Society* (Chicago: Science Research Associates, 1972), a book including twelve full ethnographies. Also useful are Michael Agar, *The Professional Stranger: An Informal Introduction to Ethnography* (New York: Academic Press, 1980); Dell Hymes, *Foundations in Sociolinguistics: An Ethnographic Approach* (Philadelphia: U of Pennsylvania P, 1974); and Gerry Philipsen, "Linearity of Research Design in Ethnographic Studies of Speaking," *Communication Quarterly* 25 (1977): 42–50. See also Philipsen's studies, e.g., "Speaking 'Like a Man' in Teamsterville: Culture Patterns of Role Enactment in an Urban Neighborhood," *Quarterly Journal of Speech* 61 (1975): 12–22; and his, with Tamar Katriel, "'What We Need is Communication': 'Communication' as a Cultural Category in Some American Speech," *Communication Monographs* 48 (1981): 301–17.

13. (Prospect Heights: Waveland Press, 1984) e.g., Chapters eight and nine.

14. See pp. 174–5.

15. See pp. 206f. Marwell and Schmitt's work is "Dimensions of Compliance-Gaining Behavior: An Empirical Analysis," *Sociometry* 30 (1967): 350–64. Our source for the list is Gerald Miller, Frank Boster, Michael Roloff, and David Seibold, "Compliance-Gaining Message Strategies: A Typology and Some Findings Concerning Effects of Situational Differences," *Communication Monographs* 44 (1977): 40.

16. *Letting Go: A Practical Theory of Relationship Disengagement and Reengagement* (Albany: State University of New York Press, 1987), 20–21.

CHAPTER FIVE

1. A version of this report appeared as "The Peoples Temple: A Study in Rhetorical Indisposition," in *Oldspeak/Newspeak: Rhetorical Transformations*, ed. Charles W. Kneupper (Arlington: Rhetoric Society of America, 1985), 67–83.

2. Most factual detail on Peoples Temple activities, as well as background information on the membership and Jim Jones, are drawn from the investigation of journalist Tim Reiterman (with John Jacobs), a thorough, highly detailed and documented account of over 600 pages: *Raven: The Untold Story of the Rev. Jim Jones and His People* (New York: Dutton, 1982).

3. Reiterman, *Raven*, 9–13, 582, 17.

4. Gregory Rochlin, *Man's Aggression: The Defense of the Self* (Boston: Gambit, 1973), 22.

5. *Raven*, 18–21.

6. Excerpts from a videotape of the sermon and evidence of expressive audience response are included in Reiterman's *Raven*, 146–50.

7. "Inside Peoples Temple," *New West* 1 Aug. 1977: 30–31, 34–36, 38.

8. *Raven*, 4–5, 137, 145–46, 156, 256, *passim*.

9. *Raven*, 24.

10. *The Suicide Cult* (New York: Bantam, 1978), 68.

11. Qtd. in Charles A. Krause, *Guyana Massacre: The Eyewitness Account* (New York: Berkley, 1978), 61.

12. *Raven*, 146.

13. Qtd. in Krause, *Guyana Massacre*, 61.

14. *Raven*, 400; qtd. 430.

15. Qtd. in James Reston, Jr., *Our Father Who Art in Hell: The Life and Death of Jim Jones* (New York: Time Books, 1981), 44.

16. *Couples in Collusion* (New York: Jason Aronson, 1982), 71.

17. *Raven*, 15.

18. Qtd. in Kilduff and Javers, *The Suicide Cult*, 11.

19. Willi, *Couples in Collusion*, 63–64.

20. Barbara Easton, Michael Kazin, and David Plotke, "Desperate Times: The Peoples Temple and the Left," *Socialist Review* 9 (1979): 69.

21. *Raven, passim.*

22. *Raven.*

23. Kilduff and Javers, *The Suicide Cult*; Krause, *Guyana Massacre;* Reiterman, *Raven.*

24. Ibid.

25. *Raven*, 216, 302, 416, 441.

26. Qtd. in Kilduff and Javers, *Suicide Cult*, 76.

27. *Guyana Massacre,* 84.

28. *Guyana Massacre,* 157.

CHAPTER SIX

1. Richard H. Rovere, *Senator Joe McCarthy*, (New York: Harcourt, Brace, 1959), 86–88; Reinhard H. Luthin, *American Demagogues, Twentieth Century* (Gloucester: Peter Smith, 1959), 274; Allen J. Matusow, *Joseph R. McCarthy*, ed. Matusow (Englewood Cliffs: Prentice-Hall, 1970), 10–11.

2. Rovere, *Senator*, 92–93.

3. *The Politics of Fear: Joseph R. McCarthy and the Senate* (Lexington: Kentucky U P, 1970), 4.

4. Griffith, *Politics of Fear*, 5.

5. Matusow, *McCarthy*, 11.

6. *Senator*, 94–96.

7. *Politics of Fear*, 5–7.

8. Matusow, *McCarthy*, 121; Griffith, *Politics of Fear*, 9–12; Rovere, *Senator*, 99–104.

9. *McCarthy*, 15.

10. Griffith, *Politics of Fear*, 13.

11. Jack Anderson and Ronald W. May, *McCarthy: The Man, the Senator, the "Ism,"* (Boston: Beacon Press, 1952), 128–37; Griffith, *Politics of Fear*, 16n.

12. Matusow, *McCarthy*, 14; Luthin, *American Demagogues*, 279.

13. *Politics of Fear*, 17, 27–29.

14. Anderson and May, *McCarthy*, 172–73; see also Eric F. Goldman, *The Crucial Decade—And After: America, 1945–1960* (New York: Vantage Books, 1960), 139–41.

15. See Athan G. Theoharis, *Seeds of Repression: Harry S. Truman and Origins of McCarthyism* (Chicago: Quadrangle Books, 1971).

16. *The Truman Doctrine and the Origins of McCarthyism* (New York: Alfred A. Knopf, 1972), 3–12; see also Theoharis, *Seeds of Repression*, 8–17.

17. Qtd. in Luthin, *American Demagogues*, 280.

18. Goldman, *Crucial Decade*, 143.

19. Anderson and May, *McCarthy*, 206–07.

20. The analysis here is of material that McCarthy had put into the Congressional Record and which he claimed was a copy of the Wheeling speech. In all probability, it is a transcript of his Reno speech. See Matusow, *McCarthy*, 19–26.

21. See Griffith, *Politics of Fear*, 48n.

22. Rovere, *Senator*, 19–20.

23. "GOP and McCarthyism," *New Republic* 30 Oct. 1950: 6.

24. Joseph R. McCarthy, "Annual Kansas Day Republican Banquet Speech," *The Rhetoric of the Speaker: Speeches and Criticism*, ed. Haig Bosmajian (Boston: D. C. Heath, 1967), 54–61.

25. Barnet Baskerville, "Joe McCarthy, Brief-Case Demagogue," *The Rhetoric of the Speaker*, ed. Bosmajian, 75.

26. McCarthy, "Text of Address by McCarthy Accusing Governor Stevenson of Aid to Communist Cause," *New York Times* 28 Oct. 1952, 26–27.

27. Edwin R. Bayley, *Joe McCarthy and the Press* (Madison: Wisconsin U P, 1981), 29.

28. Rovere, "Letter from Washington," *The New Yorker* 22 April 1950: 107–08.

29. *New York Times* 21 June 1954, 1.

30. Anderson and May, *McCarthy*, 23–24.

31. See Baskerville, "McCarthy," 66–67.

32. Qtd. in Matusow, *McCarthy*, 104.

33. Rovere, *Senator*, 246–47; Robert Griffith, "McCarthy, Joseph Raymond," *Dictionary of American Biography,* Supplement Six 1956–60; Roberta Strauss Feuerlicht, *Joe McCarthy and McCarthyism* (New York: McGraw-Hill, 1972), 148–49.

34. Anderson and May, *McCarthy*, 6–11; Feuerlicht, *McCarthy*, 10; Goldman, *Crucial Decade*, 138; Griffith, *Politics of Fear*, 2–3; Matusow, *McCarthy*, 10.

35. See H. R. Schaffer, *The Child's Entry into a Social World* (London: Academic Press, 1984), 193, 198–202, 212.

36. Anderson and May, *McCarthy*, 6–19.

37. *Politics of Fear*, 3.

38. Anderson and May, *McCarthy*, 20–24.

39. *Man's Aggression: The Defense of the Self* (Boston: Gambit, 1973).

40. Anderson and May, *McCarthy*, 14, 25, 30, 31, 53–54, 120, 125–27, 211; Feuerlicht, *McCarthy*, 12, 147–49; Griffith, *Politics of Fear*, 13–14; Rovere, *Senator*, 45–118, 150–51, 171, 217–18.

41. See Joyce McDougall, "Primitive Communication and the Use of Countertransference," *Countertransference: The Therapist's Contribution to Therapy*, ed. Lawrence Epstein and Arthur H. Feiner (New York: Jason Aronson, 1979), 267–303.

42. *Senator,* 59–60.

43. *Senator,* 59.

44. *Politics of Fear,* 14.

45. Fred J. Cook, *The Nightmare Decade: The Life and Times of Senator Joe McCarthy* (New York: Random House, 1971), 76.

46. Anderson and May, *McCarthy,* 362.

47. Luthin, *American Demagogues,* 316; Baskerville, "McCarthy," 73; Matusow, *McCarthy,* 15; Will Herberg, "No Idea, No Cause, No Program, Nothing," *McCarthy,* ed. Matusow, 123–24.

48. See Herberg, "Nothing," 124.

49. See Chapter nine.

50. Rochlin, *Man's Aggression*; Aaron Stern, *Me: The Narcissistic American* (New York: Ballantine Books, 1979).

51. Bayley, *McCarthy,* 8, 214ff.

52. *Senator,* 140–43.

53. Qtd. in Anderson and May, *McCarthy,* 358.

54. Rovere, *Senator,* 59, 20–22; see also Peter Vierick, "McCarthy and Ressentiment," *McCarthy,* ed. Matusow, 144–47 and Seymour Martin Lipset, "McCarthyism and the Ethnic Factor," *McCarthy,* ed. Matusow, 157–66.

55. See McDougall, "Primitive Communication."

56. Stern, *Me.*

57. Stern, *Me.*

58. See Rochlin, *Man's Aggression,* 254, 259–60.

59. *Senator,* 3.

60. Rochlin, *Man's Aggression.*

61. *Senator,* 266.

62. Donald W. Winnicott, *Playing and Reality* (New York: Basic Books, 1971), 10–11.

CHAPTER SEVEN

1. (London: Heineman, 1913), 420 pp.

2. See Otto F. Kernberg, "Why Some People Can't Love," *Psychology Today* June 1978: 55–59.

3. See Joyce McDougall, "Primitive Communication and the Use of Countertransference," *Countertransference: The Therapist's Contribution to Therapy,* ed. Lawrence Epstein and Arthur H. Feiner (New York: Jason Aronson, 1979), 267–303.

4. Jürg Willi, *Couples in Collusion* (New York: Jason Aronson, 1982), 66.

CHAPTER EIGHT

1. See Appian, *The Roman History of Appian,* trans. Horace White, 2 vols. (New York: Macmillan, 1899), 2: I, 9; Plutarch, *The Lives of Noble Grecians and Romans,* trans. John Dryden (New York: Random House, 1932), 999; Donald R. Dudley, *The Civilization of Rome* (New York: Mentor, 1962), 71; M. L. Clarke, *Rhetoric at Rome* (London: Cohen and West, 1965), 43.

2. Cicero, "Brutus," *On Oratory and Orators,* trans. J. S. Watson (New York: Harper and Brothers, 1875), XXVII.

3. Plutarch, *Lives*, 993.

4. See Alvin H. Bernstein, *Tiberius Sempronius Gracchus: Tradition and Apostasy* (Ithaca: Cornell U P, 1978), 42.

5. See Bernstein, *Tiberius*, 20–21; Henry C. Boren, *The Gracchi* (New York: Twayne, 1968), 23–24.

6. "Brutus," LVIII, XXVII. See also David Stockton, *The Gracchi* (Oxford: Clarendon Press, 1979), 25.

7. *Tiberius*, 29. See also Boren, *Gracchi*, 29; Stockton, *Gracchi*, 26.

8. *Lives*, 998. See also 994.

9. "Ego Distortion in Terms of the True and False Self," *The Maturational Processes and the Facilitating Environment* (London: Hogarth, 1965).

10. See Boren, *Gracchi*, 26.

11. *Lives*, 995–96.

12. See Boren, *Gracchi*, 39.

13. *Lives*, 997.

14. *Tiberius*, 69.

15. See Stockton, *Gracchi*, 29–30.

16. *Lives*, 997.

17. See *Tiberius*, 83–101; Boren, *Gracchi*, 18–22; Stockton, *Gracchi*, 6–22.

18. *Lives*, 998.

19. See *Appian*, I, 7–10; Plutarch, *Lives*, 998.

20. Plutarch, *Lives*, 998; see Truesdell S. Brown, "Greek Influence on Tiberius Gracchus," *Classical Journal* 42 (1947): 471–74; see Donald R. Dudley, "Blossius of Cumae," *Journal of Roman Studies* 31 (1941): 94–99.

21. Hugo Last, "Tiberius Gracchus," *The Cambridge Ancient History, vol. 9, The Roman Republic, 133–44, B.C.,* ed. S. A. Cook, F. E. Adcock, and M. P. Charlesworth (Cambridge: Cambridge U P, 1951), 21.

22. *Lives*, 998.

23. *Tiberius*, 229–30.

24. Boren, *Gracchi*, 56–57; see also *Tiberius*, 164–66.

25. *Appian*, I, 17; see also F. E. Adcock, *Roman Political Ideas and Practice* (Ann Arbor: U of Michigan P, 1959), 54; *Tiberius*, 158; Frank Burr Marsh, *A History of the Roman World from 146 to 30 B.C.* (London: Methuen, 1963), 34–37.

26. "Brutus," XXVII.

27. See H. H. Scullard, *From the Gracchi to Nero* (London: Methuen, 1959), 25–27.

28. *Appian*, I, 9.

29. See Stockton, *Gracchi*, 40.

30. *Lives*, 999.

31. *Lives*, 999.

32. *Appian*, I, 10; Plutarch, *Lives*, 998–99; Stockton, *Gracchi*, 62–65.

33. Stockton, *Gracchi*, 65.

34. *Lives*, 1000; Stockton, *Gracchi*, 65.

35. *Appian*, I, 11.

36. *Tiberius*, 180–81.
37. Plutarch, *Lives*, 1000; see also Marsh, *Roman World*, 40–41.
38. See Boren, *Gracchi*, 58; Stockton, *Gracchi*, 83.
39. See Stockton, *Gracchi*, 66–67; Marsh, *Roman World*, 41.
40. *Tiberius*, 207, 211.
41. *Lives*, 1002–1004; see Boren, *Gracchi*, 58, 67.
42. See Marsh, *Roman World*, 44.
43. *Tiberius*, 213.
44. *Appian*, I, 2; see also Plutarch, *Lives*, 1006.
45. "Tiberius Gracchus: A Role Analysis," M. A. thesis, California State University, Hayward, 1984.
46. *Tiberius*, 165.
47. See Scullard, *Gracchi to Nero*, 30, 39; *Tiberius*, 64; Stockton, *Gracchi*, 74.
48. Evan T. Sage, "A Note on the Tribunate of T. I. Gracchus," *Classical Journal* 9 (1913): 50, 52.
49. Last, "Tiberius," 35.
50. *Roman World*, 37, 49.
51. Theodor Mommsen, *The History of Rome: Vol. 3*, trans. William Purdie Dickson (London: Richard Bentley, 1894), 333.
52. See *Tiberius*, 231–32; *Appian*, I, 17.
53. See Mommsen, *Rome*, 322; see also Stockton, *Gracchi*, 69–74. Cf. Berstein, *Tiberius*, 157–58.
54. *Gracchi*, 61–62; see also Finley Hooper, *Roman Realities* (Detroit: Wayne State U P, 1979), 161; *Tiberius*, 209.
55. *The Restoration of the Self* (New York: International Universities Press, 1977), 88.
56. "Transitional Objects and Transitional Phenomena," *Playing and Reality* (New York: Basic Books, 1971), 10–11.
57. "An Overview of the Concept of Narcissism," *Social Casework* Mar. 1977: 141.
58. *Seven Roman Statesmen of the Late Republic* (London: Edward Arnold, 1910), 13.
59. "Ego Distortion," 146–47; *The Child and the Outside World: Studies in Developing Relationships*, ed. Janet Hardenberg (London: Tavistock, 1957), 140.
60. Stockton, *Gracchi*, 85.
61. "Introduction," *Tiberius Gracchus, Destroyer or Reformer of the Republic?*, ed. Riddle (Lexington: D. C. Heath, 1970), viii–ix.
62. *Tiberius*, 198; see also 213, 230.
63. Hooper, *Roman Realities*, 167.

NOTES TO CHAPTER NINE

1. *Civilization and Its Discontents*, trans. James Strachey (New York: W. W. Norton, 1961).
2. *The Sane Society* (New York: Rinehart, 1955).

3. "Distance and Relation," *Psychiatry* 20 (1957): 94–104.

4. *Civility and Disobedience* (Cambridge: Cambridge U P, 1975), 82.

5. Lawrence W. Rosenfield, Laurie Schultz Hayes, and Thomas Frentz, *The Communicative Experience* (Boston: Allyn and Bacon, 1976).

6. *Technology and Civility: The Skill Revolution in Politics* (Stanford: Hoover Institution Press, 1977), 22–25.

7. Lewis A. Coser, "The Notion of Civility in Contemporary Society," *Archives of Europeenness de Sociologie* 21 (1980): 13.

8. *After All* (New York: Knopf, 1936), 221.

9. See Roderick P. Hart and Don M. Burks, "Rhetorical Sensitivity and Social Interaction," *Speech Monographs* 39 (1972): 75–91.

10. Richard Sennett, *The Fall of Public Man* (New York: Vantage, 1978).

11. *The Magic Mountain*, trans. H. T. Lowe-Porter (New York: Modern Library, 1927), 652.

12. Colwyn Trevarthen, "Conversations with a Two-month-old," *New Scientist* 2 May 1974: 235; Donald W. Winnicott, *The Child and the Family: First Relationships* (London: Tavistock, 1957), 63.

13. Robert M. Bramson, *Coping with Difficult People* (New York: Ballantine, 1981).

14. Neil Postman, "TV's 'Disastrous' Impact on Children," *U. S. News & World Report* 19 Jan. 1981: 46–48.

15. Charles Derber, *The Pursuit of Attention: Power and Individualism in Everyday Life* (New York: Oxford U P, 1979).

16. Lionel Trilling, *Sincerity and Authenticity* (Cambridge: Harvard U P, 1972).

17. Norman Cousins, *Human Options* (New York: W. W. Norton, 1981).

18. Willard Gaylin, *The Rage Within: Anger in Modern Life* (New York: Simon and Schuster, 1984), 24–26, 31, 66, 73, 157.

19. Christopher Lasch, *The Culture of Narcissism: American Life in an Age of Diminishing Expectations* (New York: W. W. Norton, 1979) and *The Minimal Self: Psychic Survival in Troubled Times* (New York: W. W. Norton, 1984).

20. "Civility and Psychology," *Daedalus* 109 (1980): 140–41.

21. *Me: The Narcissistic American* (New York: Ballantine, 1979), 183.

22. *The Prose of the World*, trans. John O'Neill, ed. Claude Lefort (Evanston: Northwestern U P, 1973), 143–44.

23. Charles M. Rossiter, Jr. and W. Barnet Pearce, *Communicating Personally: A Theory of Interpersonal Communication and Human Relationships* (Indianapolis: Bobbs-Merrill, 1975), 161.

24. *Griefs and Discontents: The Forces of Change* (Boston: Little, Brown, 1965), 15, 30–31 and *Man's Aggression: The Defense of the Self* (Boston: Gambit, 1973), 49, 83, 256–7.

25. Rossiter and Pearce, *Communicating Personally,* 27–33.

26. *The Cinderella Complex* (New York: Pocket Books, 1981), vi.

27. *Man's Aggression,* 50.

28. *The Moral Judgment of the Child* (London: Routledge & Kegan Paul, 1960), 407–08.

29. *Disturbed Communication: The Clinical Assessment of Normal and Pathological Communicative Behavior* (New York: W. W. Norton, 1957), 77, 145.

30. *The Restoration of the Self* (New York: International Universities Press, 1977), 187–88.

31. *Me*, 11.

32. *Man's Aggression*, 206.

33. *Disturbed Communication*, 145.

34. "Rhetoritherapy Versus the Medical Model: Dealing with Reticence," *Communication Education* 26 (1977): 39. See also Phillips, David E. Butt, and Nancy J. Metzger, *Communication in Education: A Rhetoric of Schooling and Learning* (New York: Holt, Rinehart and Winston, 1974).

35. *Moral Judgment*, 407–12.

36. "Toward a Theory of Thinking," *The Organization and Pathology of Thought: Selected Sources*, trans. and comment, Rapaport (New York: Columbia U P, 1951), 724.

37. Thomas Gordon, *Leader Effectiveness Training, L.E.T.* (New York: Wyden, 1977).

Name Index

Subject Index

Acheson, Dean, 108, 110, 115
Adversity, in infancy, 33–34
Aeschines, 2
Affect attunement, 22–23: and
consubstantiality, 23, 31; and good
audience, 160; and good enough
environment, 23, 36; in intersubjectivity, 22–23, 25, 29
Aggressor, identification with, 119
America of 1950s: abuse of by J.
McCarthy, 115–17, 118–20, 151;
and confirmation of J. McCarthy,
111–12, 116, 118, 119–20, 151;
defensiveness in, 116–20; and identification with aggressor, 119; as
inadequate audience, 116, 119–20,
151; individualism in, 152; loss of
civility in, 120, 146, 150–51;
motivation of, 118–20; narcissistic
needs of, 116, 118–20; regression
of, 118; rhetorical indisposition of,
116, 118–20, 146, 151; seeking
confirmation in, 118; values of,
107; vulnerability of to J. McCarthy message, 107–08, 115–20, 151
Analysis and criticism, of rhetorical
indisposition, 67–88, 121: and
biographical awareness, 70, 80, 88;
and consubstantiality, 67–68; and
critic as pathologist, 67–68; enthymeme in, 68; evidence for, 80;
of fiction, 72–73, 77–78, 80, 121,
124; interdisciplinary nature of,
70–71; message content in, 68, 69;

methods in, 73–75, 79–88; and narcissistic collusion, 86; personal narratives and, 85; primary sources in,
79; roles in, 68; rubrics of, 67–72;
standards for, 68, 80–81; subjects
for, 73–78, 79, 88, 121
Anomie, oppressiveness of, 50, 98,
160
Aristotelian logic, and realism, 163
Army-McCarthy hearings, 111, 116
"As if" personality, 52, 55: and
rhetorical servicing, 66
Athenian Agora, 154
Athletes, unfavorable narcissism of,
75
Audience: in Aristotelian theory, 163;
in classroom, 161; consciousness
of, 28–29, 30–31; and enthymeme,
2, 4; and free choice, 47; inadequacy of, 98, 99–102, 116, 119–20,
151; J. Jones selection of, 94, 96,
97, 99; of J. McCarthy, 107–08,
115–20; most vital, 165; narcissistic
selection of, 64–65; of personal
narratives, 84; primary function
of, 163; as rhetor, 67, 154, 159;
rhetorical indisposition of, 119–20;
in rhetorical interaction, 2, 3, 4, 7,
11, 29, 40–41, 46, 48, 50; and
rhetorical rules, 46–47, 57; and
role message, 68; and roots of Mc-
Carthyism, 103, 120; Tiberius'
alienation of, 145; as ultimate
judge, 63, 154; and unfavorable